BRIAN INGLIS

The Power of Dreams

PALADIN
GRAFTON BOOKS
A Division of the Collins Publishing Group

LONDON GLASGOW
TORONTO SYDNEY AUCKLAND

Paladin
Grafton Books
A Division of the Collins Publishing Group
8 Grafton Street, London W1X 3LA

Published in Paladin Books 1988

First published in Great Britain by
Grafton Books 1987

Copyright © Brian Inglis 1987

ISBN 0-586-08709-5

Printed and bound in Great Britain by
Collins, Glasgow

Set in Bembo

Contents

Acknowledgements   iv

Introduction: Horn – or Ivory?   1

1. Inspiration from Dreams   6
2. Problem-solving in Dreams   29
3. Second Sight in Dreams   63
4. Dreaming the Future   98
5. Lucid Dreaming   170
6. Dream Interpretation   176
7. Burnished Horn   202

Bibliography   208

Source References   211

Index   215

Acknowledgements

Under the heading 'Can you help?', an appeal went out in the *Telegraph Sunday Magazine* in 1985 for accounts of unusual dreams, 'especially those which have predicted an event in real life, solved waking problems, or come up with an idea for use in people's work'. The Koestler Foundation, it explained, felt that this was an important, and so far sadly underestimated, area for research. The Foundation's Research Officer, Joanna Trevelyan, has since received hundreds of accounts, demonstrating that many people agree. I have used some of them in *The Power of Dreams*, but the Foundation would like to collect more, with a view to providing a springboard for further research. They should be sent to Joanna Trevelyan at the Koestler Foundation, 10 Belgrave Square, London W1. My thanks to her, and to all those who responded to the initial appeal. My thanks also to Bernard Levin and Morton Schatzman, who scrutinised the proofs.

Introduction

Horn – or Ivory?

'Lady,' replied the subtle Odysseus, 'nobody could force any other meaning on this dream; you have learnt from Odysseus himself how to translate it into fact. Clearly, the suitors are all of them doomed; there is not one who will get away alive.'

'Dreams, Sir,' said the cautious Penelope, 'are awkward and confusing things; not all that people see in them comes true. For there are two gates through which these insubstantial visions reach us: one is of horn, the other of ivory. Those that come through the ivory gate cheat us with empty promises that never see fulfilment; while those that issue from the gate of burnished horn inform the dreamer what will really happen.'

I grew up accepting certain prevalent assumptions about dreams. However long they seemed to be when recalled on awakening, they were really 'all over in a flash' – in a fraction of a second. If they meant anything, they went by opposites; to dream of failing an examination presaged passing it. Still, to dream of passing it did not necessarily mean impending failure. Dreams were not to be taken seriously. 'Only a dream' was a standard form of consolation.

My faith in this conventional wisdom was first shaken by reading J.W. Dunne's *An Experiment with Time*, published in 1927 and periodically reissued in editions revised by the author. 'Dreaming the future' was not regarded as an occult experience – as a curiosity, rather; and Dunne was careful to provide an hypothesis to account for it which, he hoped, would keep it within the confines of physics (the idea of Time as an additional dimension had been given an extensive airing). He also suggested that the time-slips which his theory sought to explain were of a nature that any of us could explore, simply by having a pad and a pencil beside the bed and making sure, first thing on waking every morning, to jot down everything we could remember about our dreams. Although nothing came of this when I tried it, I would hear from time to time of people for whom the method had worked. In any case, my interest had been aroused; and it was to be nourished in the later 1930s by J.B. Priestley's *Time and the Conways* and *I Have Been Here Before*, both produced in West End theatres in London, and both inspired by Dunne's book.

At university, Sigmund Freud's *The Interpretation of Dreams* (1900) was required reading, along with Marcel Proust, T.S. Eliot and W.H. Auden, for anybody who wished not to be identified as one of the hearties. The sexual symbolism attracted amused comment; to relate even the most innocent-sounding of dreams was to risk ribald interpretations; but we took it seriously. And later, when I became immersed in the history of medicine and of paranormal phenomena, I came to appreciate the remarkable influence of dreams not only in both those fields, but on the whole course of history, on account of the reliance placed upon them for guidance. Admittedly the reliance was often misplaced, because it was based on faulty interpretation. But there was an abundance of evidence to show how useful dreams can be, and had been, to those shrewd enough or lucky enough to interpret them wisely.

It was with some irritation, then, that I came across a newspaper report in 1983 that two molecular biologists had been undertaking research which demonstrated to their satisfaction that the dismissive view was correct. The function of dreaming, they claimed, is to endow us with 'a cleaning-up action to remove potentially parasitic modes'. Without this cleansing drainage, evolution would have been unable to manufacture 'the highly-refined neo-cortex we have today'. Attempts to remember dreams, therefore, 'should perhaps not be encouraged, because such remembering may help to retain patterns of thought which are best forgotten.'

Had the date been 1 April, I would have suspected a spoof; but according to the report, the biologists' contention had been published in *Nature*, and their identity meant that their curious theory was quite likely to be taken seriously by *Nature*'s readers. Francis Crick, from the Salk Institute in California, is one of the very few scientists whose name is familiar to the public, following his unravelling of the genetic code and his Nobel Prize. And Graeme Mitchison works in the Medical Research Council's prestigious molecular biology laboratories at Cambridge University.

What they were offering was the latest reductionist model, derived from their neurobiological research. Other types of model, from other disciplines, evidently did not concern them. A few years earlier Christopher Evans had put forward a theory which had interesting similarities with theirs; on the analogy of a computer, he suggested, the brain's programming must periodically be updated, and dreaming may be one of the ways by which redundant programs are cleared while the brain is 'off-line', in sleep. But Evans, although internationally respected as an authority on computers, was by training a psychologist, a species despised in reductionist circles. Crick and Mitchison did not even mention his pioneering ideas.

Still less were they likely to mention the historical evidence about dreams, even when it was derived from scientific research. In *The Double Helix* (1968) James Watson, Crick's colleague and fellow Nobel Laureate, had little to say about the work of their predecessors, on which they had built; for a reason which Sir Peter Medawar has attributed not to any lack of generosity but to 'stark insensibility'. Such matters 'belong to scientific history, and the history of science bores most scientists stiff.'

As it happened, I had just been asked by John Anstey, the veteran editor of the *Telegraph Sunday Magazine*, whether there was any topic I was itching to write about. Yes, I replied: the influence of dreams on the course of history. Reductionists might deride the evidence as anecdotal; but they could hardly dispute its profound effects.

Take the development of religions. In early civilisations it was taken for granted that dreams were a vehicle which the gods used to pass their instructions, exhortations and warnings, as the Lord so frequently does in the pages of the Old Testament. In the Gospels, a dream tells Joseph that no mere mortal has cuckolded him; another warns him to flee with Mary and the infant Jesus to escape the massacre of the innocents. A dream set Siddhartha Gautama on the course which was to make him the Buddha. A dream convinced Mahomet that he had been chosen to join Abraham, Moses and Jesus among the prophets.

But there was a catch. Considering the misery that religions have brought in their wake – wars, pogroms, human sacrifice, the Inquisition, terrorism – surely the world would have been a better place if those dreams *had* been forgotten? Reductionists and rationalists would presumably insist that we would have been far better off if science, rather than religion, had been dominant.

Instead, I concentrated in the article on dreams which had been valuable on a more down-to-earth level, citing testimonials from eminent historical figures, distinguished scientists among them. To this Mitchison replied, upon being shown a copy, 'Of course, no one would deny that dreams may occasionally be amusing, or even give accidental insight, but the evidence scarcely warrants the notion that dreams systematically convey useful information.' Needless to say, I had not suggested that there is anything systematic in the process – far from it. My contention was simply that they have conveyed useful information too often for the process to be dismissed as 'accidental'.

Accompanying the article, when it was published on 26 May 1985, was a note to say that the Koestler Foundation would be interested to receive accounts of dreams of an unusual nature along the lines of those referred to, such as dreams which had foretold future events or solved working problems. The Foundation, of which I am a trustee, was set up in Arthur Koestler's lifetime to promote the exploration of regions on the borders of orthodox science, dreams among them. Dreaming, he claimed in *The Act of Creation* (1964), in its literal as well as its metaphorical sense, 'seems to be an essential part of psychic metabolism'. The contributions which flowed in to the Foundation show that there must be a considerable measure of agreement with him; but at the same time, people are a little embarrassed about admitting they take their dreams seriously. A few even admitted they had never before told the dreams they recounted to anybody else.

Priestley had found the same thing after he had been interviewed on the subject of Time on the BBC arts programme *Monitor* in 1964. In the course of the interview the suggestion was thrown out that viewers might like to send in accounts of experiences they had had which seemed to contradict conventional notions about Time. Priestley found himself inundated with letters – after the first thousand, he stopped counting. The majority were precognitive dreams, or dreams which gave information of a kind which could be checked, but which the dreamers could not have known about in the ordinary way. But far from this being regarded as an asset, many of the correspondents were clearly uneasy, fearing that they might be considered odd or unbalanced.

Twenty years on, that impression appears still to be widespread, giving rise to a curious ambivalence on the subject. Many people take their dreams seriously, at least to the point of worrying about them. Stories of dreams which have 'come true' are a commonplace. Yet the impression lingers that to believe such things is a superstition, which cannot really be defended. My aim is to show not merely that it can be defended, but that the evidence from historical and biographical sources, and to a limited extent from research, shows how valuable dreaming can be, if both its potential and its limitations are better appreciated.

The evidence is necessarily anecdotal – a term of reproach in scientific circles. But so is the great bulk of evidence from history; and we do not reject it simply because it cannot be reproduced in a laboratory. This raises a point which I feel is important: accounts of dreams are just as reliable (or unreliable) if they were recorded a hundred years ago or if they were recorded yesterday. The test is the trustworthiness of the dreamers, and the attestation. Naturally accounts of dreams in, say, Homer, or the Old Testament cannot be relied upon – though they can give a very useful indication of the influence of dreams, at the time, and of what people thought about their sources. But in some periods, notably towards the close of the nineteenth century, dreams were recorded and attested with greater care than they usually are today.

It is not always possible to tell from an account whether the description is of a dream, a vision, or a day-dream – a reverie. A rough test is whether the conscious mind has been aware of what is being perceived; but as everybody knows, in the process of falling asleep and of waking up, the distinction is blurred, as it can also be in day-dreaming. I have tended to accept the dreamer's own attribution. I have also included some instances of the very common experience of 'sleeping on it': going to bed with a problem on the mind, and waking up with the solution *in* the mind. Is it presented in a dream which has been forgotten? Or the result of some process of unconscious deliberation which occurs in dreaming? We do not know; but unquestionably it can be an asset – as can its allied helper: the ability many people possess of telling themselves to wake at a certain specified time, confident that they will not need an alarm call.

I have concentrated on the types of dream which have proved to be useful, or which carry the potential for usefulness when the mechanism of dreaming is better understood: dreams which have provided inspiration for writers, composers and artists; problem-solving dreams; dreams which appear to have shown the mind can travel, in space or in time; lucid dreams, in which a measure of conscious control has been achieved; and dreams which, when correctly interpreted, have provided prognostic and diagnostic information about the dreamer's health. And in conclusion, a survey of the views and the hopes of explorers of this still undervalued region.

1

Inspiration from Dreams

As I walked through the wilderness of this world, I lighted on a certain place where there was a den; and I laid me down in that place to sleep; and as I slept I dreamed a dream. I dreamed, and behold I saw a man clothed with rags, standing in a certain place, with his face from his own house, a book in his hand, and a great burden upon his back. I looked and saw him open the book, and read therein; and as he read he wept and trembled: and, not being able longer to contain, he brake out with a lamentable cry, saying 'What shall I do?'

The Pilgrim's Progress is only one of hundreds of renowned stories and poems which the writers chose to present in the form of a dream. From Piers Plowman to Alice in Wonderland, the device has proved invaluable. The debt owed to dreams, Walter de la Mare claimed, by poetry, and 'by all imaginative literature, is beyond computation'. Yet their value as sources of inspiration – as distinct from vehicles by which inspiration can be conveyed – is much less widely recognised.

This must surely be because most of us have been conditioned not to take our dreams seriously. Writers may understandably fear that their work will be discounted if they disclose its dream source. There may also be a feeling of the kind D.H. Lawrence expressed in a letter to Edward Garnett in 1912. 'I can never decide whether my dreams are the result of my thoughts, or my thoughts the result of my dreams,' he mused. 'But my dreams make conclusions for me. They decide things finally. I dream a decision. Sleep seems to hammer out for me the logical conclusions of my vague days, and offer them as dreams.' Yet Lawrence went on to say it was 'a horrid feeling, not to be able to escape from one's own – what – self-daemon? – fate? – or something ... ?' To rationalists, the notion that some undiscovered source of intelligence may be responsible for inspiration remains repugnant; H.G. Wells apparently did not care to reveal that dreams had provided him with one of his stories, but he confided this to his friend, Edmund Haynes.

We will consequently never know how much literature owes to dreaming. But there is some striking evidence for our indebtedness from a few writers, as well as from musicians and painters, to confirm its value in the past and its potential for the future.

Writers

The most explicit avowal of dreaming as the source of his inspiration is Robert Louis Stevenson's, in the essay on the subject which he included in his *Across the Plains* (1892). 'There are some amongst us,' he asserted,

> who claim to have lived longer and more richly than their neighbours; when they lay asleep they were still active; and among the treasures of memory that all men review for their amusement, these count in no second place the harvest of their dreams.

In childhood, Stevenson recalled, he had been 'an ardent and uncomfortable dreamer', the discomfort predominating. But as he grew older, he found that 'the little people who manage man's internal theatre', who previously had played about in it like children, could be trained to assist him as a professional story-writer when he began to try to sell his tales.

> Here was he, and here were the little people who did that part of the business in quite new conditions. The stories must now be trimmed and pared and set upon all fours, they must run from a beginning to an end and fit (after a manner) with the laws of life; the pleasure, in one word, had become a business; and that not only for the dreamer, but for the little people of his theatre. These understood the change as well as he. When he lay down to prepare himself for sleep, he no longer sought amusement, but printable and profitable tales; and after he had dozed off in his box-seat, his little people continued their evolutions with the same mercantile designs.

Sometimes, if he fell too deeply asleep, the 'Brownies' – his other word for the Little People – produced rubbish; 'and yet how often have these sleeping Brownies done him honest service, and given him, as he sat idly taking his pleasure in the boxes, better tales than he could fashion for himself!'

'Little People', 'Brownies', sound mawkish today. It was not mawkish to Celts, nor to those who, like Stevenson, accepted the Celtic assumption that there are 'powers' which can influence our lives; that they can take human, or other, forms – fairies, banshees, nymphs; and that they can be invoked in their spirit capacities to help people, as they had helped him. He was not prepared to defend his belief in them or to attempt to describe them; when asked to explain precisely what he meant by his Little People:

> what shall I say they are but just my Brownies, God bless them! who do one-half of my work for me while I am fast asleep, and in all human likelihood, do the rest for me as well, when I am wide awake and fondly suppose I do it for myself. That part which is done while I am sleeping is the Brownies' part beyond contention; but that which is done when I am up and about is by no means necessarily mine, since all goes to show the Brownies have a hand in it even then. Here is a doubt that much concerns my conscience. For myself – what I call I, my conscious ego, the denizen of the pineal gland unless he has changed his residence since Descartes, the man with the conscience and the variable bank-account, the man with the hat and the boots, and the privilege of voting and not carrying his candidate at the general elections – I am sometimes tempted to suppose he is no story-teller at all, but a creature as matter of fact as any cheesemonger or any cheese, and a realist bemired up to the ears in actuality; so that, by that account, the whole of my published fiction should be the single-handed product of some Brownie, some Familiar, some unseen collaborator, whom I keep locked in a back garret, while I get all the praise and he but a share (which I cannot prevent him getting) of the pudding.

Stevenson gave himself the credit only for being an excellent *adviser*. He knew when to cut material, or dress it up a bit; he held the pen; and he made the arrangements for publication, which gave him some claim to a share in the proceeds – though not, he feared, as large as he actually took.

To illustrate how the little people worked for him, he cited *The Strange Case of Dr Jekyll and Mr Hyde* (1886). He had long been trying to find a vehicle for a story about 'that strong sense of man's double being', without success. Then, in urgent need of funds, he spent two days racking his brains for a plot of any sort; 'and on the second night I dreamed the scene at the window, and a scene afterward split in two, in which Hyde, pursued for some crime, took the powder and underwent the change in the presence of his pursuers'. The rest Stevenson made up consciously, 'though I think I can trace in much of it the manner of my Brownies.' For the most part, he concluded, his Brownies were 'somewhat fantastic'. They liked passion and the picturesque; and 'they have no prejudice against the supernatural.'

Nor did Anna Kingsford's. Hers was one of the most remarkable stories in the history of what has come to be called Women's Lib; irritated by the way in which the medical profession in Britain blocked entry to women, she went to Paris in 1874, qualified there as a doctor, and became one of the leading writers on medical and other scientific subjects – including dreams, whose significance she felt had been given inadequate recognition. 'The priceless insights and illuminations I have acquired by means of my dreams have gone far to elucidate for me many difficulties and enigmas of life, and even of religion, which otherwise might have remained dark for me,' she claimed, 'and to throw upon the events and vicissitudes of a career filled with bewildering situations, a light which, like sunshine, has penetrated to the very causes and springs of circumstances, and given meaning and fitness to much in my life that would else have appeared to me incoherent or inconsistent.'

Anna Kingsford left no details to substantiate this claim; but before she died she compiled a book from those of her dreams which, for her, fell into the category of short stories.

The most remarkable features of the experiences I am about to record are the methodical consecutiveness of their sequences, and the intelligent purpose disclosed alike in the events witnessed and in the words heard or read. Some of these last, indeed, resemble, for point and profundity, the apologues of Eastern scriptures; and, on more than one occasion, the scenery of the dream has accurately portrayed characteristics of remote regions, city, forest, and mountain, which in this existence at least I have never beheld, nor, so far as I can remember, even heard described, and yet every feature of these unfamiliar climes has revealed itself to my sleeping vision with a splendour of colouring and distinctness of outline which made the waking life seem duller and less real by contrast.

Published in 1888 – at her insistence, only after her death – the dreams cannot convey that 'splendour'; but they are sufficiently absorbing to suggest that had she wanted to she could easily have dressed them up and sold them as fiction. For her, however, their importance lay in their influence on her career. They had come to her, she recalled, whenever she was most deeply involved in her work, such as when she was preparing to take her examinations while she was a medical student, or in the course of her medical practice after she had qualified. It had seemed to her almost as if their function had been to supply what other people obtained from light bedtime reading, sparing her from having to read herself to sleep.

Understandably, short story writers appear to have had fewer inhibitions about recalling the dream origins of their works. 'Long years have elapsed, and my memory is feeble through suffering,' Edgar Allan Poe admitted, but he was very clear about the way he had obtained the inspiration for his favourite among all his tales, 'The Lady Ligeia' (1838). He had encountered her in a dream, in which her eyes, in particular, left an indelible impression on him.

They were, I must believe, far larger than the ordinary eyes of our own race. They were even fuller than the fullest of the gazelle eyes of the tribe of the valley of Nourjahad. Yet it was only at intervals – in moments of intense excitement – that this peculiarity became more than slightly noticeable in Ligeia. And at such moments was her beauty – in my heated fancy thus it appeared, perhaps – the beauty of beings either above or apart from the earth ...

Above all, it was their expression which had remained with him. 'How for long hours I have pondered upon it! How have I for the whole of a midsummer night struggled to fathom it!'

'I *dreamed* a short story last night,' Katherine Mansfield noted in her journal on 10 February 1918,

even down to its name, which was *Sun and Moon*. It was very light. I dreamed it all – about children. I got up at 6.30 and wrote a note or two because I knew it would fade. I'll send it some time this week. It's so nice. I didn't dream that I read it. No, I was in it, part of it, and it played round invisible me. But the hero is not more than 5. In my dream I saw a supper table with the eyes of 5. It was awfully queer – especially a plate of half-melted ice-cream.

'Three of my essays are literal records of dreams,' J.B. Priestley told the author Rodolphe Megroz, whose *The Dream World* (1939) remains a useful collection. 'The Dream', 'The Berkshire Beasts' and 'The Strange Outfitter' were three 'real dreams that I wrote down as I remembered them, especially the last two, which are both comic but very queer, rather like *Alice in Wonderland*.'

A few novelists have been prepared to admit that they owe certain characters or situations to their dreams, notably Jack Kerouac. His *Book of Dreams* (1961) – 'Just a collection', as he explained, 'that I scribbled as I woke up' – is of little interest for the scribbled material; but for avid readers of his books, if there are any survivors of that once well-populated territory, he reveals how they provided the key to many of the characters. A more impressive testimonial has been offered by Graham Greene. 'The genesis of my novel *It's a Battlefield* was a dream', he has recalled in *Ways of Escape* (1981),

and *The Honorary Consul* began too with a dream. Sometimes identification with a character goes so far that one may dream his dream and not one's own. That happened to me when I was writing *A Burnt-Out Case*. The symbols, the memories, the associations of that dream belonged so clearly to my character Querry that next morning I could put the dream without change into the novel, where it bridged a gap in the narrative which for days I had been unable to cross. I imagine all authors have found the same aid from the unconscious. The unconscious collaborates in all our work: it is a *nègre* we keep in the cellar to aid us. When an obstacle seems insurmountable, I read the day's work before sleep and leave the *nègre* to labour in my place. When I wake the obstacle has nearly always been removed: the solution is there and obvious – perhaps it came in a dream which I have forgotten.

'Sleeping on it' is rather easier to admit as a vehicle for inspiration than actual dreaming; especially for the removal of 'writer's block'. When Mrs Gaskell asked Charlotte Brontë if she had ever taken opium, because her description of the sensations which followed so closely resembled those Mrs Gaskell had herself experienced,

She replied that she had never, to her knowledge, taken a grain of it in any shape, but that she had followed the process she had always adopted when she had to describe anything which had not fallen within her own experience; she had thought intently on it for many and many a night before falling to sleep – wondering what it was like, or how it would be – till at length, sometimes after the progress of her story had been arrested at this one point for weeks, she wakened up in the morning with all clear before her, and then could describe it, word for word, as if it had happened.

Sir Walter Scott, too, whenever he was in difficulties with a story – he noted in his Journal in 1826 – it 'was always when I first opened my eyes that the desired ideas thronged upon me. This is so much the case that I am in the habit of relying upon it, and saying to myself, when I am at a loss, "Never mind, we shall have it at seven o'clock tomorrow morning".'

In one instance, 'sleeping on it' was hardly adequate to account for Scott's achievement. To his biographer John Gibson Lockhart, *The Bride of Lammermoor* was 'the most pure and powerful of all the tragedies that Scott ever penned'; and rather than subject it to formal criticism, Lockhart preferred to recall how it had been written, as recorded by James Ballantyne, Scott's friend and printer. Scott, who had been seriously ill at the time – 1819 – dictated the book from his bed, sometimes getting up and acting it out as if in a somnambulistic state. The book, according to Ballantyne, had not only been written but actually published, before Scott recovered; 'and he assured me, that when it was first put into his hands in a complete shape, he did not recollect one single incident, character or conversation it contained!' The original story he had known from his boyhood – the general facts about the parents, the children, the rival lovers, the forced marriage, and the final catastrophe;

but he literally recollected nothing else: – not a single character woven by the romancer, not one of the many scenes and points of humour, nor anything with which he was connected as the writer of the work. 'For a long time,' he said, 'I felt myself very uneasy in the course of my reading, lest I should be startled by meeting something altogether glaring and fantastic. However, I recollected that you had been the printer, and I felt sure that you would not have permitted anything of this sort to pass.' 'Well,' I said, 'upon the whole, how did you like it?' 'Why,' he said, 'as a whole, I felt it monstrous gross and grotesque; but still the worst of it made me laugh, and I trusted the good-natured public would not be less indulgent.'

Fascinated though Scott was with the supernatural, he wanted to keep it (as, later, did Dickens) in his fiction, not in his life; and doubtless realising that he might have been disturbed to hear in detail how he had composed the tale, Ballantyne did not broach the subject to him again. But on his deathbed in 1821 Ballantyne felt that it ought to be made known. His recollection, he claimed, was as clear as if he had taken it down in shorthand; and he believed Lockhart would agree with him 'in thinking that the history of the human mind contains nothing more wonderful'.

As our appeal for accounts of dreams for the Koestler Foundation was not specifically directed at writers, it is not surprising that there was relatively little response from them. But one from Alec L. Glasfurd is of considerable interest. At around the age of ten he had a vivid dream, which seemed important at the time.

I was taken down some steps, as a small child in appearance but before I was born, and introduced into a cavernous, low-ceilinged stone-built room. At the far end sat a Catholic potentate of the Middle Ages who, I vaguely understood, had been a pope – dark robe, a strange white close-fitting cap with side-flaps, and a very unusual face with a pointed beard, long hooked nose and dark piercing eyes, an 'Eastern' face more like my idea of an Old Testament prophet's. Several monks were around him. He told me that one of the tasks in my coming life would be to tell the truth about him which had been obscured and distorted by prejudice. I answered that I was not a Catholic, and surely someone else could do it better. But he insisted.

In 1959, some 35 years later, Glasfurd – who by this time had moved from Presbyterianism to 'a rather militant agnosticism' – was travelling through Spain, and stopped off at Peñíscola, a town 100 kilometres north of Valencia. There, he learned that in the early 1400s the castle had belonged to Pedro de Luna, the first 'Pôpe Benedict XIII', chosen by the French cardinals in 1394 and recognised as Pope by his fellow countrymen, but repudiated by the Italians, and Catholics in many other countries, as the antipope. Glasfurd's knowledge of the schism was limited, and he had no clear memory of de Luna.

But the spectacular castle and the story of the old antipope making his last stand there made an unexpected impression on me, and when I got home, I looked him up. And then I was hooked. From general histories I moved to the original sources. I perceived that he had been an honest and sympathetic character, and that his life was a marvellous illustration of Spanish obstinacy and a *reductio ad absurdum* of papal claims.

It seemed extraordinary to Glasfurd that nobody with better qualifications had written a book about de Luna; so he decided to write it himself.

In preparing the book I searched long for a possible portrait of him, and at last I found a marginal sketch in a contemporary account of a council held at Perpignan. As soon as I saw it, I recognised the potentate of my childhood dream. The face was at a slightly different angle – my dream was not a prevision of the drawing – but it was unmistakably the same face.

The face was to be the frontispiece of *The Antipope*, published in 1965. Glasfurd fears that it made little impression on the mandarins of church history; 'as I saw at the time, he should have chosen a better champion'. The antipope could in fact have done far worse. Glasfurd's account is not only readable, but well documented and convincing – except to mandarins. It is written in the colloquial manner of a historical novel ('On a blustery January morning in the year 1376, while flurries of almost horizontal rain slashed down ... '), a form of presentation anathema to the academic historian.

Playwrights

Playwrights have found it rather more difficult to incorporate dream sequences into their works, though there have been exceptions, such as Priestley's *Time and the Conways* (1937). But there are examples of a dream providing the inspiration for the writing of a play – including one which must be counted among the most influential, in its effect on the subsequent course of events, that has ever been written.

In 1902 the brothers Frank and W.G. Fay, soon to help to launch the Abbey Theatre, were looking for a play to put on in Dublin to supplement

A.E.'s *Deirdre*, which was not long enough. They asked W.B. Yeats if he would let them have his *Land of Heart's Desire*. No, he told them, 'but he had a little play which he would give them, *Cathleen ni Houlihan*, and he thought he could persuade Maud Gonne to play the leading part in it', Ulick O'Connor has recalled in his *Celtic Dawn*. 'At first the Fays were a little depressed when Yeats told them that the theme for *Cathleen ni Houlihan*, inspired by an old Irish legend, had come to him in a dream. But they cheered up when he assured them that it was the traditional name for Ireland in the form of a woman who requires young men to sacrifice themselves for her.'

The two plays were put on at St Teresa's Temperance Hall, which seated only 300 spectators; but the impact, particularly of Maud Gonne as Cathleen, was powerful – and lasting. Arthur Griffith's journal, *United Irishman*, predicted that it would be the beginning of a new national theatre; so it proved, as the outcome was the establishment of the Abbey company, with its repertory soon supplemented by J.M. Synge, Lady Gregory and Sean O'Casey. Simply in terms of the theatre, Yeats' dream could be held to be artistically highly influential; but as he realised, its political importance also had to be considered, as helping to nourish the mood of readiness for a blood sacrifice which was to culminate in the Easter rising in 1916. The leaders of the rising were the kind of men who would have been stirred by the legend, and moved by Yeats' version of it; and this was later to disturb him.

> All that I have said and done
> Now that I am old and ill
> Turns into a question till
> I lie awake night after night
> And never get the answers right
> Did that play of mine send out
> Certain men the English shot?

Even if *Cathleen ni Houlihan* could not be held responsible, there can be no question that it was one of the fateful steps on the path to 1916.

Another remarkable instance of a dream's inspiration in the theatre is the story of William Archer's *The Green Goddess*, produced in 1921. Archer had made an impressive reputation in London as a journalist and theatre critic; but during the First World War, when he reached his sixties, he had begun to wonder whether he could maintain his output and, if not, how he could maintain his income. He had become interested in dreams after reading Freud on the subject, and had begun to record his own, which were posthumously to be fused into a book. 'Practice no doubt made him expert in the art of remembering and noting, for many of the dreams recorded in his voluminous notes are long and complicated,' his biographer Lt. Col. C. Archer observed. 'But the dream of September 1-2, 1919, which changed the course of his life, was a comparatively simple one.'

A week afterwards, Archer had written, 'What do you think I was doing all yesterday? Sketching a play which came to me in a dream!' For all his experience of writing his dreams out in detail, he was not sure how much of what he remembered had actually been in the dream. But he was certain it was responsible for the root idea – 'the idea that constitutes the originality (if any) of the theme', and he was able to complete a draft without difficulty.

More than thirty years before, he had collaborated with Bernard Shaw to try to write a play; Shaw's forte being dialogue, Archer's, construction. It had not worked; Shaw converted Archer's draft into a different and almost, from Archer's point of view, unrecognisable version, which was subsequently to launch Shaw's dramatist career as *Widowers' Houses*. Their friendship had nevertheless survived; and now Archer diffidently sent Shaw a draft of his new play, again suggesting collaboration. Shaw lightly rebuked him for being lazy. Archer then tried Harley Granville-Barker; Granville-Barker passed the draft to the producer Winthrop Ames in America; Ames picked George Arliss to play the lead as the suave Rajah who exploits an idol's powers; and a year after Archer had completed *The Green Goddess* it became the success of the season in New York – as it was again to be in London three years later.

'The fixed idea, which had obsessed him for thirty-five years and had become almost an article of faith, that he was incapable of producing theatrically effective dramatic work, could not be uprooted in a moment,' his biographer commented. But it had to yield to the heady experience of turning up at the theatre in New York and hearing that there might be no spare seat for him: the theatre, holding 1700 people, was sold out. So his ambition – 'simply a desire for filthy lucre' he insisted – 'I want an Old-Age Pension' – was massively fulfilled.

Archer's other dreams, however, as related in the compilation made of them after his death, are a disappointment. 'A noted and devastating variety of the genus bore is the habitual dream-narrator,' he had admitted, and his own confirmed that judgment. Contrasting them with the collection of Anna Kingsford's reveals the reason. Archer's were of the familiar type, departing from the constraints of real life, fascinating to the dreamer for the strange courses they take, but tedious to hear unless the story they tell is satisfying in its own right – that is, readable to somebody who is not aware that it is the product of a dream.

'I do not believe the inspiration falls from heaven,' Cocteau wrote in 1937 at the time he was producing his *Knights of the Round Table* – a distinctly bisexual version of the Arthurian legend. 'I think it rather the result of a profound indolence, and of our incapacity to put to work certain forces in ourselves.' These unknown forces, however, would occasionally take the opportunity to break through 'the kind of somnolence in which we indulge ourselves'. The poet, he insisted, 'is at the disposal of the night. His role is humble, he must clean house and await its due visitation.' In his own case, *The Knights of the Round Table* had been a visitation of this kind. 'I was sick and tired of writing when, one morning, after having slept poorly, I woke with a start and witnessed, as from a seat in the theatre, three acts which brought to life an epoch and characters about which I had no documentary information, and which I regarded as forbidding.' Only later had he been able to check his inspiration with the sources.

Of the major film directors of the recent past, Luis Buñuel, in his autobiography *My Last Breath* (1982), has paid tribute to the inventive power of his dreams. *Un Chien Andalou* (1928) – his first film, which scandalised audiences – 'was born of an encounter between my dreams and Dali's', he recalls in one chapter entitled 'Dreams and Reveries'. 'If someone were to tell me I had twenty years left, and ask me how I'd like to spend them, I'd reply "Give me two hours a day of activity, and I'll take the other twenty-two in dreams"' – provided, he wisely adds, he can remember them.

Poets

Young writers uncertain whether to concentrate upon prose or verse, Charles Lamb once advised, should decide by examining the texture of their dreams; 'if these are prosaic, they may depend upon it they have not much to expect in a creative way from their artificial ones.'

Certainly the list of works by poets which have come to them in dreams would be even longer than that of authors – and in one respect even more remarkable; the number of times they have been delivered as if by dictation, or on a video screen. Using the third person, Coleridge recalled in 1816 how, nearly twenty years earlier, Kubla Khan had materialised –

> all the images rose up before him as things, with a parallel production of the correspondent expressions, without any sensation or consciousness of effort. On awakening he appeared to himself to have a distinct recollection of the whole, and taking his pen, ink and paper, instantly and eagerly wrote down the lines that are here preserved. At this moment he was unfortunately called out by a person on business from Porlock, and detained by him above an hour, and on his return to his room, found, to his no small surprise and mortification, that though he still retained some vague and dim recollection of the general purport of the vision, yet, with the exception of some eight or ten scattered lines and images, all the rest had passed away like the images on the surface of a stream into which a stone has been cast, but, alas! without the restoration of the latter!

Doubts have been cast on the reliability of Coleridge's memory in relation to this episode; but there is no question about his reliance on dreaming. For him, 'there was no conscious division between day and night, between not only dreams and intuitions, but dreams and pure reason,' the critic and poet Arthur Symons insisted; 'we find him, in almost all his great poems, frankly taking not only his substance, but his manner, from dreams, as he dramatises them after a logic and a passion of their own.' It was this capacity for infusing the dream material with his personal logic, Symons went on, which distinguishes Coleridge from Blake, where the verse is 'literally unconscious'. There is a sense in which all Blake's verse was dreamed up. He regarded himself as a medium through whom the divine force poured, rather than a creative dreamer.

Goethe believed he owed some of his facility in verse to the 'invisible genius' which Wilhelm, in *The Travelling Years* (1821), described as 'whispering something rhythmical to me, so that on my walks I always keep step to it.' Sometimes his poems were composed in what, if his protégé Peter Eckermann's version of his words is to be trusted, amounted to automatic writing.

They have been preceded by no impressions or forebodings, but have come suddenly upon me, and have insisted on being composed immediately, so that I have felt an instinctive and dreamy impulse to write them down on the spot. In such a somnambulistic condition, it has often happened that I have had a sheet of paper lying before me all aslant and I have not discovered it till all has been written, or I have found no room to write any more.

Trying to write a ballad with the refrain 'Only the song of a secret bird', Swinburne found to his irritation, according to his biographer Edmund Gosse, that it would not come for him, and went disconsolately to bed. In the morning, he was able to write it out without so much as a pause. In Swinburne's case, he was not aware of dreaming. The first three stanzas of 'A Vision of Spring in Winter', he noted, came in the course of a night when he was neither dreaming nor on the borderline of sleep, but in a sound sleep from which he awoke to write them down. The next morning he feared to find them nonsense, but they needed no alteration.

John Masefield's poem 'The Woman Speaks' came to him in a dream in which he became aware of 'a tall lady dressed for out-of-doors with furs and a picture hat'. In the dream he knew of her past, and that she was in Lincoln's Inn Fields on a Sunday morning. As she moved out of the dream, 'the whole of the poem appeared in high relief on an oblong metal plate', from which he wrote it down.

> Bitter it is, indeed in human fate
> When life's supreme temptation comes too late.
> I had a ten years' schooling, where I won
> Prizes for headache and caparison.
> I married well; I kept a husband warm
> With twenty general years of gentle charm.
> We wandered much, where'er our kind resort,
> But not till Sunday to the Inns of Court.
> So then imagine what a joy to see
> The town's grey, vast and unappeaséd sea
> Suddenly still, and what a hell to learn
> Life might be quiet, could I but return.

A.C. Benson's curious verse 'The Phoenix', written in 1884, relates how the fabled bird propagated its species by flying off to die by fire, the next generation rising from the ashes. It consisted of four quatrains in a jingling eccentric metre.

> By feathers green, across Casbeen
> The pilgrims track the Phoenix flown
> By gems he strewed in wastes and wood
> And jewelled plumes at random thrown

Asked how he came to write it, Benson explained, 'I dreamed the whole poem in a dream, in 1884, I think, and wrote it down in the middle of the night on a scrap of paper by my bedside.' He had never had a similar experience, before or after; nor was it in a style he ever attempted at any other time. 'I can really offer no explanation either of the idea of the poem or its interpretation.' As it had come to him with no volition of his own he could neither understand the symbolism nor interpret it.

Verses poured from Anna Kingsford in her dreams; all she had to do was write them down.

> Eyes of the dawning in heaven?
> Sparks from the opening of hell?
> Gleams from the altar-lamps seven?
> Can you tell?
>
> Is it the glare of a fire?
> Is it the breaking of day?
> Birth-lights, or funeral pyre?
> Who shall say?

A cynic might comment that the world would not be a poorer place if her verses, and for that matter Benson's 'Phoenix', had remained unrecorded; and there are many examples of dream poems which, on awakening, have turned out to be absurd. As the German poet Friedrich Hebbel noted in his diary in 1838, when he was working on his tragedy Judith he had dreamed a poem, and was pleased with it in his dream, but as he got closer to awaking became dissatisfied with it, and could not recollect it when he awoke. For his part, though, he felt certain that 'the strange stirrings of self-consciousness that always precede waking, and

cause us to look mistrustfully at the dream-state we are in, are responsible
for numbing the psyche's poetic working and killing off the very living
germ of that precious idea, like a sudden blast of cold air, so that when I
awoke the idea was paralysed.' Poems of value could be lost, he believed,
because the critical jealous awakening mind blocked recollection of them.

   Although there is no method by which the role of forgotten dreams can
be assessed – whether, or to what extent, they are essential to the process
by which the mind provides us with information or inspiration during
sleep, to be available on waking – there is plenty of evidence, in the form
of dreams which are not remembered on waking but are recalled later, of
their possible role. In his essay on poetry's symbolism W.B. Yeats recalled
an occasion when, while engaged upon a poem, he had to stoop to pick up
a pen he had dropped; the action triggered remembrance of dreams he had
had for several nights, so striking that when he came out of what had
resembled a trance state, he could not for a time recall what he had been
doing that morning. In the making and understanding of a work of art, he
decided, 'we are lured to the threshold of sleep, and it may be far beyond
it, without knowing that we have ever set our feet upon the steps of horn
or of ivory.'

   Of his poem 'The Cap and Bells', Yeats recalled that he had dreamed the
story 'exactly as I have written it'.

> The jester walked in the garden
> The garden had fallen still
> He bade his soul rise upward
> And stand on the window sill.

The young queen, behind the window, would not listen to his soul; nor
to his heart when he offered that, too. But she was touched when, after his
death, she found he had left her his cap and bells.

> She opened her door and her window
> And the heart and the soul came through.

He had not been sure, at first, whether to put the dream – 'beautiful and
coherent, it gave me the sense of illumination and exaltation that one gets
from visions' – into prose or verse; but he had settled for the poem, which

had always meant a great deal to him. How did it come to him? 'Blake would have said, "the authors are in eternity", and I am not quite sure they can only be questioned in dreams.'

Artists

The most celebrated of dreams in the history of art – aside, that is, from those in which celebrated artists have tried to portray what they have seen in their dreams – is the one which proved to be the making of William Blake, according to his biographer Alexander Gilchrist.

By the end of 1788, the first portion of that singularly original and significant series of poems, by which of themselves Blake established a claim, however unrecognised, on the attention of his own, and after generations, had been written; and the illustrative designs in colour, to which he wedded them in inseparable loveliness, had been executed. The *Songs of Innocence* form the first section of the series he afterwards, in grouping the two together, suggestively named *Songs of Innocence and Experience*. But how publish? For standing with the public, or credit with the trade, he had none.

Blake knew he could be his own engraver, but not his own compositor; and for a time he could think of no solution. Inspiration at last came in 'a vision of the night' in which his dead brother Robert told him what to do.

On his rising in the morning, Mrs Blake went out with half-a-crown, all the money they had in the world, and out of that laid out 1s 10d. on the simple materials necessary for setting in practice the new revelation. Upon that investment of 1s 10d. he started what was to prove the principal means of support of his future life – the series of poems and writings illustrated by coloured plates, often highly finished afterwards by hand – which became the most efficient and durable means of revealing Blake's genius to the world.

—the method consisting of engraving words, as well as designs.
Blake's painting, like his writing, was so intimately bound up with his dreams that it would be futile to try to unravel the different strands, conscious and unconscious. With Turner this is a little easier as, according

to his biographer Philip Gilbert Hamerton, his landscapes bore 'about the same relation to reality that our dreams do when we dream of some place that we have visited'. Although a church, say, might be recognisable in the picture, it would lack certain features – not because of any lapse of memory on Turner's part, but because his work 'is not remembering, it is *dreaming*, and drawing or painting the dream.'

And now let us ask, what are the nature and qualities of the dream? Is it mere confusion, or is it orderly with an order of its own, which is not the order of reality? The answer is, that the dream has great order and unity. Let us think then of Turner henceforth simply as a poet who is not to be bound down by topographic facts of any kind ... He paid as much attention to truth of all kinds as poets generally do. He lived in a world of dreams, and the use of the world of reality, in his case, seems to have been only to supply suggestions and materials for the dreams.

In his *Les Rêves et les moyens de les diriger* (1867) the Marquis Hervey de Saint-Denys referred to an artist friend who had been following Hervey's experiments – designed to discover how to make better use of dreaming – and one night had a dream in which he was at work on a religious painting which he was, in fact, working on and which was giving him difficulties:

Suddenly an unknown person of majestic appearance entered his studio, took from him his palette and brushes, erased half the figures he had sketched in, changed the rest and added some others – in a word, transformed the whole composition of the picture. In a moment, the canvas was miraculously finished and the spectral painter had disappeared.

When Hervey's friend woke up he could not remember the whole composition; 'nevertheless he was able to derive considerable profit from the vision he had had, and thus owed one of his best canvasses to the inspiration he had received while asleep.'

Painters have occasionally acknowledged dreams as sources of inspiration since then. Gauguin's recumbent Tahitian girl in 'The Spirit Watches' (1899) was an embodiment of a dream. It was only with the arrival of surrealism, however, that artists began to regard dreams as an essential ingredient of their paintings, which were often designed to point the contrast between the real world and the dream world. André Breton's aim, as stated in the 1924 Surrealist manifesto, was 'to reconcile the contradiction which has hitherto existed between dream and reality in an absolute reality, in a super-reality'. But even dedicated surrealists, or their admirers, will find it hard to claim that reconciliation has been satisfactorily effected.

Musicians

The compositions of the 18th-century Italian violinist and composer Giuseppe Tartini are no longer often heard in concert halls or on the radio. But if any one of them is on a programme, it is likely to be the *Trillo del Diavole*, the 'Devil's Trill'; and the programme notes are likely to record one of his accounts of how he came to write it, when he was only twenty-one. In his dream, he had managed to make the devil his slave:

how great was my astonishment when I heard him play with consummate skill a sonata of such exquisite beauty as surpassed the boldest flights of my imagination. I felt enraptured, transported, enchanted; my breath was taken away, and I awoke. Seizing my violin I tried to retain the sounds I had heard. But it was in vain. The piece I then composed, The Devil's Sonata, was the best I ever wrote, but far below the one I had heard in my dream!

On a journey to Vienna in 1821, Beethoven dreamed that he had gone even further afield, to the Middle East; and while he was travelling there, a canon came into his head.

But scarcely did I awake when away flew the canon, and I could not recall any part of it. On returning here however, the next day, in the same carriage ... I resumed my dream journey, being on this occasion wide awake, when lo and behold! in accordance with the laws of association of ideas the same canon flashed across me; so being now awake I held it as fast as Menelaus did Proteus, only permitting it to be changed into three parts ...

In 1853, Wagner, describing how he composed, insisted that although he needed complete absorption in what he was doing, this was not the same as concentration: 'the only way to achieve my end is to let my mind rove back again into the realms of dreams.' And the French composer Vincent d'Indy disclosed that often, on waking, he had a faint memory of a composition, which he had to concentrate on remembering so that it would not be lost to him.

A possibility that remains to be explored is whether people who are not musical, or who regard themselves as being, say, tone deaf, could be prompted by dreams to gain or regain their musical faculties. Serjeant Edward Cox, a leading barrister in London in the 1870s, was a keen amateur psychologist who kept an open mind about bizarre phenomena, and was prepared to investigate them whenever they were brought to his attention. In one instance, his curiosity was directed to something which to him was inexplicable, which had occurred in his own life. He had a poor ear, he explained in his account of what happened, and no memory for music. Yet he dreamed he heard an entire opera of his own composition, 'overture and all, with a full band and half a dozen characters, each acting his own part, and the stage, the scenery, machinery and decoration, as perfect as any I have ever beheld'. Had he been a musician, this might have been attributed to wishful thinking. As it was, he could not help feeling that his mind, 'free to act without the encumbrances of the sleeping body and exercising its unfettered faculties far beyond their capacity in waking life, had made me a musician.'

'A certain reason'

'I am in no way facetious, nor disposed for the mirth and galliardize of company,' Sir Thomas Browne remarked in *Religio Medici* (1635), 'yet in one dream I can compose a whole comedy, behold the action, apprehend the jests, and laugh myself awake at the conceits thereof; were my memory as faithful as my reason, I would never study but in my dreams.'

This has been the snag. Even when our galliardizing, as recollected on wakening, is recalled as brilliant, it can only rarely be exploited. That the *potential* for more effective exploitation is there, however, has often been claimed, notably by Ralph Waldo Emerson. We should study our dreams for self-knowledge, 'yet not the details, but the quality', he argued in his essay on demonology (1838). They had a poetic integrity and truth. 'Limbo and dust-hole of thought' though dreams might appear, they were presided over by a certain reason, too. Their extravagance from nature is yet within a higher nature. They seem to us to suggest a certain abundance and fluency of thought not familiar to the waking experience. They pique us by independence of us, yet we know ourselves in this mad crowd, and owe to dreams a certain divination and wisdom. My dreams are not *me*, they are not Nature, or the Not-me; they are both. They have a double consciousness, phantoms that rise the creations of our fancy, but they act like mutineers and fire on their commander ...

Robert Graves would have agreed. *The Meaning of Dreams*, published in 1924, is disappointingly slight, but it was an attempt to demonstrate what he described as 'the constructive and direct powers of this fantastic method of thought, a proof of the value of dreams on their own account.'

'Everybody takes his own dreams seriously, but yawns at the breakfast table when somebody else begins to tell the adventures of the night before,' Helen Keller realised when she embarked on her 'Dream World' chapter in *The World We Live In* (1933). Yet she felt compelled to deal with the subject because so often people – particularly scientists – had assumed that somebody who is blind, almost from birth (in her case, deaf as well) dwell in a world that was 'flat, colourless, without perspective, with little thickness and less solidity – a vast solitude of soundless space'. Her dreams seemed to her to be little different from those of others: some coherent, some inconsequent, some amoral ('the moral inconsistency of dreams is glaring. Mine grow less and less accordant with my proper principles,' she admitted. 'I ascribe to those I love best acts and words which it mortifies me to remember, and I cast reproach after reproach upon them,' so that sometimes she longed to dream no more.) 'Oh, dreams, what opprobrium I heap upon you – you, the most pointless things imaginable,' she lamented.

Yet remove the dream-world and the loss is inconceivable. The magic spell which binds poetry together is broken. The splendour of art and the soaring light of imagination are lessened because no phantom of fadeless sunsets and flowers urges onwards to a goal. Gone is the mute permission or contrivance which emboldens the sound to mock the limits of time and space, forecast and gather in harvests of achievement for ages yet unborn. Blot out dreams, and the blind lose one of their chief comforts; for in the visions of sleep they behold their belief in the seeing mind and their expectation of light beyond the blank, narrow night justified.

She could recall 'few fine thoughtful poems, few works of art, or any system of philosophy,' Helen Keller concluded, 'in which there is no evidence that dream-fantasies symbolise truths concealed by phenomena.'

Yet perhaps the most impressive tributes to dreams as the source of inspiration have come from two 19th-century physicians, John Addington Symonds – father of the author of that name – and Henry Maudsley. Symonds gave two lectures on the subject of sleep and dreams in Bristol in 1851; and in the second of them, he was concerned to emphasise the significance of the similarity between the imagination in dreams and in our waking lives. The essential difference, he pointed out, is simply that our minds in dreams do not actively and artificially go to work on the materials which the imagination provides: what we witness is forced upon us whether or not we desire it. But the imagination's powers are all the greater for that; Symonds went on to claim that what distinguished a genius from the rest of us is the ability to allow the imagination the free play it has in dreams, while making it serve his creativity. A clever man may put ideas together, but this requires conscious effort; 'In the works of genius we perceive no such marks of elaboration, unless in the finishing off.' He cited Milton's *Paradise Lost* as an example. 'The imagination of the genius, and that of the dreamer, are thus clearly allied in so far as they work by "an art unteachable, untaught".'

Maudsley had made his name as a physician who was skilled at handling nervous breakdowns; and his *Pathology of Mind*, first published in 1867, was for the most part a conventional survey of the neurophysiology of the time. On dreams, however, he declined to accept the prevailing view that they were meaningless. He did not attempt to deny 'the fantastical deviations from the ordinary tracks of association of ideas, the loss of volitional power over the ideas, the suspension of conscience, the distraction of the ego, and the seeming reality of dreams'; but he rejected totally the common notion that in dreaming there is a loss of the faculty of combining and arranging ideas.

True it is that there is usually a loss of the faculty of combining and arranging them as we do when we are awake; but one of the most remarkable features of dreaming, which has hardly had the consideration which it deserves, is the singular power of combining and arranging ideas into the most vivid dramas. It would be no great exaggeration to say that the dramatic powers of a dunce, in dreaming, exceed that which is displayed by the most imaginative writer in his waking state. When we reflect upon the extraordinary creations of dreams, and consider that the most stupid and unimaginative person often constructs scenes, creates characters, and contrives events with a remarkable intensity of conception, distinctness of outline, and exactness of details, putting into the mouths of his dramatic persons dialogues suited to their several characters, we might well conclude that there is, independently of will or consciousness, a natural tendency of ideas, however stirred, to combine and arrange themselves into a kind of drama, even though they have no known associations and appear quite independent of, if not antagonistic to, one another.

'Of all vanities,' Maudsley claimed, 'metaphysics is the vanity of vanities'; he regarded himself as a hard-headed pragmatist, a characteristic adopted enthusiastically by the school of psychiatry in London which bears his name. But in his views on dreams he was ahead of his time.

2

Problem-Solving in Dreams

'A good part of our sleep is peered out with visions and fantastical objects, wherein we are confessedly deceived,' Sir Thomas Browne observed in his essay on dreams. 'The day supplieth us with truths; the night with fictions and falsehoods.' Nevertheless he believed that 'divine impressions' might come through.

> That there should be divine dreams seems unreasonably doubted by Aristotle. That there are demoniacal dreams, we have little reason to doubt. Why may there not be angelical? If there be guardian spirits, they may not be inactively about us in sleep, but may sometimes order our dreams, and many strange hints, instigations or discourses, which are so amazing to us, may arise from such foundations.

The emergence of rationalism in the 18th century and positivism in the 19th made belief in guardian angels unfashionable; dreams themselves became suspect because of their longstanding occult associations. Still, a few writers were prepared to stand up for them, notably John Abercrombie, physician to Queen Victoria in Scotland, and author of *Inquiries Concerning the Intellectual Powers*, which went through some 16 editions between 1830 and 1855. Facts on record, he insisted, showed that there were mental operations in dreams of a more intellectual character than was generally appreciated; and he cited a testimonial from a colleague whom he admired, who had claimed that thoughts which he had in dreams, and even the way they were put, were so good in point of reasoning, illustration and language 'that he has used them in his college lectures, and in his written lucubrations'. The Marquis de Condorcet, too, a brilliant mathematician before he had made his name as philosopher and statesman at the time of the French Revolution, had 'related of himself that when engaged in some profound and obscure calculations, he was often obliged to leave them in an incomplete state, and retire to bed to rest; and that the remaining steps, and the conclusion of his calculations, had more than once presented themselves in his dreams.'

At the time when Abercrombie was writing, psychology and psychiatry had still to evolve into recognised disciplines; and it was left to physicians to deal with all the problems of the kind that would now be regarded as psychosomatic. Orthodoxy had not then hardened into the assumption that physical symptoms must have an organic cause; there was still a willingness to investigate the possibility of some emotional component in illness; and the role of sleep (or sleeplessness) and dreams received the kind of careful consideration that John Addington Symonds gave them in his Bristol lectures in 1851. Like Abercrombie, he emphasised that dreams had been useful to scientists; according to Benjamin Franklin's friend the physician Pierre Cabanis, Franklin 'so often formed correct and highly important conceptions of persons and political events in his sleep that he was inclined to view his dreams with superstitious reverence'; while the real fact was 'that the philosopher's acute and sagacious intellect was operating even in his sleep.' And in 1867 the Marquis Hervey de Saint-Denys, in his book on dreams, listed three philosopher-scientists who had credited their dreams with help in their work: the 17th century naturalist, mathematician and sage Jerome Cardan; the 18th century philosopher Étienne Connot de Condillac; and Jean Baptiste Biot, a noted French astronomer physicist in the early 19th century, who had himself told Hervey that 'on several occasions he had done useful work in his sleep.'

The leading London surgeon of the mid-19th century, too, Sir Benjamin Brodie, cited cases he knew about where dreams had presented answers to questions which had baffled the dreamers. He presented his *Psychological Inquiries* in the form of an argument between 'Crites' and 'Eubulus', but on this issue, at least, they were in agreement. 'I have heard of mathematicians who have solved problems in their sleep,' 'Crites' observed. 'An acquaintance of mine, a solicitor, was perplexed as to the legal management of a case which concerned one of his clients. In a dream he imagined a method of proceeding which had not occurred to him while he was awake and which he afterwards adopted with success.' 'Eubulus' concurred: 'A friend of mine, a distinguished chemist and natural philosopher, has assured me that he has more than once contrived an apparatus for an experiment which he proposed to make, in a dream; and another friend, who combines mathematical with all sorts of knowledge besides, has solved problems in his sleep, which had puzzled him when awake.'

Although these testimonials to the value of dreams were provided by men with established reputations, they were not sufficient to banish the stigma which had attached itself to dreaming on account of its past associations with the supernatural. 'It has been decided by the scientists,' Frederick Greenwood lamented in 1894, 'that dreams are entirely profitless.' Greenwood was one of the ablest and most influential of London newspaper editors at the time – under him, Francis Williams noted in *Dangerous Estate* (1957), 'the *Pall Mall Gazette* brought wit, lightness, urbanity and intellectual polish back into journalism at a time when the morning press had turned staid and dull' – and his *Imagination in Dreams* remains among the most perceptive of works on the subject. The dismissive attitude of scientists irritated him. 'My suggestion is that this is an undiscriminating mistake; and that imagination, which is a teaching faculty, reveals in dreams an originality and force far beyond all that it displays when we are awake,' he asserted. Dream imagination might mislead; but it was only necessary to look at the historical record 'to see that what imagination has done for Science (usually under the name of "inspiration") goes so far beyond all that Science could do for itself, that Reason is quite unable to explain its ways and means.' It had been the common experience of men of genius 'that their noblest thoughts, their keenest intuitions, seem to flash into the mind from without, rather than to spring up from within. They seem to proceed from some independent agency external to mind and yet at home in it; which is just what might be said of dreams.' By this time, however, scientists were unlikely to listen to anybody who was not himself a scientist, let alone a journalist, however distinguished.

The extent to which Greenwood's contentions were (and are) justified will never be known, as so many dreams which have played their part in the development of science may never come to light because the dreamers did not care to reveal them – or if they did, declined to describe the dream or identify themselves. 'The cases are numerous where questions have been answered, or problems solved, in dreams or during unconscious sleep,' Oliver Wendell Holmes observed in his *Mechanism in Thought and Morals* (1878), a pithy attack on the materialist creed which scientists had come to worship. Two of his most distinguished scientific colleagues in Harvard had admitted to Holmes that they had benefited from problem-solving in dreams; but they would not allow him to name them.

Biographers of eminent scientists, too, have often omitted all reference to stories of the way in which their subjects have had their inspiration from a dream. 'The whole of modern physics and its applications,' Louis Pauwels and Jacques Bergier claimed in their *Le Matin de Magiciens* (1960), is derived from a dream which Nils Bohr had when he was a student. He was on a sun, consisting of burning gas; 'planets whizzed by, whistling as they passed. They were attached to the sun by thin filaments, and revolved around it.' When he awoke, it dawned upon him that what he had seen was the long-sought-after model for the atom. That Bohr had such a dream has often been claimed, but the accounts of it differ wildly – the weirdest coming from Jeremy Taylor in *Dream Work* (1983). Bohr's dream, according to Taylor, was of 'a pleasant day at the races', after which Bohr realised 'that the marked lanes on the race track within which the horses are required to run were analogies of the fixed and specific orbits that electrons are required to follow.' Small wonder that Bohr's admirers have felt they can ignore what many of them feel is a put-down – the notion that so important and influential a theory should have come to him in a dream.

Still, there is a sufficiency of well-attested cases of scientists obtaining valuable insights from dreams. There is little reason to doubt that in some ways the most important single contribution to the development of modern science, Cartesian philosophy, was triggered by the succession of three dreams which René Descartes had in 1619.

Descartes' dreams

Descartes, then aged 23, was in Ulm, at the winter quarters of the Prince of Nassau's army. He was already an accomplished mathematician, but his ambition was to be much more: a philosopher who would demonstrate that the precision of mathematics could be extended to embrace metaphysics. Progress had eluded him. Then on the night of 10 November, he had the dreams, 'the most important thing in my life'.

According to Adrien Baillet's biography – published in 1641, when Descartes was still living – in the first of the dreams Descartes was confronted by some ghosts who frightened him so much that he could hardly stand upright, and had to lean to his left to disguise the weakness in his right side. 'Embarrassed at having to walk in this way, he tried to straighten up; but a kind of whirlwind spun him round. He nearly fell with each step, until eventually, seeing a college open on his way, he went in to look for shelter and a cure for his pains.' His first idea was to go to the college chapel to pray; 'but finding he had just passed somebody he knew without giving him a salutation, he was about to return to greet him when he was driven violently back by the wind towards the chapel.' There, a man in the courtyard called him by name, telling him that Monsieur N. had something for him. Descartes assumed it must be a melon, brought from abroad. But he was disturbed to see that the people around were finding no difficulty in standing upright, though he himself was still wavering about, in spite of the fact the wind had gone down.

At this point he woke up, feeling a real pain in his side, 'which he feared meant that some evil spirit might be trying to seduce him.' He turned on his right side, 'and prayed to God to keep him from the evil influence of the dream, and all the calamities that he could expect as punishment for his sins.' Falling asleep again, 'he immediately had another dream, in which he believed he heard a loud explosion which he took to be a clap of thunder.' When he woke up, frightened, the room appeared to be full of sparks – something that had happened to him before, but on this occasion he decided 'to look to philosophy for an explanation'; and this calmed his fears. He was able to relax and fall asleep again.

In the third dream, Descartes saw a book on a table, without knowing how it had come to be there. 'Opening it, he was glad to find it was a dictionary, as he hoped it would prove to be useful.' He then realised that his hand was on another book, which he also had not seen before. He had no idea where it could have come from. It turned out to be a collection of poems by various authors. The dream then became confused, with the book of poems vanishing and reappearing.

The impact of the dreams was such that Descartes was trying to interpret them as they went along. God, he decided, remained his only refuge – but this was not the God of his childhood. The God of his adult self must surely be chiding him for his weakness, driving him forward to his destiny. The clap of thunder was an intimation that the spirit of Truth had descended upon him: the books, that poetry, as well as philosophy, had a role to play in the acquisition of wisdom. And the melon? Coyly, Descartes suggested it invoked 'the charms of solitude, but presented by purely human solicitations'. Freud was to be more explicit: 'if we make allowances for the language of the day, it is obvious that it is a question of fantasies about women conducive to masturbation.' (In pornographic lore, a melon is the most valued of masturbatory adjuncts.)

Surveying the dreams and Descartes' interpretation, Raymond de Becker came to the conclusion in his *Understanding of Dreams* (1968) that it does not matter whether it was correct. The important point was that Descartes believed in it, and from it 'received the illumination of what he later considered to be the greatest of his discoveries: the unity of all the human sciences.' More than that: 'the centuries since Descartes would have been quite different if, on the night of 10 November, 1619, the unilateralism of the philosopher's first approaches had not been counter-balanced by three dreams expressing his unconscious anguish and revolt.'

This is not a view that has commended itself to Christians, who feel that true enlightenment does not come in so slipshod a manner. Jacques Maritain, the Catholic philosopher-propagandist, surmised that the dreams had been excited in a philosopher's brain by malign Rosicrucian influences. Rationalists have found the dreams even more embarrassing. Although Descartes' theories about dreaming have been endlessly discussed and dissected by philosophers since, it is rare for them even to mention the three which, that November night, changed the course of his life.

'Let us learn to dream'

In a few cases it has been difficult for sceptics to discount the evidence for the importance of dreams for science, such as those of Friedrich Kekulé, Professor of Chemistry at the University of Ghent, in the later years of the 19th century. His were a little unusual, in that they came in reveries during which he seemed to be able to shut off consciousness for a time, so that he could let the solutions to his problems come through and then catch them before they slipped from memory. There was no doubt in his mind, though, that they were dreams.

One fine summer evening while Kekulé was living in London, he was returning home by the last bus through the deserted streets when

I fell into a reverie and lo! the atoms were gambolling before my eyes. Whenever hitherto, these diminutive beings had appeared to me, they had always been in motion; but up to that time, I had never been able to discern the nature of their motion. Now, however, I saw how, frequently, two smaller atoms united to form a pair, how a larger one embraced the smaller ones; how still larger ones kept hold of three or even four of the smaller; whilst the whole kept whirling in a giddy dance.

He saw, too, how 'the larger ones formed a chain'; and he spent part of the night sketching these 'dream forms', which were to provide him with his theory of the constitution of molecules.

These reveries were periodically to assist him for years; in particular the last of them. While he was dozing in a chair in front of a fire, atoms began to gambol before his eyes.

This time the smaller groups kept modestly in the background. My mental eye, rendered more acute by repeated visions of this kind, could now distinguish larger structures of manifold confirmation; long rows, sometimes more closely fitted together; all twining and twisting in snakelike motion. But look! What was that? One of the snakes had seized hold of its own tail, and the form whirled mockingly before my eyes. As if by a flash of lightning I awoke.

Kekulé's realisation that the molecules of certain compounds are closed chains was to prove of crucial importance. 'Let us learn to dream, gentlemen,' he felt justified in asserting, 'and then perhaps we will discover the truth.'

A comparably notable advance was the discovery of a way to classify the elements with reference to their atomic weights. One night in 1869 the Russian chemist Dmitri Mendeleev, weary after fruitless attempts to find the answer, went to bed and dreamed that he saw a table of the elements, in which they 'fell into place as required.' Waking, he was careful to record it. Only in one place, he was to find, was a correction necessary in what came to be known as the periodic table of the elements – another of the decisive developments in 19th-century science.

The greatest of 19th-century naturalists, Henri Fabre, asserted in his *Souvenirs entomologiques* that in his case, at least, sleep did not suspend mental activity, but enhanced it. He might wrestle in vain with a problem during the day; but at night 'a brilliant beacon flares up in my brain, and then I jump from my bed, light up my lamp and write down the solution the memory of which would otherwise be lost; like flashes of lightning these gleams vanish as suddenly as they appear.'

The most elaborate single case of problem-solving through a dream is
the one reported in 1883 by H.V. Hilprecht, Professor of Assyrian at the
University of Pennsylvania. He had spent a weary evening 'in a vain
attempt to decipher two small fragments of agate which were supposed to
belong to the finger-rings of some Babylonians', a task made the more
wearisome by the fact that he did not have the originals, only a hasty sketch
made by somebody who had been on the expedition which had found
them. For the book he was preparing, the best he could do was to surmise,
as one of the fragments had 'KU' on it, that it might be ascribed to King
Kurigalzu; the other, he decided, was unclassifiable. Baffled, weary and
exhausted, he went to bed, and was soon asleep.

Then I dreamed the following remarkable dream. A tall, thin priest
of the old pre-Christian Nippur, about forty years of age and clad in
a simple abba, led me to the treasure chamber of the temple, on the
south-east side. He went with me into a small, low-ceilinged room
without windows, in which there was a large wooden chest, while
scraps of agate and lapis lazuli lay scattered on the floor. Here he
addressed me as follows: 'The two fragments which you have
published separately upon pages 22 and 26, belong together, are not
finger-rings, and their history is as follows. King Kurigalzu [circa
1300 BC] once sent to the temple of Bel among other articles of agate
and lapis lazuli, an inscribed votive cylinder of agate. Then we priests
suddenly received the command to make for the statue of the god
Ninib a pair of earrings of agate. We were in great dismay, since
there was no agate as raw material at hand. In order to execute the
command there was nothing for us to do but cut the votive cylinder
into three parts, thus making three rings, each of which contained a
portion of the original inscription. The first two rings served as
earrings for the statue of the god; the two fragments which have
given you so much trouble are portions of them. If you will put the
two together you will have confirmation of my words. But the third
ring you have not yet found in the course of your excavations, and
you never will find it.' With this, the priest disappeared.

Hilprecht woke up at the conclusion of the dream, and immediately
related it to his wife, for fear he might forget it. In the morning, he
examined the fragments, and found that when he put them together as

instructed, allowing for some missing letters, he was able to read off the inscription: 'To the god Ninib, son of Bel, his Lord, has Kurigalzu, pontifex of Bel presented this.' His wife confirmed his story, and further confirmation was to come a few weeks later when he was able to examine the agate fragments themselves. They were in two different cases, as the curator had also not realised they were linked. When they were put together, they fitted.

Jean Louis Agassiz, the Swiss naturalist who became professor of Natural History at Harvard in 1848 and was one of the most bitter critics of Darwin, had a similar experience. In her biography of her husband, his widow recalled an occasion when he had been striving unsuccessfully to solve a problem which bothered him:

He had been for two weeks striving to decipher the somewhat obscure impression of a fossil fish on the stone slab in which it was preserved. Weary and perplexed, he put his work aside at last, and tried to dismiss it from his mind. Shortly after, he waked one night, persuaded that while asleep he had seen his fish with all the missing features perfectly restored. But when he tried to hold and make fast the image it escaped him. Nevertheless, he went early to the Jardin des Plantes, thinking that on looking anew at the impression he should see something which would put him on the track of his vision. In vain – the blurred record was as blank as ever.

The next night he saw the fish again, but with no more satisfactory result. When he awoke, it disappeared from his memory as before. Hoping that the same experience might be repeated on the third night, he placed a pencil and paper beside his bed before going to sleep.

Accordingly, toward morning, the fish reappeared in his dreams, confusedly at first but at last with such distinctness that he had no longer any doubt as to its zoological characters. Still half dreaming, in perfect darkness, he traced these characters on the sheet of paper at the bedside.

The next morning, Agassiz found that his sketch had given him the information he needed. Of much greater importance was the dream of the German pharmacologist Otto Loewi, one night in 1920. It had been assumed that control of bodily functions was maintained by the transmission of electrical impulses. But it had been found that certain drugs could have a similar effect; and nearly twenty years earlier, Loewi had speculated whether the electrical impulses might imitate a chemical action to act on muscles or glands. As he could not think of any experiment which would enable him to test this hypothesis, he had put it out of his mind until (by his own account)

> I awoke, turned on the light, and jotted down a few notes on a tiny slip of thin paper. Then I fell asleep again. It occurred to me at six o'clock in the morning that during the night I had written down something important, but I was unable to decipher the scrawl. The next night, at three o'clock, the idea returned. It was the design of an experiment to determine whether or not the hypothesis of chemical transmission that I had uttered seventeen years ago was correct. I got up immediately, went to the laboratory, and performed a simple experiment on a frog's heart according to the nocturnal design ...

The results of the experiment 'became the foundation of the theory of chemical transmission of the nervous impulse' for which sixteen years later Loewi received his Nobel Prize. And at least one recent Nobel Laureate, Albert Szent-Gyorgi, has credited 'sleeping on them' as the solution to his research problems: 'My brain must continue to think about them when I sleep because I wake up, sometimes in the middle of the night, with answers to questions that have been puzzling me.'

In some ways the most remarkable of all the cases of scientific inspiration in dreams is the career of Srinivasa Ramanujan. His name is not now familiar, and indeed he was never a public figure; he was always a 'mathematician's mathematician', according to James R. Newman, co-author of 'Mathematics and the Imagination', an article in the *Scientific American* in 1948. But within that circle, he was generally regarded as the most remarkable phenomenon of his generation.

Born in India in 1887 of a poor family, he showed himself as quite a prodigy at school; but it was the loan of G.S. Carr's *Synopsis of Pure Mathematics* (1886) when he was fourteen that 'awakened his genius'. The book offered him no more than its title suggested, summarising known theorems up to the 1870s; yet when he came to Britain in 1914 it was found that he was 'abreast, often ahead of, contemporary mathematical knowledge. Thus in a lone, mighty sweep he had succeeded in re-creating in his field through his own unaided powers, a rich half century of European mathematics.' It was doubtful, Newman thought, whether 'so prodigious a feat had ever before been accomplished in the history of thought'.

How was it accomplished? The boy's mother had been unable to bear a child until her father interceded for her with a local goddess. It was the goddess, Ramanujan used to assert, who inspired him by providing him with the formulae in dreams. When he woke up 'he would frequently note down results and verify them' – where he could: sometimes they were too far ahead of his waking mind. This pattern 'repeated itself throughout his life'; but it was to be cut off when he died of TB at the age of 31.

Mathematicians appear to have been among the most fortunate beneficiaries of assistance from dreams. In her *Studies in Dreams* (1921) Mary Arnold-Forster gave examples – including the case of her father, whose experience had been similar to Condorcet's:

> The mathematical problem that had baffled him came into the treatise on crystallography on which he was engaged. After working at it for many hours he was obliged to leave it unsolved and to go to bed. He fell into a deep sleep, and in the course of a long dream the answer to the problem came to him. He often described this to me and told me how in an early hour of the morning he awoke and wrote down the solution that the dream had given him, and anxiously tested its correctness.

Seeking support in the 1860s for the contention that dreams could provide useful information, the Marquis Hervey de Saint-Denys asked around among his friends; and one of them said that when he had been trying to solve a chess problem, which involved reaching checkmate from an unusual position in six moves,

> he dreamed that he had the chessboard in front of him, with each piece in its correct place. He continued his study of the problem, but this time the solution he was looking for appeared with marvellous lucidity. The game was continued and ended, and he clearly saw the disposition of the pieces on the board after each move.

So clear were the moves in his mind when he awoke that he promptly went back to his chessboard and played them by memory. The solution, he found, was correct.

But the most engaging of all such accounts, surely, concerns Ernst Chladni of Wittenberg who in the latter part of the 18th century became Europe's leading authority on acoustics. As related in *Such Stuff as Dreams*, (1967) edited by Brian Hill, the story is that one evening in 1789, tired after a walk, Chladni sat down to take a nap.

> Scarcely had he closed his eyes, when the image of an instrument such as he wished for, seemed to present itself before him, and terrified him so much that he awoke as if he had been struck with an electric shock. He immediately started up in a kind of enthusiasm; and made a series of experiments which convinced him that what he had seen was perfectly right – that he now had it in his power to carry it into execution. He made his experiments, and constructed his first instrument in so private a manner that no person knew anything of it. On the 8th March, 1790, his first instrument of this kind was completed, and in a few days he was able to play on it some easy pieces of music. To this instrument he gave the name of Euphon, which signifies an instrument which has a pleasant sound.

So the euphonium, or tenor tuba, was born.

Do scientists dream?

'Do visionary experiences lead to scientific breakthroughs?' *The Brain/ Mind Bulletin* asked on 28 July 1986 under the heading:

THE GREAT KEKULÉ DEBATE: DO SCIENTISTS DREAM?

Scientists, the article observed, have begun to discuss the issue in their professional journals. Predictably the reductionist camp is dismissive. 'Chemist John Wotis and molecular researcher Susanna Rudofsky think the famous story [of Kekulé] presents a damaging picture of scientists – and chemists in particular.' Chemists, they say, 'don't dream things up. They get hard facts, then formulate a chemical structure.'

It is futile to confront such people with the historical evidence, because for them history is anecdotal, and anecdote is not science. But some scientists today are no longer prepared to dismiss the evidence out of hand. In a 27-page review cited in the *Brain/Mind Bulletin*, 'the most extensive discussion of the origins of the benzene theory ever to appear', Alan Rocke and Bertrand Ramsay point out that Kekulé would hardly have publicly revealed the source of his inspiration as a joke; it could only have prompted ridicule. Telling the story when he did – as an elder statesman, at a gathering in his honour – indicated that he was anxious for it to be taken seriously.

Outside the neurobiological enclave, there has recently been a greater willingness on the part of commentators on dreams to accept their potential value as problem-solvers. Even Christopher Evans – though his theory that they fulfil the function of computer 'program clearance', allowing unwanted material to be removed, is not far from Crick's – was well aware that it failed to explain the kind of dreams which helped Kekulé and Fabre. Citing a psychologist's claim that if a person is consciously working on a problem, 'it is very likely that his or her unconscious will continue working in the dream state', Evans had to admit that deeply though he mistrusted 'the Freudian ring of the "unconscious"', its general thesis 'seems to be irrefutable; dreams continue the work begun during consciousness.' And in his *Dreams and Nightmares* (1954) James Hadfield was even more explicit. 'The function of dreams is, by the reproduction of the problems of the day, subjective or objective, to work towards their solution.' Sometimes the dreams simply call attention to the problems. Sometimes they offer inadequate answers. But in some cases, 'they offer real solutions to the practical problems of life.'

'Prompting' in dreams

If mathematicians and scientists can receive abstruse calculations in their dreams, should not the rest of us occasionally obtain a similar benefit? The answer is that some of us have been, and are still being, beneficiaries. Probably the luckiest – and also one of the most influential, in view of what the dream prompted him to do – was Elias Howe. The precise course which his dream took has been variously described; but the best known version is W.B. Kaempffert's, in his history of American inventions (1924).

Like many of his contemporaries, Howe had been trying fruitlessly to work out how a lockstitch sewing machine could be made. In his dream, in 1844, he was captured by savages who threatened him with death if he could not finish the machine.

Cold sweat poured down his brow, his hands shook with fear, his knees quaked. Try as he would, the inventor could not get the missing figure in the problem over which he had worked so long. All this was so real to him that he cried aloud. In the vision he saw himself surrounded by dark-skinned and painted warriors, who formed a hollow square about him and led him to a place of execution. Suddenly he noticed that near the heads of the spears which his guards carried, there were eye-shaped holes! He had solved the secret! What he needed was a needle with an eye near the point! He awoke from his dream, sprang out of bed, and at once made a whittled model of the eye-pointed needle, with which he brought his experiments to a successful close.

Although Howe promptly patented his invention, he had to spend seven years in poverty fighting off imitators. Still, he finally was able to enjoy the proceeds.

A friend of Mary Arnold-Forster assured her that he had been able to rely on his dreams to help him with mathematical problems, as she related in her *Studies in Dreams* (1921):

On more than one occasion when studying for examinations I worked for two or three days at a problem without arriving at the solution, and finally worked it in my dreams with such clearness that I was able to write down the correct result quite easily on awaking. On occasions during my schooldays the same thing used to happen, and if I met with very hard sums and riders I used to put pencil and paper by my bedside so as to be ready to write down the answer if it came to me in my sleep.

In her experience, Mary Arnold-Forster asserted, such cases might not be common, but they were not isolated.

To judge from the contributions to the Koestler Foundation, they still occur. While W.H. Moss, a Fellow of the Institute of Chartered Accountants, was serving in the army as a bombardier in Persia during the war he had three precognitive dreams, something that had not happened to

him before and has not happened since. Two of them simply foretold
something that was about to occur; but the third was surprising.

A man on duty with radar equipment woke me one night and told me
that the diesel engine power unit was malfunctioning. I suggested that
he 'tickled' the motor with a six-volt battery; he said he would do so
and left.
    Later on the man woke me again, and reported trouble with the
generator. I asked him if he'd tried the remedy I'd suggested. He
asked me what I was talking about; he had only just reported the
trouble. This was confirmed by others there, and I was astounded to
find that I had dreamt the first awakening. He tried the remedy and
it was successful.

Bombardier Moss, strangely enough, would not have suggested the
'tickling' had he been awake at the time; 'although I had heard of it during
training, about three years earlier, I had never used it or thought about it
after.'
As a student, Dr E.G. West, OBE, now a consultant metallurgical
engineer,

found that struggling to solve problems, particularly in mathematics
and design, I could sleep on them and frequently obtain a solution
during dreaming. However, if I did not immediately make a note on
waking, I forgot the vital points of my solution in the morning. I
therefore adopted the practice of taking a note pad and pencil to bed
and making a note of the essential elements of my dreamt solutions as
soon as I awoke from the dream. The results always seemed to be
satisfactory, and I used the technique on many occasions.

This technique, he then found, continued to be useful during his
professional career, 'not so much solving mathematical problems, but
obtaining useful indications of how particular aspects of consulting jobs
could be tackled and reports of evidence could be presented' – a form of
dreaming which, he came to believe, is 'simply an extension of one's
waking thought processes' conducted without the accompanying distraction of working life.
This extension of waking thought-processes, clearly, can take many

different forms. It has been known to act as a tutor. In *Le Sommeil et les rêves* (1861) the science writer Alfred Maury described how, many years earlier when he was learning English,

> I was above all trying to come to grips with verbs followed by prepositions. I had the following dream: I was speaking English and, wanting to tell somebody that I had visited her the previous evening, I used the expression 'I called for you yesterday.' That's not quite right, came the reply; we say 'I called on you yesterday.' The next day, when I awoke, the memory of that detail of my dream was very clear. I took the grammar which lay on the table by my bed and checked; the imaginary person had been quite correct.

Once, at least, in recent times, by correcting an error the dream 'prompter' has been the means of restoring a despondent individual to confidence and back to fame and fortune. The American golfer Jack Nicklaus was playing so badly at one point in his career that he was not dissatisfied if he managed to get round a course in 76; but one night he dreamed about his golf swing. 'I was hitting them pretty good in the dream and all at once I realised I wasn't holding the club the way I've actually been holding it lately,' he told a reporter.

> I've been having trouble collapsing my right arm taking the club head away from the ball, but I was doing it perfectly in my sleep. So when I came to the course yesterday morning, I tried it the way I did in my dream and it worked. I shot a 68 yesterday and a 65 today and believe me it's a lot more fun this way. I feel kind of foolish admitting it, but it really happened in a dream. All I had to do was change my grip just a little.

The memory-jogger

If scientific and technical problems can find solutions in dreams, could problems of other kinds also be solved? The first writer to examine the issue in some detail was John Abercrombie, who devoted a section of his *Inquiries Concerning the Intellectual Powers* to a discussion of the way the powers operated during sleep. The main characteristics of dreaming, he admitted, were that the impressions received appeared to be real – 'the belief is not corrected, as in the waking stage, by comparing the conception with the things of the external world;' and that the impressions follow each other in ways 'over which we have no control; we cannot, as in the waking stage, vary the series, or stop it at our will.' But this did not mean that the impressions were necessarily unreliable. On the contrary, they could be extremely helpful – in particular, he argued, as memory-joggers; and he cited an example which had occurred to a particular friend of his, which could be relied upon in 'its most minute particulars'.

At a time when his friend was working as a bank-teller, an irritating client pushed ahead of the other people waiting to be attended to and demanded to be paid six pounds. He was trying to explain why, but with such a ferocious stammer that eventually one of the people behind him suggested that the teller should accede to the demand, simply to get rid of him. He did, and then forgot about the episode. Eight or nine months later, when the books had to be balanced, the teller was confronted with a deficiency of six pounds.

After a week of fruitlessly trying to find how the error arose, he returned home exhausted and went to bed.

He dreamt of being at his place in the bank – and the whole transaction with the stammerer passed before him in all its particulars. He awoke under a full impression that the dream was to lead him to the discovery of what he was so anxiously in search of; and on examination soon discovered that the sum paid to this person had been neglected to be inserted in the book of interests, and that it exactly accounted for the error in the balance.

To Abercrombie, the case appeared 'exceedingly remarkable', considering the time interval. Still, the teller had eventually remembered the episode; unlike the dreamer in a case which had intrigued Sir Walter Scott. The dreamer, 'Mr R.' (checking on the tale later, Robert Dale Owen was able to identify him as Mr Rutherford) was 'a gentleman of landed property' known to Scott, who was being prosecuted for arrears of *teind* – tithe – by a neighbouring nobleman. Rutherford was sure that his father had bought out the nobleman; but a search through his father's papers and the records of his lawyers revealed no trace of the receipt. Rather than fight the case in the courts, he had decided to go to Edinburgh and see if he could effect a compromise.

He went to bed with this resolution, and, with all the circumstances of the case floating upon his mind, had a dream to the following purpose. His father, who had been many years dead, appeared to him, he thought, and asked him why he was disturbed in his mind. In dreams men are not surprised at such apparitions. Mr Rutherford thought that he informed his father of the cause of his distress, adding that the payment of a considerable sum of money was the more unpleasant to him because he had a strong consciousness that it was not due, though he was unable to recover any evidence in support of his belief. 'You are right, my son,' replied the paternal shade: 'I did acquire right to these *teinds*, for payment of which you are now prosecuted. The papers relating to the transaction are in the hands of Mr – a writer (or attorney), who is now retired from professional business and resides at Inveresk, near Edinburgh. He was a person whom I employed on that occasion for a particular reason, but who never, on any other occasion, transacted business on my account. It is very possible,' pursued the vision, 'that Mr – may have forgotten a matter which is now of a very old date, but you may call it to his recollection by this token, that when I came to pay his account, there was difficulty in getting change for a Portugal piece of gold, and we were forced to drink out the balance at a tavern.'

Inveresk happened to be near at hand and Rutherford, instead of going to the capital, was sufficiently impressed by his dream to walk across and call on the retired attorney.

Without saying anything of the vision, he inquired whether he ever remembered having conducted such a matter for his deceased father. The old gentleman could not, at first, bring the circumstance to his recollection; but on mention of the Portugal piece of gold, the whole returned upon his memory. He made an immediate search for the papers, and recovered them; so that Mr Rutherford carried to Edinburgh, the documents necessary to gain the cause which he was on the verge of losing.

Walter Scott had maintained that there was nothing supernatural about the dream, and Abercrombie agreed; there was every reason to believe, he argued, 'that the gentleman had heard the circumstances from his father, but had entirely forgotten them, until the frequent and intense application of his mind to the subject with which they were connected, at length gave rise to a train of association which recalled them in the dream.' But sometimes this kind of explanation is less plausible.

Horace Hutchinson – better known for his writing on golf, but an assiduous collector of dreams – recalled how in 1870 a friend of his, an engineer, had been put in charge of a stretch of road, part of his routine being to ensure that the bridges on it were safe. The engineer reported:

One day I dreamt in a most vivid manner that I saw an exact picture of a certain small bridge. All the surroundings were complete, and left no doubt as to which bridge it was. A voice at the same moment said to me, 'Go and look at that bridge.' This was said distinctly three times. In the morning the dream still persisted in my mind, and so impressed me that I rode off at once about six miles to the bridge. Nothing was to be seen out of the ordinary. The small stream was, however, coming down in flood. On walking into the water, I found to my astonishment that the foundations of the bridge had been entirely undermined and washed away. It was a marvel that it was still standing. Of course, the work necessary for preserving the bridge was done.

He told Hutchinson that but for his dream the bridge would have collapsed, as ordinarily he would not have made such an inspection. He had never in his life had a similar experience: 'I have no doubt,' he concluded, 'that a special warning was given me by a higher intelligence.'

At that time, the existence of the subconscious mind had yet to be accepted, or it might have been nominated as the 'higher intelligence' involved. But this would hardly account for the experience of William Cavendish-Bentinck, sixth Duke of Portland, when he was concerned in the preparations for the Coronation of King Edward VII in 1901.

The State coach had to pass through the Arch at the Horse Guards on the way to Westminster Abbey. I dreamed that it stuck in the Arch, and that some of the Life Guards on duty were compelled to hew off the crown upon the coach before it could be freed. When I told the Crown Equerry, Colonel Ewart, he laughed and said, 'What do dreams matter?' 'At all events,' I replied, 'let us have the coach and

Arch measured.' So this was done, and to my astonishment, we found that the Arch was nearly two feet too low to allow the coach to pass through. I returned to Colonel Ewart in triumph, and said, 'What do you think of dreams now?' 'I think it's damned fortunate you had one,' he replied. It appears that the State coach had not been driven through the Arch for some time, and that the level of the road had since been raised during repairs.

That dreams still occasionally spare people from embarrassment or worse, is clear from some of the Koestler Foundation's correspondents; notably Gordon Pearson, a chartered surveyor.

A few years ago I spent several weeks working late each night in order to prepare tender documents for a large building project.
    One night, asleep in bed, I was awakened by a severe jolt, which left me temporarily frightened. I had dreamed that I had made an error in the work that had kept me so busy for so long. I was unable to go to sleep again until I had made a written note of the possible error. Upon awakening the following morning I found the note, so I checked my work when I got to the office. I found I had made a major error which, had it not been corrected, would have cost the client dear, and caused severe embarrassment to my employer.

Often the memory-jogging has been done by a vision of a deceased parent or loved one, as if to emphasise the significance of the information imparted. A correspondent of Frederick Greenwood's (whom he did not identify; but he asserted in his *Imagination in Dreams* (1894) that she was 'honourably known to the world') told him that when her father died his business and his house had been left to her mother who, having no experience in such matters, was easily robbed. The daughter barely knew the house, as earlier she had been either at boarding school or in the family's holiday home. One night she had stayed up reading by candlelight in the drawing room.

Even now, looking back, I cannot be convinced that I fell asleep, or decide that what was perhaps a dream was not a vision. On hearing a church-bell ring the first quarter past one I looked up from my book. Opposite was my dead father's favourite armchair. To my astonishment a black veil seemed to lie over it. While I rubbed my eyes and again stared, the veil lightened till it became gray; and in the ugly mist a shape became visible. With a slowness which still fills me with horror to remember, the shape took the lineaments of my father: not as I had seen him dead, but grayer, thinner, and with a dreadful clayey look about him. Taking up the candle he told me to follow him and learn the secret of the robberies, which, he said, were greater than they were supposed to be; and at the same time he named as culprit a man-servant whom we all trusted and were attached to. As for me, I should as soon have suspected my mother as this man. I followed my father downstairs into parts of the house that were unfamiliar to me. He opened the doors without any difficulty, though the keys were upstairs in my mother's room.

She was certain she had never even heard the word 'sky-light' until her father then used it, showing one to her. In his time it had always been locked at night. Since his death this had been neglected, 'and by means of this dream it was soon proved that thieves who were the accomplices of a trusted servant used to come in, and go out, through this skylight.'

When Mrs Patrick Campbell – Liza Doolittle in the first production of *Pygmalion*, a part which Bernard Shaw had written for her – was growing old, she lost her charm and most of her former friends; but when she fell ill, one who looked after her in the 1930s was Sara Allgood, who had made her name at the Abbey Theatre in Dublin. Shortly before the outbreak of the Second World War 'Mrs Pat' thought she was going to die; but she recovered, and decided to live out her remaining days in Paris. Before she left, she gave Sara a teapot and a framed water-colour of a heron as mementoes.

Sara was one of a number of members of the Abbey Company who were eventually lured to Hollywood, there to earn more in a week than she might have expected to earn at the Abbey Theatre in a year. She had grown up with the belief that the first dream to be dreamt in a new home will come true; and according to her friend Patrick Mahoney, the first dream she had in a house she had bought in Beverly Hills

had the same exaggerated clearness as is characteristic of stereoscopic vision. On the horizon there appeared, as though by magic, a locomotive which whistled by at full speed. Everything was in its logical place as in a real view, but the absolutely distinctive feature was the emotion aroused when the train came to an abrupt halt some distance after it had passed the station. Mrs Campbell alighted and came running up to her old friend. She was looking pale and wan, as though she had been undergoing a great strain.

Before Sara could express her astonishment, Mrs Campbell held a hushed finger to her lips. 'Have you found my gift from the grave? Look behind the picture.' These words were uttered with that sublime air of boredom which had been one of her admired feats on the stage.

The next morning Sara took down the water-colour. Removing its backing, she found a caricature of 'Mrs Pat' by Max Beerbohm – worth, it was reckoned, rather more than $1,000. She had known that Mrs Pat had moved from Paris to Pau, in the south-west of France where she found herself in 1940 under the German occupation; but it had been reported that all was well with her. A few days after the dream Sara read the news of her death.

One of the contributors to Oliver Stevens' *Mystery of Dreams*, a collection mainly from American sources published in 1950, came from an old friend of his whom he did not identify, but evidently trusted. Her husband had died in the summer of 1929, just after they had put down 10 per cent, $5,000, for a house; and she asked the Trust which was in charge of the money to sell whatever bonds seemed best to them, to complete the payment. They did not do so, perhaps because the value of stock was surging up. She had found that the Trust held fifty shares in First National Bank Stock; when she first looked up the price it was $650 a share, and by the end of August it had topped the $1,000 mark.

At this time I was sleeping very badly and on this particular night I remember getting to sleep very late. Before I awakened I had a dream – the most vivid one that I have ever had. Up to that time (not three months after his death) I had never dreamed of my husband, and rarely dreamed at all. I dreamed that he was standing in front of his dresser, tying his necktie, then combing his hair, dressed ready to go down for breakfast. (I usually had a tray upstairs and he and my daughter, a hearty breakfast downstairs together.) He said to me: 'I am going to put in a call to E.W.C. and ask him what's doing in First

National Bank Stock. That stock only pays $175.00 three times a year (I did not know what it paid) and it is now selling for $1,050 a share. Unless they are going to give a split-up I think it's the best thing to sell to pay for our new home.' As he turned to go out of the room he smiled at me and said, 'I'll see you later,' and as the door closed, it awakened me! For a moment I believed he had been there just as usual! It was all so amazingly real to me – his voice and looks, and gestures, and personality! It was cruelly heart-breaking to accept the fact that it was just a dream.

When she had recovered from the shock she rang a friend at First National, who told her that an hour before, shares were selling at $1,375. As he thought the price over-inflated, he agreed with her that her shares should be sold to buy the house. Her brother-in-law, too, was persuaded to give his agreement; and she then called a Vice-President of the Trust to ask him to put the sale through immediately. He was reluctant, but eventually agreed. As it turned out, she sold at the top of the market. Friends of hers, who hung on to their shares, lost every dollar in the great crash.

In a case sent to the Foundation, a parent's prompting may have had a decisive influence on a career – though as it happened, Colin Forrest was destined to move on to another one, as a professional baritone. At the time, he was anxious to qualify as a nurse, and was working to pass his next examination. In a dream

I saw my dead father (a naval surgeon) looking about 25 years old, in a brilliant white gown; and he said 'the thyroid gland'. My first nursing exam was next day at the Royal West Sussex Hospital, Chichester, and I was so struck with the dream that I looked up the thyroid that morning. There it was, in the exam, so I could answer it well.

Lost and found

Probably the most frequently reported 'prompting' dreams are those in which some valued lost object has been retrieved, as a result of the information provided. Again, it has often been given by the vision of someone who, when the dreamers awake, they know to be dead.

The most valuable of all the possessions found in this way must surely be the missing last thirteen cantos of Dante's *Paradiso*. According to Boccaccio, Dante's family and friends were unable to find them in spite of a careful and protracted search, and had begun to assume that he had left *Paradiso* unfinished. Some eight months after Dante's death, however, one of his disciples, Piero Giardino, was woken up one night by Dante's son Jacopo

who told him that that night while he was asleep, his father Dante had appeared to him, clothed in the purest white, and his face resplendent with an extraordinary light; then he, Jacopo, asked him if he lived, and that Dante had replied: 'Yes, but in the true life, not our life.'

Then he, Jacopo, asked him if he had completed his work before passing into the true life, and if he had done so, what had become of that part which was missing, which none of them had been able to find. To this Dante seemed to answer: 'Yes, I finished it,' and then took him, Jacopo, by the hand and led him into that chamber in which he, Dante, had been accustomed to sleep when he lived in this life; and, touching one of the walls, he said: 'What you have sought for so much is here;' and at these words both Dante and sleep fled from Jacopo at once.

Jacopo, unable to sleep, had decided to rouse Giardino so that they could conduct the search together, to find whether the directions (which were very clear in Jacopo's memory) were the work of a true spirit, or a delusion.

For which purpose, though it was still far in night, they set off together, and went to the house in which Dante resided at the time of his death. Having called up its present owner, he admitted them, and they went to the place thus pointed out; there they found a mat fixed to the wall, as they had always been used to see it in past days; they lifted it gently up, when they found a little window in the wall, never before seen by any of them, nor did they even know that it was there.

In it they found several writings, all mouldy from the dampness of the walls, and had they remained there longer, in a little while they would have crumbled away. Having thoroughly cleared away the mould, they found them to be the thirteen cantos that had been wanting to complete the *Commedia*.

Boccaccio was of Jacopo's generation, and had every opportunity to hear the story from those concerned in it. How fortunate, he unkindly commented, that the discovery had relieved Jacopo of an ambition to finish the *Paradiso* himself.

Such messages, Andrew Lang – historian, folklore expert, classicist – noted in his *Book of Dreams and Ghosts* (1897), can provide information which subsequently turns out to be correct, of a kind which the dreamer 'did not know that he knew, and was very anxious to know.' He cited the case of a barrister of his acquaintance who sat up late one night to write letters, and after midnight went out to post them.

On undressing he missed a cheque for a large sum, which he had received during the day. He hunted everywhere in vain, went to bed, slept, and dreamed that he saw the cheque curled round an area railing not far from his own door. He woke, got up, dressed, walked down the street and found his cheque in the place he had dreamed of. In his opinion he had noticed it fall from his pocket as he had walked to the letterbox, without consciously remarking it, and his deeper memory awoke in slumber.

In 1884 Herbert J. Lewis sent an account to the Society for Psychical Research of an episode four years previously, when he had lost the landing order of a ship carrying iron ore to Cardiff, which

had to commence discharging at six o'clock the next morning. I received the landing order at four o'clock in the afternoon, and when I arrived at the office at six I found that I had lost it. During all the evening I was doing my utmost to find the officials of the Custom House to get a permit, as the loss was of the greatest importance, preventing the ship from discharging. I came home in a great degree of trouble about the matter, as I feared that I should lose my situation in consequence.

That night I dreamed that I saw the lost landing order lying in a crack in the wall under a desk in the Long Room of the Custom House.

At five the next morning I went down to the Custom House and got the keeper to get up and open it. I went to the spot of which I had dreamed, and found the paper in the very place. The ship was not ready to discharge at her proper time, and I went on board at seven, and delivered the landing order, saving her from all delay.

One of the cases investigated by the Society for Psychical Research in 1889 was of a dream which had led to the recovery of a lost gold brooch. On a visit to London Mrs A.M.Bickford Smith found, when she returned to her hotel after shopping, that it had vanished; and as she had been trying on clothes in a fitting room in Swan & Edgar's, she felt sure that she must have left it there, and asked them to look for it. They did, but could not find it.

I was very vexed, and worried about the brooch, and that night I dreamed that I should find it shut up in a number of the *Queen* newspaper that had been on the table, and in my dream I saw the very page where it would be. I had noticed one of the plates on that page. Directly after breakfast I went to Swan & Edgar's and asked to see the papers, at the same time telling the young lady about the dream, and where I had seen the brooch. The papers had been moved from that room, but were found, and to the astonishment of the young ladies, I said: 'This is the one that contains my brooch;' and there at the very page I expected I found it.

Mrs Bickford Smith's brother-in-law, who had been at the hotel and was involved in the search, confirmed her account.

Horace Hutchinson gave a number of cases in his 1901 collection, including one from 'C.H.H.' in America concerning the finding of a lost ring which he had been given by his sister when he was a youth. He and some friends had rigged up a swing in woodland by the Delaware, 'and they enjoyed themselves on it'. One evening he found that the ring was missing, and he spent much of the following day searching for it without success.

Went to bed thinking very seriously of the ring. Along towards morning had a very impressive dream. I saw the ring, covered by a little ridge of sand, between two footprints under the swing. That dream was so vivid that on awaking I could see the road, buildings, fences, trees, swing and sand, with the footprints therein, the same as in the dream, and as soon as it was light enough to see I started for that swing, not attempting to look for it on the way. On arriving at the swing I walked deliberately into the sand until I reached the before-mentioned ridge, between said footprints, and with the top of my boot, removed a little sand from the top of the ridge, and out rolled the ring. The birds were singing overhead in the trees, the river was rushing on its way to the sea, a train of cars on the York and Erie R.R. across the river passed along. I banged my head several times with my fist to make sure I was not still in the land of dreams; no, I was there, standing in the sand. And there lay the ring. There was no hallucination about that, but a good, square, honest, useful dream.

R.L. Megroz's *The Dream World* (1939) contained an unusual variant on the dream-finding of lost objects. The dreamer, a woman, would not allow him to use her name, but he had satisfied himself that her story was genuine.

In her home in Florence she had lost a ring which for her was of value both for its worth and for its associations. It had belonged to her grandmother, whose husband had given it to her; it had seven diamonds, for luck – 'and indeed luck had followed my grandparents, so that the ring had taken on a special significance.' The fact that she had left it on a table while workmen were in the house only made the loss more bitter; she feared that luck would desert her. But she was determined not to be morbid or superstitious about it, and by the time five months had passed she was resigned to her loss.

On the night of her dream she felt as she once had when under the influence of an anaesthetic, lifted on to another plane. There, she met a man who she had known when she was a child, about thirty years before, and who had been killed in a railway accident. He took a gold ring from his wedding finger, and placed it on the third finger of her right hand. It was loose; and holding on to it, so as to be sure not to lose it, she gradually became conscious that she was in her bedroom, and that what she had on her finger was her diamond ring. Contented, she fell asleep again. But when she woke up the ring had disappeared.

She could not believe that the ring had been a figment of her imagination. In some manner, she felt certain, it meant that she was destined to find it. She set out in search of it – to the derision of her friends, when she told them what had happened.

> For three days I covered old ground inquiring in shops to which stolen objects had sometimes been traced. I visited the only pawn office, a Government institution, but all in vain. Then while crossing the Ponte Vecchio towards evening on my way home, still glancing into the windows as I passed, in one of them I caught sight of my ring!
>
> Of the formalities that had to be gone through before my treasure was restored to me it would take too long to relate. But some details may be of interest. The ring had been taken to Venice and sold to a dealer there. He in his turn disposed of it to another who brought it back to Florence. It had changed hands many times before it was purchased by the dealer in whose window I had discovered it.
>
> But what seems to me a strange coincidence is that he had had it in his possession only three days – as his register, in perfect order, proved – only a few hours, in fact, before I had felt the ring on my finger.

Was it coincidence, she wondered? Was it not possible that she had had an experience of a kind which orthodox science rejected? 'Had the fact that the ring, holding certain magnetic qualities in affinity with other qualities in me because of long association and contact, made materialisation easy and possible as soon as it came into my close environment – for it was within a stone's throw of my house that I discovered it?' As far as she was concerned, this did not matter. The dream had done its work; 'the essential is that the ring is in my possession, whatever the explanation of the matter may be.'

In *The Invisible Picture* (1981) Louisa Rhine related the case of a 16-year-old Oregon girl who was just starting on her first job as an assistant to a dentist. He had asked her to collect a package containing gold foil, and to lock it in his cabinet. While she was removing the wrapping, there was a knock on the door and she left it to admit 'Frenchie', one of the town's 'characters', who had come to pick up something which the dentist had left for him. She went into an inner office and brought it out to him. When he left, she turned to the shallow drawer in which she had put the foil. It had gone.

'Frenchie', she knew, had often been in the local jail for disorderly conduct, but never for any serious crime. She had a vague recollection that she had heard the drawer being closed, softly; but to accuse him, she realised, would destroy him.

Worried nearly sick, she went to bed praying for guidance. Early, before dawn, she awoke from a vivid dream. She thought a voice had told her how to open the bottom drawer of the cabinet, pull it out and release a certain catch, push forward the drawer above and find the gold foil wedged against the back wall of the cabinet.

At daylight she rushed to the office, followed the directions – and found the envelope with the gold intact.

The next time she met 'Frenchie' he told her to be more careful: 'You just can't tell who might come wandering in.' Seeing the open drawer with the gold in it, he had closed it, and somehow in the process had tipped the envelope off the back into the recess.

In the hundreds of accounts of dreams which flowed in to J.B. Priestley following the *Monitor* programme in 1964, a number were of the discovery of lost objects. A woman who had lost her umbrella dreamed that she returned to a restaurant where she had had a meal; in reply to her inquiry about it, she was told in her dream, 'Mother took it upstairs and said she would keep it if nobody asked after it as she liked the bird-head handle.' On the strength of the dream she went to the restaurant and, according to her husband, a girl there *'spoke the very words in the dream'* and handed over the umbrella.

Research

In his *Second Sight in Daily Life* (1951) W.H.H. Sabine gave an instance of a dream which, he insisted, showed in 'the clearest possible way' that it should *not* be put in the extra-sensory category. Rather it pointed the way to a line of research which would be profitable: the use of dreams to solve problems.

Looking through a second-hand bookseller's catalogue, Sabine had come across a book published in 1801 purporting to elucidate the mysteries of Masonry: and he noted that on the title page there was a code

Ziydvjxyjpix

ty Qxzf & Oivjjxg Qvwgzjpix

Intrigued, he tried to break the code using the method prescribed in Poe's *Gold Bug* (1843), which he happened to have read not long before, based on the frequency with which letters appear in the English language – 'e', in particular. The sentence, however, was not long enough for this technique to be productive, and Sabine gave up the task as hopeless.

During the night he had a dream consisting of a single picture: the word

ARCHITECTURE

in violet coloured letters on a black ground. It did not occur to him to link it to the code when he woke up, until he happened to notice the catalogue, 'and it suddenly flashed across my mind that maybe "architecture" was that long word in code. 'So, to my considerable excitement, it proved,' and the rest of the solution was easy.

mc Seal and Written Signature

– 'mc', presumably, being short for 'masonic code'.

When, later in the 1950s, William Dement was conducting research into dreams at Stanford University, he decided he would investigate whether students there could use their dreams to help them to solve problems. He posed certain questions which, he suggested, they should study before going to sleep: for example

> The letters O.T.T.F.F. form the start of an infinite sequence. How are the successive letters determined, and what are the next two?
> H.I.J.K.L.M.N.O. form a word. What is it?

The answer to the first is that the initial letters represent One, Two, Three, Four, Five; the next two will be Six and Seven, and so on. The answer to the second is WATER; the sequence is 'H' to 'O' – H_2O.

Of over a thousand entries, in 87 cases dreams appeared to have some relevance, and although only seven students had direct 'hits', they were revealing. One student dreamt of being in a gallery.

> As I walked down the hall, I began to count the paintings – one, two, three, four, five … But as I came to the sixth and seventh, the paintings had been ripped from their frames! I stared at the empty frames with a peculiar feeling that some mystery was about to be

solved. Suddenly I realised that the sixth and seventh spaces were the solution to the problem.

In other cases, the dream information was not diagnosed correctly. One dreamer had a succession of dreams about water – swimming, sailing, watching rain – without realising that they were offering clues to the solution of 'H_2O'.

In 1983 the *New Scientist* suggested that its readers might like to take part in an experiment to see whether dreams can solve problems of a kind which would ordinarily baffle the waking mind. One of them was mathematical.

Using six line segments of equal lengths, can you construct four equilateral triangles such that the sides of the triangles are the same lengths as the line segments?

Eleven people wrote to Morton Schatzman, who was conducting the experiment, to relate how a dream had helped them to solve the problem. One, a student, dreamed that she was running her hand along some railings when six of them came together 'to form a kind of wigwam'. Later, her chemistry teacher appeared in the dream and said '109°28'.' The student knew that 109°28' was connected with tetrahedral molecules; and on waking, she realised that tetrahedrons consist of four equilateral triangles. That and the 'wigwam' gave her the clue to the solution, which was that the model would be a three-sided pyramid.

This student knew about tetrahedrons; but one of the solvers had no mathematical or scientific abilities. Her dream had been directly about the puzzle. In it, she had asked a scientist for help. In reply the scientist had jumped up and down, and eventually 'flown to the top of a cupboard'. When the dreamer woke up, it occurred to her that the triangles must be given lift-off. She drew what this suggested, and her colleagues told her it was a tetrahedron. 'For a non-mathematical person like me to come up with the right answer was a great thrill,' she told Schatzman. 'I don't think I'd have solved it without the dream, because I am not a person who thinks in that sort of way.'

The second brain-twister was easier, at least to people with no mathematical knowledge.

What is remarkable about the following sentence: 'I am not very happy acting pleased whenever prominent scientists overmagnify intellectual enlightenment'?

– the kind of puzzle that looks so simple when it is explained, but often eludes conscious effort. A sixth-form student got the answer in a dream in which he was lecturing to scientists sitting around at small tables. When he awoke, it struck him that there had been five tables, with one, two, three, four and five scientists respectively. 'I realised that it is the number of letters in each word that was important. I counted the letters, and arrived at the sequence 1, 2, 3 – 13.'

Another dreamer had typed 'The quick brown fox jumps over the lazy dog' – the sentence that includes every letter in the alphabet; but his supervisor told him to type 123456789 instead. When he woke up, he had the clue to the solution. In another dream, there was a nod of approval to Freud. In it there was a nobleman – a Count. The pun gave the clue.

Nearly all the correspondents who had solved the problems claimed that they had woken up from their dreams at the usual time in the morning. Going to sleep with the problem on the mind, in other words, did not entail being woken up in the night with the solution. The conclusion from the admittedly small experiment, Schatzman thought, was that 'contrary to Francis Crick and Graeme Mitchison's hypothesis that we dream to "unlearn" irrelevant information, it is apparent that dreams can help to solve problems.' Some dreams give the answer; some give hints which might easily be overlooked, unless the dreamer expects to find a hint in the dream and searches the dream for it. We may be getting answers to our problems without being aware of it, if we do not pay sufficient attention to our dreams.

The form and the source

In many cases of dream-prompting and problem-solving, the explanation which Walter Scott provided for Rutherford's dream – that it was 'only the recapitulation of information which Mr Rutherford had readily received from his father while in life', but had forgotten – is plausible; more plausible, in a sense, than it was in Scott's time, because research has been revealing the range of memory which can be tapped in the subconscious, in experiments with hypnotic regression. Similarly Hilprecht's dream solving the problem of the Babylonian agate fragments was accounted for by Professor W. Romaine Newbold, whose commentary on it was published in the *Journal of the Society for Psychical Research* in 1893. He thought that all the information which it had provided was within the reach of 'the processes of associative reasoning which Professor Hilprecht daily employs'.

Another possibility has also to be taken into account, in any assessment of the source of the material which reaches us in dreams. Before any claim that it comes through extra-sensory perception can be seriously entertained, Edmund Gurney, Joint Honorary Secretary of the SPR with Frederic Myers, pointed out in 1886, an objection has to be considered.

Millions of people are dreaming every night; and in dreams, if anywhere, the range of possibilities seems infinite; can any positive conclusion be drawn from such a chaos of meaningless and fragmentary impressions? Must not we admit the force of the obvious *a priori* argument, that among the countless multitude of dreams, one here and there is likely to correspond in time with an actual occurrence resembling the one dreamed of; and that when a dream 'comes true', unscientific minds are sure to note and store up the fact as something extraordinary, without taking the trouble to reflect whether such incidents occur oftener than pure chance would allow?

This line of argument is still often heard. It was cogently presented by Christopher Evans in a book he was working on at the time of his death, which has since been edited and completed by his namesake Peter Evans, BBC radio's science correspondent, and published in 1983 as *Landscapes of the Night*. What we mistake for ESP, Christopher Evans believed, are simply indications that our minds are more astute than we realise; and to illustrate the point, he cited an experience of his own.

A watch he owned had been stolen; but when he went to report the theft he found to his embarrassment (a very common experience) that he could not remember the make, in spite of the fact that it was on the watch face.

That night I woke suddenly in the midst of a vivid dream. It seemed that I had been looking at the face of my watch, in a kind of expanded close-up. The hands, numbers and other features, even the metallic sheen of the casing, were brilliantly visible. So too was its name, clearly spelt out in capital letters in the centre of the face – BIFORA.

Many people would have classified this as psychic, Evans commented, and that would be a possible explanation. But he felt it was much more likely that the name had been lodged in his memory and 'could be dredged up in a dream'.

It was a reasonable explanation of *this* dream; but Evans, who could not bring himself to accept the reality of ESP, had selected as his example a dream which could easily be accounted for without it. He did not care to cite the more impressive examples of 'striking correspondences' which the SPR began to record, and which have continued to appear since. But one useful step was taken by the Swiss psychologist Theodore Flournoy, a man greatly admired both by his contemporary, the philosopher-psychologist William James, and by his protégé, Jung ('my revered and fatherly friend', as Jung was to describe him). Sceptical by temperament but meticulously careful to present both sides of the case, Flournoy devoted much time and thought to the problems which were being thrown up by psychical researchers; and a point he made in his *Spiritism and Psychology* (1911) helped him to remove some of the confusion.

The form in which information is presented in dreams is not a reliable guide, Flournoy insisted, to its *source*. Thus, the theatrical embellishments in Hilprecht's dream – the tall, thin priest, the room littered with agate and lapis lazuli – did not imply that the priest had actually existed: they were there because these were the associations which the information contained in the dream called up in Hilprecht's imagination. If Agassiz had happened to have Spiritualist leanings, Flournoy surmised, the fossil fish which he had seen in his dream might have been presented 'with appropriate setting, by some messenger from the other world, or by a fisherman from prehistoric times.' But as it happened, Agassiz was a positivist.

Nevertheless Flournoy felt compelled to admit that in some cases, the information provided in a dream could not readily be accounted for by the fact that the dreamer's subconscious mind, holding all the scattered pieces of information, had sorted them out and presented them in the form of the solution to a problem which had baffled the conscious mind.

3

Second Sight in Dreams

Today, the issue whether extra-sensory communication occurs in dreams – indeed, whether it occurs at all – remains in dispute. Yet both historically and in our own times, there is evidence of its occurrence which cannot be accounted for by chance coincidence. Although chance cannot be ruled out in individual cases, for the accounts as a whole it is an implausible explanation.

Often what is communicated is of little or no intrinsic interest – *except* as evidence of ESP, when its very triviality may strengthen the case. A good example has been given by one of the co-authors of *Dream Telepathy* (1973) – Alan Vaughan, recalling how in 1970 he watched Kurt Vonnegut, an author whose work he greatly admired, on a television programme. A couple of nights later he had a dream about Vonnegut. On an impulse, Vaughan wrote it out and sent it to him: 'You were planning to leave soon on a trip. Then you mentioned that you were moving to an island named Jerome. (As far as I know there is no such place so perhaps the name Jerome or initial "J" has some related meaning?)' A fortnight later he received Vonnegut's reply. 'Not bad. On the night of your dream, I had dinner with Jerome B. (an author of children's books), and we talked about a trip I made, three days later, to an island named England.'

Granted that this was an instance of ESP, why should information of such unimportance have reached Vaughan? A hypothesis has been put forward recently by the psychiatrist Jan Ehrenwald, harking back to Henri Bergson's claim that the main function of the human brain is to act as a filter.

All of us are constantly being bombarded by messages from our senses; the brain seeks to ensure that only those most relevant to our needs get through. When we cross a road, our eyes and ears are tuned to pick up the presence of traffic; we see a tree on the other side, but are not aware of it; we hear birds singing, but are not aware of them. As sixth-sense communications have to a great extent been made redundant by the messages from the five more specialised senses, Bergson argued, they have even lower priority – in much the same way as the sense of smell in human beings has been largely made redundant.

Extra-sensory communications, Ehrenwald maintains, reach our conscious minds through the filter in two ways. One is 'flaw-directed'. ESP messages are flowing in all the time; occasionally the filter fails in its function, and lets one through, though it may be of no importance. The other, however, *is* important. It is 'need-directed', and the filter mechanism may let it through for that reason.

The fact that the conscious mind is not intervening during sleep makes it easier for information from outside sources to slip through, occasionally to be recalled on waking. If this is accepted, the presumption is that communication between people who are close, by ties of family or love, will often be encountered in reports of dreams. It is. Accounts of one curious variety of inter-communication are particularly common: 'shared' dreams.

Shared dreams

In many cases, the dreamers appear to have picked up the thoughts of somebody close to them. In one of the accounts checked in the 1880s by Edmund Gurney for the SPR, Jean Eleanora Fielding, a clergyman's wife, described how one night when she was sleeping badly, she whiled away the time recalling in detail her childhood home in Scotland, where she had not been for twenty years; and this had brought up recollections of a neighbour there, Harvey Brown. Her husband, who was asleep, knew her family home, but knew of Brown only by name. They had never spoken of Brown in all the twenty years. But 'He and I awoke at 6. Before a word of any kind was said, he said to me, "I have had such a strange dream about Harvey Brown, and been at the old home, wandering about it."'

Mrs Naomi Harris of the Peabody Trust in London has told the Foundation of a rather similar experience; except that in her case she was the dreamer, and what she dreamed actually answered a question in her husband's mind. In 1986 she had an unusually vivid dream about being shown around Kenwood House by Lady Iveagh. She knew of the Guinness connection with Kenwood House, but did not know whether any such person as a Lady Iveagh existed. Still, the dream was so realistic, and Lady

Iveagh featured so strongly in it, that she mentioned it to her husband the next morning.

'Thank goodness!' was his reply. 'That's the name I have been trying and trying to remember!' He, a doctor, during the previous day, and that night, had been racking his brains for the name in connection with one of his patients.

In these instances the sharing could be explained away as the product of chance coincidence, without too much stretching; but it becomes less plausible as the explanation for the type of 'sharing' recorded by another of Gurney's collection, in the category which he thought 'might reasonably be regarded as telepathic'. In January 1882, the Rev. A.B. McDougall, a scholar at Lincoln College, Oxford, was staying in a house in Manchester when one night he felt 'an unpleasantly cold something slithering down my right leg'. It turned out to be a rat. The following morning, 11 January, a cousin of his who happened to be staying in his room at his home

came down to breakfast and recounted a marvellous dream in which a rat appeared to be eating off the extremities of my unfortunate self. My family laughed the matter off. However, on the 13th a letter was received from me giving an account of my unpleasant meeting with the rat and its subsequent capture. Then everyone present remembered the dream my cousin had told, certainly 48 hours before.

In some families, 'sharing' of the kind where husband and wife both have the same or a very similar dream the same night are so common that they almost cease to be remarked upon; unless, as in an example Jeremy Taylor has given in his *Dream Work* (1983), what is shared is far too odd to be put down to the fact that husbands and wives must occasionally be thinking, and consequently dreaming, along similar lines. Had both husband and wife been thinking about elephants, for both to dream of elephants would not have seemed strange; but one night they both had dreams

involving full-sized elephants, with correspondingly large human hands at the ends of their forefeet. In my dream the elephant had been a woolly mammoth, while in Kath's it had been a circus elephant, but in both dreams the elephants sat back on their haunches and waved their gigantic hands at us, in a gesture similar to hand gestures in a vaudeville routine.

Chance also offers an implausible explanation for a shared dream reported to the Foundation by Mrs M.R. Elliot, of Derby.

I was in a lovely house, sunny and open, lots of people about, in particular a young man who came to me and said 'I love you.' I replied 'I love you, too.' He had dark hair and brown eyes. I felt he was completely trustworthy and good.

When I met my mother, who lives nearby, she told me she had dreamed of a lovely young man who she met at a party who said 'I love you' and she replied 'I love you, too.' Her dream man even matched the description of mine.

Mrs Elliot could think of no logical reason why she and her mother should both have been in the same frame of mind at the time.

That dreams are so often shared among people close to each other has significant implications for psychology. It is possible, too, that sharing may indicate an unexpected or undeveloped closeness between people who do not know each other, as in a case recounted by Louisa Rhine in *The Invisible Picture* (1981).

A man in New Jersey dreamed he was out with a gun and a woman companion, a person whom he knew only slightly. He thought they were both shooting at different objects, but the targets that impressed him most were some cows in a field. He remembered the dream in the morning, partly because the woman was no one he was particularly interested in, but one of the people in his home town whom he knew only casually.

The next day he happened to meet her in a store. When she saw him she said she wanted to tell him about a 'crazy' dream she had about him the night before. 'I was stunned for a moment when she said she had been dreaming that she and I were out shooting cows.'

Might investigation have shown that there was some as yet unexplored affinity?

There are even weirder accounts of sharing, notably one culled from the classics by Aubrey in his *Miscellanies* (1696).

A certain gentleman named Prestantius, had been entreating a

Philosopher to solve him a doubt, which he absolutely refused to do. The night following, although Prestantius was broad awake, he saw the Philosopher standing full before him, who just explained his doubts to him, and went away the moment after he had done. When Prestantius met the Philosopher the next day, he asks him why, since no entreaties could prevail with him the day before, to answer his question, he came to him unasked, and at an unseasonable time of night, and opened every point to his satisfaction. To whom thus the Philosopher: 'Upon my word it was not me that came to you; but in a dream I thought my own self that I was doing you such a service.'

Hearing about an equally extraordinary case involving the Drummonds of Drumquaigh in Scotland and their dog Fanti, Andrew Lang took the trouble to have it confirmed by the family. Mrs Ogilvie, her son the Laird, and her eldest daughter were at home at the time; their two younger daughters away with friends.

One morning Miss Ogilvie came down to breakfast and said to her brother, 'I had an odd dream; I dreamed Fanti went mad.'

'Well, that *is* odd,' said her brother. 'So did I. We had better not tell mother; it might make her nervous.'

Miss Ogilvie went up after breakfast to see the older lady, who said, 'Do turn out Fanti; I dreamed last night that he went mad and bit.'

In the afternoon the two younger sisters came home.

'How did you enjoy yourselves?' one of the others asked.

'We didn't sleep well. I was dreaming that Fanti went mad when Mary wakened me, and said she had dreamed Fanti went mad, and turned into a cat, and we threw him into the fire.'

Fanti did not go mad, living out the rest of his days in tranquillity. Knowing the family, Lang had no doubt that their account was genuine; but he was reluctantly to concede that it was nothing more than 'a curiosity of coincidences'.

The most grotesque of all reported cases of dream sharing, though, is surely one which was related by Robert Graves. He had been discussing J.W. Dunne's *An Experiment With Time* with some friends; and, obeying Dunne's instructions to record every detail of a remembered dream, he took care to record what he remembered of one which had left a vivid impression on him when he awoke. In it he had met Oscar Wilde in a cocktail bar with two other writers whom Graves disliked (but did not identify); an episode followed in the dream by a queer word appearing in capitals – 'TELTOE, PELTOE, or TELSOE or something like that' – which left him baffled.

The dream as a whole meant nothing to him, but he recounted it to his friends the following day. The day following that, a letter arrived for him from a total stranger, a Mr Roberts, forwarded from Islip where he had previously lived. It included the lines

> Attercop, the all-wise spider
> The poet at Islip scrawled – Re
> Oscar Wilde at the tipplers;
> Whistler, do let's appreciate
> Walter Pater's polish, deceit.

'Something is wrong with these anagrams, I fancy,' the letter continued. 'I lack the monkey-wit to worry them out. What did you intend? I can think of dozens more. It must be pure chance.'

To Graves it was pure gibberish – except the first line, which came from one of his poems. Eventually it dawned on him that his correspondent must have assumed that 'Attercop' was an anagram, prompting him to try to find the meaning by trying out anagrams of the whole line. It was *not* an anagram. 'Attercop' is an old Scots word for spider (as the tale was originally told, it was 'Bruce and the Attercop').

'But the business about Oscar Wilde,' Graves told R.L. Megroz, who used the tale in *The Dream World*,

> – the two literary friends – a mad story originating with the anagrams – someone invaded my dream and the word *teltoe, peltoe* or *telsoe* seems to have been a residue of letters that Mr Roberts tried to make use of in an anagram by allowing them to form a proper name (and I had been to the trouble of trying to find the word in the *Times Atlas* and Larousse's *Dictionary of Names!*)

Roberts' letter, Graves pointed out, had been posted two days before the dream, and arrived two days after it.

I was probably myself responsible for the whole incident. For I had written (but not published) a poem about the curious effect of anagrams, and had it strongly in my mind about the time that Roberts wrote his letter to me. In it I coined the word 'Anagrammagic'. My wireless vibrations, it seems, somehow affected him while he was reading the Attercop poem, and his, in revenge, disturbed my dream.

If necessary, Graves concluded, he would furnish Megroz with proof, in the form of the documents and attestation by his friends.

Shared dreams, then, are flaw-directed in that they are not let through the brain's filter on account of their importance. Yet it can be argued that they may be need-*prompted*, to some extent, when the sharing is between two people who are emotionally close to each other. And this lends them a significance which the trivial content so often obscures, in so far as they show that there is communication at a deeper level than conventional psychology has been prepared to recognise.

The existence of need-directed dreams is of even greater significance, indicating as it does the ability of the brain's filter to recognise signals marked 'urgent'. Reports of 'crisis' dreams, as they are sometimes described, fall into four main categories: 'disaster' dreams, which appear to have been triggered by some major calamity, such as a plane crash or an assassination; 'farewell' dreams, which provide a notification of the death of a relative or loved one; 'call' dreams, in which it is as if a telepathic link has been established by somebody who is longing to communicate with the recipient; and what might be described as 'unfinished business' dreams, where the vision of somebody who has died comes in a dream with a request for forgiveness, or for the righting of some wrong.

'Disaster' dreams

The more calamitous the event, the more likely it should be that people will pick it up telepathically; and although this is not something which can be tested statistically, some support is lent to it by investigations such as the one pursued in the late 1950s by Professor Ian Stevenson of the University of Virginia into the sinking of the *Titanic*. Of the dreams which he records, one stands out from the rest.

A New York woman had a nightmare of her mother in a lifeboat so overcrowded that it was in danger of sinking. She related it to her husband the next morning, but as they assumed her mother was still in Europe, he reassured her. The next day they read of the sinking, and she found to her horror her mother's name on the passenger list. As it happened, her mother survived. She had not told her daughter of her intention of sailing on the *Titanic*, hoping to surprise her. She described how in the lifeboat, at the time of her daughter's dream, she had feared the worst, thinking that at any moment it would capsize; 'and all the while her thoughts were concentrated on the daughter, whom she expected never to see again.'

Graham Greene was one of the dreamers that night, though he does not feature in Stevenson's collection. Describing how important dreams have been to him in *A Sort of Life*, Greene notes that they have often given him hints of dire events.

On the April night of the *Titanic* disaster, when I was five and it was Easter holiday time in Littlehampton, I dreamt of a shipwreck. One image of the dream has remained with me for more than sixty years: a man in oilskins bent double beside a companion-way under the blow of a great wave. Again in 1921 I wrote home from my psycho-analyst's: 'A night or two ago I had a shipwreck dream, the ship I was on going down in the Irish Sea. I didn't think anything about it. We don't have papers here as the usual thing, and it was not till yesterday, looking at an old paper, I saw about the sinking of the *Rowan* in the Irish Sea. I looked at my dream diary and found that my dream had been Saturday night. The accident had happened just after Saturday midnight.' Again in 1944 I dreamed of a V1 missile some weeks before the first attack. It passed horizontally across the sky flaming at the tail in the very form it was to take.

Louisa Rhine has recorded how on 7 December 1941 a man who had been having a siesta in his Alabama home suddenly jumped to his feet and told his wife he had just heard the President announce that the Japanese had attacked Pearl Harbor. Nonsense, she told him; he was dreaming. The radio had been on; if there had been any such announcement, she would have heard it. While they were arguing, there was a news 'flash' – Roosevelt had announced that the Japanese were bombing Pearl Harbor.

During the 1968 presidential election campaign, Louis Heren, the distinguished Foreign Editor of *The Times*, spent a couple of weeks covering the Oregon and California primaries, the main contenders being Robert Kennedy and Eugene McCarthy. As he has described in his account to the Koestler Foundation,

I did not particularly like Kennedy, he had a mean streak as well as the conviction that the Presidency was his by right, and I applauded – not in the columns of *The Times*, of course – when he lost to McCarthy in Oregon. It was a bitter blow for Kennedy, but California was the bigger state and he had more money than his rival. He campaigned like a man possessed, and it soon became apparent that he would win the State.

As this made the campaign there of less significance and interest than if there had been a chance of Kennedy's losing, Heren returned to Washington, where he watched the coverage of the election the following Tuesday evening on television.

Knowing that I had a hard day ahead of me I went to bed before the inevitable result was announced. As usual I quickly fell asleep, but had a terrible nightmare. Somebody was trying to assassinate Kennedy, and I was trying to defend him, swinging my portable typewriter. I fell out of bed in a sweat; my wife comforted me, and then went downstairs to make a pot of tea. Being a good correspondent's wife, she turned on the radio, as the announcer was saying that Kennedy had been killed.

Many disaster dreams can be attributed to chance, because such dreams are so common. But sometimes the coincidence of detail is impressive, as in a case recorded by G.N.M. Tyrrell in his *Science and Psychical Phenomena* (1938). One night in 1928 Dudley Walker, one of Tyrrell's correspondents, dreamed he was present as an observer when a train crashed into a smaller one on the same line.

I saw the express and its coaches pitch and twist in the air, and the noise was terrible. Afterwards I walked beside the wreckage in the dim light of dawn viewing with a feeling of terror the huge overturned engine and smashed coaches. I was now amid an indescribable scene of horror with dead and injured people, and rescue workers everywhere.

Most of the bodies lying by the side of the track were those of women and girls. As I passed, with some unknown person leading me, I saw one man's body in a ghastly state, lifted out and laid on the side of an overturned coach.

A train accident actually occurred that night in a town a few miles from where Walker lived, the result of a collision between two trains of the kind he had seen. Of the eight people killed, seven were women, one of them a young girl, and a newspaper report noted that 'one gruesome sight was that of a man's body lying on top of one of the carriages.' Nor could this be explained away by suggesting that Walker's recollection of his dream had been influenced by the newspaper accounts. So shaken had he been by it that he had described it in detail to his mother when he came down for breakfast (which he was too shocked to eat); later, he had related it to his employer; and he had actually written an account of it before reports of the crash began to appear in the evening papers.

This is a common characteristic of the disaster category – a nightmare quality which makes a deeply disturbing impression upon the dreamers, especially if ordinarily they rarely remember their dreams. Reporting such an experience to the Foundation, Mrs Marion Yau of Cheadle in Cheshire has described how she awoke one night in 1967, 'sweating profusely and in a terrible state; I was shaking, my heart was pounding very fast and I was very frightened.' In this case, it was the husband who came to the rescue with a cup of tea. She told him she had witnessed a terrible sea disaster, 'the ship listing to the side, oil pouring into the sea, waves lashing the ship, but most of all the struggling birds covered in oil fighting to stay above the waves.' The morning paper brought the news of the *Torrey Canyon* disaster, the first one of its kind off the British coast, with its immense oil spillage from the crippled tanker, and its destructive consequence for sea birds.

'Farewell' dreams

The second category of crisis dreams, also very commonly reported, are those which seem to anticipate a death notice in the newspapers. The dream performs this in various ways – sometimes showing the dead in their coffins, sometimes in visions as if the dead were coming to pay their last respects to the living. Although it is not uncommon to dream of the death of friends or relatives, in some cases the timing, where the dream coincides with the death, and in others the circumstantial detail, suggest clairvoyance.

The death of somebody well-known is often 'seen' in dreams, as in another of the Foundation's cases. Mrs Marie L. Freeman was staying with her family in a chalet in Cornwall, when early one morning she dreamt that she saw Professor Bronowski – familiar through his television series – flying overhead, dressed quite normally. 'He looked down at me and said "I died early this morning." I replied that I felt very sorry, but he just flew on.' Mrs Freeman told her husband and her teenage children about the dream when they woke up. When her husband switched on the radio, they heard the announcement that Bronowski, whom she had never met, had died.

In many cases it can be argued that the dreamers could have subconsciously become aware that somebody was about to die; but when they have been living at a distance, for a long time, this becomes unlikely. Lying in his cabin during a fierce storm in the Pacific, in 1852, during one of his prolonged periods of exile, Giuseppe Garibaldi dreamed of his mother and a funeral. He had been away for months, and it was to be months before, on his return to Italy, he heard she had died on the night of his dream. Similarly Henry Morton Stanley, before he achieved lasting fame as an explorer, had been living for some years in America out of contact with his family in Wales, when he had a dream which made a profound impression on him. As he recalled in his *Autobiography*, while serving with the Confederate forces he had been captured at Shiloh, and sent to a prisoner-of-war camp near Chicago. One morning in 1862 he was relaxing after completing his chores

when, suddenly, I felt a gentle stroke on the back of my neck, and in an instant, I was unconscious. The next moment I had a vivid view of the village of Tremeirchion, and the grassy slopes of the hills of Hiraddog, and I seemed to be hovering over the rook woods of Brynbella. I glided to the bed-chamber of my Aunt Mary. My aunt was in bed, and seemed sick unto death. I took a position by the side

of the bed, and saw myself, with head bent down, listening to her
parting words, which sounded regretful, as though conscience smote
her for not having been so kind as she might have been, or had wished
to be. I heard the boy say, 'I believe you, aunt. It is neither your fault,
nor mine. You were good and kind to me, and I knew you wished to
be kinder; but things were so ordered that you had to be what you
were. I also dearly wished to love you, but I was afraid to speak of it,
lest you would check me, or say something that would offend me. I
feel our parting was in this spirit. There is no need of regrets. You
have done your duty to me, and you had children of your own, who
required all your care. What has happened to me since, was decreed
should happen. Farewell.'

I put forth my hand and felt the clasp of the long thin hands of the
sore-sick woman. I heard a murmur of farewell, and immediately I
woke.

His aunt, Stanley found later, was dying in Wales at the time. 'I believe,'
he commented, relating the story in his autobiography,

that the soul of every human being has its attendant spirit – a nimble,
delicate essence, whose method of action is by a subtle suggestion
which it contrives to insinuate into the mind, whether asleep or
awake. We are too gross to be capable of understanding the
signification of the dream, the vision, or the sudden presage, or of
divining the source of the premonition, or its import. We admit that
we are liable to receive a fleeting picture of an act, or a figure, at any
moment, but, except being struck by certain strange coincidences
which happen to most of us, we seldom make an effort to unravel the
mystery. The swift, darting messenger stamps an image on the mind,
and displays a vision to the sleeper; and if, as sometimes follows,
among tricks and twists of the errant mind, by reflex acts of memory,
it happens to be a true representation of what is to happen, we are left
to grope hopelessly as to the manner and meaning of it, for there is
nothing tangible to lay hold of.

There are many things relating to my existence which are
inexplicable to me, and probably it is best so; this death-bed scene,
projected on my mind's screen across four thousand five hundred
miles of space, is one of these mysteries.

Apart from demonstrating affection, dream visions of the dying rarely perform any particular service – though the producer David Belasco, after whom the New York theatre is named, felt that he owed one of his most successful plays to his crisis dream of his mother.

One night, after a long and exhausting rehearsal, I went to bed, worn out, in my Newport home, and fell at once into a deep sleep. Almost immediately, however, I was awakened and attempted to rise, but could not, and was then greatly startled to see my dear mother (whom I knew to be in San Francisco) standing close by me. As I strove to speak and to sit up she smiled at me a loving reassuring smile, spoke my name – the name she called me in my boyhood – 'Davy, Davy, Davy,' then, leaning down, seemed to kiss me; then drew away a little and said: 'Do not grieve. All is well and I am happy;' then moved toward the door and vanished.

The following day he told his family of his mother's appearance, and said he was sure that she must have died.

A few hours later (I was still directing rehearsals of Zoza) I went to luncheon during a recess, with a member of my staff, who handed me some letters and telegrams which he had brought from the box-office of the theatre. Among them was a telegram telling me that my darling mother had died the night before, at about the time I had seen her in my room. Later I learned that just before she died she roused herself, smiled, and three times murmured, 'Davy, Davy, Davy.'

'Thought transference,' Belasco felt, was an inadequate explanation. He was sure he had actually seen his mother, and this and other experiences had convinced him that 'what we call supernatural is, after all, at most supernormal.' This determined him to write a play on the subject and *The Return of Peter Grimm* (1911) was the profitable outcome.

A case where it was the details, rather than the precise timing, that were impressive, was provided, and vouched for, by Robert Dale Owen, in his *Footfalls* (1860). In 1836 Captain Clarke, in charge of a schooner trading between New York and Cuba, dreamed that he was present at the funeral of his grandmother in Lyme Regis; and all went as he would have expected it to do until, to his surprise, the procession did not go to the family burial place, but to a different part of the churchyard. There – according to Owen, who checked the story with Clarke – 'he saw the open grave, partially filled with water, as from the rain; and looking into it, he particularly noticed floating in the water two drowned field-mice.' Shaken by the dream, Clarke made a note of the date, and in due course found his grandmother had been buried on the same day. Later, his mother told him that the old lady had herself selected the place where she wanted to be buried; and it turned out to be where he had seen it in his dream. 'Finally, on comparing notes with the old sexton, it appeared that the heavy rain of the morning had partially filled the grave, and that there were actually found in it two field-mice, drowned.'

The vision of Samuel Clemens – Mark Twain – of his brother Henry's death in 1858 has often been cited as one of the most striking of crisis dreams. Henry was about twenty at this time; according to Samuel's biographer, Albert Bigelow Paine, he was 'a handsome, attractive boy of whom his brother was lavishly fond and proud', and was training to become a pilot on one of the Mississippi steamboats; Samuel was to follow in his footsteps. One night while staying with his sister in St Louis, Samuel dreamt that he saw Henry lying in a metal coffin supported on two chairs in a living room, with a bouquet of white flowers, and one crimson flower, on his breast. He told his sister of his dream, but then put it aside – until he heard that the steamboat Henry was on had blown up, sixty miles below Memphis. When Samuel arrived, he saw his brother lying as in the dream, in a metal coffin, 'lacking only the bouquet of white flowers with its crimson centre – a detail made complete while he stood there, for at that moment an elderly lady came in with a large white bouquet and in the centre of it was a single red rose.'

It was easy for sceptics to claim that as a writer of popular fiction, Mark Twain was not to be relied upon. Had he not established his reputation, he might not have cared to tell the tale. How difficult it was, at that time, to publish such accounts without fear of derision was to be admitted by another firmly established author, Rider Haggard, who gave his account of a remarkable crisis dream in *The Times* in 1904. 'Perhaps you will think with me that the following circumstances are worthy of record, if only for their scientific interest,' he wrote. 'It is principally because of this interest that, as such stories should not be told anonymously, I have made up my mind to publish it over my own name, though I am well aware that by so doing I may expose myself to a certain amount of ridicule and disbelief.'

Twelve days before, he explained, on the Saturday night, he had had a nightmare.

I was awakened by my wife's voice calling to me from her own bed upon the other side of the room. As I awoke, the nightmare itself, which had been long and vivid, faded from my brain. All I could remember of it was a sense of awful oppression and of desperate and terrified struggling for life such as the act of drowning would probably involve. But between the time that I heard my wife's voice and the time that my consciousness answered to it, or so it seemed to me, I had another dream. I dreamed that a black retriever dog, a most amiable and intelligent beast named Bob which was the property of my eldest daughter, was lying on its side among brushwood, or rough growth of some sort, by water. My own personality in some mysterious way seemed to me to be arising from the body of the dog, which I knew quite surely to be Bob and no other, so much so that my head was against its head, which was lifted up at an unnatural angle. In my vision the dog was trying to speak to me in words, and, failing, transmitted to my mind in an undefined fashion the knowledge that it was dying. Then everything vanished, and I woke to hear my wife asking me why on earth I was making those horrible and weird noises.

His wife told the story to the company over breakfast, and he confirmed it, but thought no more about it until he was told that the dog was missing. He then embarked on a search, finding the body of the dog floating against a weir more than a mile down the river nearby. Investigation revealed that a train had knocked it off the railway bridge into the river on the Saturday night.

'Both in a judicial and a private capacity,' Rider Haggard's letter continues,

I have been accustomed all my life to the investigation of evidence, and, if we may put aside our familiar friend 'the long arm of coincidence', which in this case would surely be strained to dislocation, I confess that that available upon this matter forces me to the following conclusions:

The dog Bob, between whom and myself there existed a mutual attachment, either at the moment of his death, if his existence can conceivably have been prolonged till after 1 in the morning, or, as seems more probable, about three hours after the event, did succeed in calling my attention to its actual or recent plight by placing whatever portion of my being is capable of receiving such impulses when enchained by sleep, into its own terrible position. That subsequently, as that chain of sleep was being broken by the voice of my wife calling me back to a normal condition of our human existence, with some last despairing effort, while that indefinable part of me was being slowly withdrawn from it (it will be remembered that in my dream I seemed to rise from the dog), it spoke to me, first trying to make use of my own tongue, and, failing therein, by some subtle means of communication whereof I have no knowledge telling me that it was dying, for I saw no blood or wound which would suggest this to my mind.

Rider Haggard went on to speculate whether a form of telepathy had been responsible; or, as his dream appeared to have occurred three hours after the dog had been hit by the train, 'it would seem that it must have been some non-bodily but surviving part of the life or of the spirit of the dog' (telepathy, at the time, had received a measure of recognition which was not yet extended to communications forward or backward in time). Whatever the interpretation of the facts – attested by all those concerned: his family, a vet, some railwaymen and so on – Rider Haggard felt that 'it does seem to suggest that there is a more intimate ghostly connection between all members of the animal world, including man, than has hitherto been believed, at any rate by Western people; that they may be, in short, all of them different manifestations of some central, informing life, though inhabiting the universe in such various shapes.'

A dream of a death led one deep-dyed rationalist to begin to realise that his positivism had misled him about the nature of reality. One night in 1872 George J. Romanes, a Fellow of the Royal Society, had a dream which so disturbed him that he wrote it down, and told his wife the following morning:

I imagined that I was seated in the drawing-room near a table, about to read, when an old lady suddenly appeared seated on the other side, very near the table. She did not speak nor move, but she looked at me fixedly, and I looked at her in the same way for at least twenty minutes. I was very much struck with her appearance: she had white hair with very black eyebrows, and a penetrating expression. I did not recognise her all at once, and I thought she was a stranger. My attention was attracted in the direction of the door, which opened and (still in my dream) my aunt entered. Upon seeing the old lady she cried out with great surprise, and in a tone of reproach, 'John, do you not know who that is?' and without leaving me time to answer she added 'It is your grandmother.'

Romanes feared the worst, but heard nothing for some days. Then his father wrote to tell him of the sudden death of his grandmother; 'it had taken place on the very night of my dream,' he recalled, 'and at the same hour.' He was prompted to take psychic phenomena seriously, and eventually to shed his positivist beliefs altogether.

'Farewell' dreams are still commonly reported. In *Working with Dreams* (1979) Montague Ullman and Nan Zimmerman record one from a woman who dreamed that when she answered the telephone by her bed it was her husband, with whom she had lived for over twenty years but had divorced five years earlier because of his alcoholism. Her bedroom dresser had twin mirrors, and while she was talking to him, he started walking out of one of them, fixing his tie.

I put the phone down, got out of bed (still dreaming), and I said 'Roger, what are you doing here?' He answered, 'I just wanted to see you.'

She woke up, feeling depressed. That morning her brother-in-law rang to tell her that her husband had died of a stroke during the night. 'I believe he told me good-bye.'

The artist Louis le Brocquy – Irish, despite his name and the fact that he lives in France – recalls a farewell dream of a curious nature which he had shortly after he had held his first exhibition in Dublin in 1942. It was a 'flying' dream, the 'flight' taking him out of Dublin into the country, where he began to walk along a road. Behind him he heard the sound of a galloping horse; when the rider came up to him, he thought he recognised her as the girl who had looked after visitors at the gallery, and he called out, 'Hello Mary.' She was not Mary, she replied severely. 'My name is

Mère Jo, and I must get on my way'; and she galloped off over the crest of the hill ahead.

When le Brocquy woke up, he recalled that his paternal grandmother, whose name was Josephine, was called 'Mère' by his parents, and 'Jo' by her husband. When le Brocquy's mother knocked at his door, a few minutes later, he at once told her he was certain his grandmother must have died during the night. 'Just five minutes previously my mother herself had learned this totally unexpected news by telephone.'

'Call' dreams

A typical 'call' dream is related in Louisa Rhine's *The Invisible Picture* (1981).

> A girl in Los Angeles one night heard her mother call her as if from the next room. She turned and, before she thought, answered 'Yes, mother.' But then she chided herself for such a lapse, when 'Mother is 3,000 miles away.'
>
> A few days later she had a letter from her mother saying that that night, 'I was so lonesome for you that I stood in the doorway of your room and called to you.'

Such cases, Louisa Rhine commented, 'tend to make an impression on people that they are unlikely to forget.'

People who are literally 'on call', such as doctors, appear to be particularly susceptible to 'call' dreams; as in a case described in some detail by Margaret Murray, the author of what for a time was regarded as the authoritative book on the development of witchcraft, though later researchers have demolished her central thesis. Sceptical though she was in general, she was sufficiently impressed by the experience of a doctor she knew to relate it in her autobiography. While practising in Calcutta, the doctor was attending one of his patients who had just had a baby, but as there were no complications had returned home and gone to bed.

> At about two o'clock in the morning, his wife woke up to find him dressing to go out. 'What *are* you doing?' she said. 'There has been no message, Chandra has not called you.'
>
> The doctor said, 'I have already sent Chandra to call the coachman to get the carriage ready, and to rouse the *durwan* [gate-keeper] to

have the gate open so that there shall be no delay. I am going to see that confinement case. Please, don't try to stop me. I feel I *must* go, and in the quickest possible time.'

When he reached the patient's house the gate-keeper there had to be roused, protesting that he had not been given any message to fetch the doctor.

The husband of the patient came running out, and exclaimed, 'What on earth are you here for? Everything is quiet upstairs. The nurse would have called me if there had been anything wrong.'

The nurse looked over the banisters and said incredulously, 'Is that the doctor? Why, doctor, whatever are you doing here at this time of night? I looked at the patient only a quarter of an hour ago, and she was sleeping peacefully.'

'I can't help it,' said the doctor. 'I *must* see her.' He was just in time, a violent haemorrhage had just set in, and had he had to wait for the delay of arousing the servants at both the houses the doctor might easily have been too late.

In *The Analysis of Dreams* (1957) the psycho-analyst Medard Boss has described a similar 'call', reported to him by a Russian doctor. One afternoon the doctor took a siesta and fell asleep around 3.30, when he dreamed that he had been sent for by a patient.

I entered a small room with dark wallpaper. On the right side of the entrance there was a chest of drawers, and on it a peculiar lamp or candlestick. I was extremely interested in this object. I had never seen anything like it before. On the left side of the door was a bed in which a woman was bleeding severely.

Shortly after he woke up,

the doorbell rang and I was called to see a patient. When I entered her room I was completely taken aback. It was remarkably similar to that of the room in my dream. An odd little petrol lamp stood on the chest of drawers on the right, and the bed was on the left. As if in a daze I approached the patient and asked her: 'Have you a violent haemorrhage?' 'Yes. How did you know?' she replied. I asked the patient at what time she sent for me. She replied that she had been feeling unwell all the morning. At one o'clock she had had a slight haemorrhage to which she had attached no importance. Only at two o'clock had she begun to be very disturbed and had gone to bed hoping the bleeding would stop. At four o'clock she had decided to send for me since her bleeding was becoming severe.

Medard Boss came across another case in which the mother of a young man who was in the course of a training analysis had two 'call' dreams about him. The son fell ill with pneumonia, and one night became delirious.

Throughout his delirium he believed that his mother was with him, and he begged her to place her cool hand on his forehead. In the course of the following morning the mother 'phoned her son's boarding-house. Instead of the usual greeting she anxiously asked the housekeeper, who had answered the telephone, whether her son was seriously ill, and whether she ought to come at once. She had dreamt of her son's illness on the previous night, but had had no other information whatsoever. In this dream she had been with her son who had been lying in bed with a high fever. He had been completely delirious and had constantly asked to be cooled.

Three years later when he was working in London, and while his mother was on holiday in Chur, he broke his right thigh on the way to his office. The following day he received another telephone call. This time the mother asked if her son's injuries were serious. She had dreamt most vividly that he was lying in a hospital bed, his right leg bandaged from top to bottom.

These were the only two occasions on which the mother, who was not well-off, had ever made a long-distance call.

It sometimes seems imperative in a dream to get a warning to the person concerned; but it is often hard to act on such an impulse on waking up. Yet with 'call' dreams it is sometimes possible for the person called to take appropriate action; as in a curious case related by Ann Bridge in her *Moments of Knowing* (1970), about a well known Anglican clergyman, Archdeacon Bevan. Bevan had been a close friend of the headmaster of

Charterhouse School; and when he died, his wife asked Bevan if he would read the lesson at the funeral service.

The night before the funeral he had a most vivid dream. He was standing in the chancel of the Charterhouse Chapel, which was full of a black-clad congregation; opposite him, in another stall, stood Mr Le Bas, the chaplain. Every detail of the chapel, which Bevan had not seen since his schooldays, was perfectly clear to him. When the time for reading the lesson approached he left his stall and went to the lectern to find the place in the Bible, but there was no Bible! – the lectern was bare. Startled and disconcerted, he stepped across to Le Bas and whispered to him 'There's no book!' To this Le Bas replied shortly – 'There never is.' Baffled, Bevan went back to the lectern and stood wondering what to do. At last he returned to Le Bas and asked him urgently – 'Then what do you do?' Gruffly, as before, Le Bas whispered – 'We always say it by heart!' Frustrated, the unhappy Archdeacon again went back to the lectern, and tried to remember the words of the lesson, but failed. In desperation, he forced himself to approach the unhelpful chaplain for the third time, and asked him – 'How does it begin?' Le Bas gave him the opening words, he went back to the empty lectern, and with an effort managed to recite the whole lesson except for one verse in which he faltered.

So deep was the impression the dream left on Bevan that he decided to take his own prayer book with him, in case it came true. No: the Bible was in its place on the lectern. Still, as he had his familiar prayer-book with him, he read from that. Afterwards he went to tea with the headmaster's widow.

After thanking him warmly for coming to perform this last service for his old friend she said – 'And I cannot tell you how thankful I was that you read it from the Authorised Version. My husband never could get to like the Revised Version. I did think of asking Mr Le Bas if the Authorised Version could not be used, but he prefers the Revised Version, and he doesn't like any alteration in his arrangements. But – you may think me very weak – but I lay awake much of last night wishing that I had the courage to ask him to let the Authorised Version be used today.

Surely, Ann Bridge commented, 'no one can doubt the telepathic element here? Le Bas's grumpiness and stubbornness transmitted from the City of London to Chelsea in such a highly dramatised form?'

In some reports of 'call' dreams it is as if a distress signal is broadcast, and picked up by people who would have come to the rescue if they had known precisely what was the matter. Mervyn Stockwood, Bishop of Southwark for a quarter of a century, has recalled in an article in *Light* how one night in 1956, when he was vicar at the University Church in Cambridge,

> I had been asleep for two or three hours when I awoke with a sense of horror. I was so frightened that I turned on the light. One thing was clear to me – I must call on the dean of King's College as soon as possible. I got up early and arrived at the college gates soon after eight o'clock. I was met by the porter, who said that the dean had committed suicide during the night by throwing himself from the turret of the chapel.

Yet Stockwood was no more than a casual acquaintance of the dean – as were a couple of other people in Cambridge, he later found, who had also, they told him, woken up that night in terror.

The 'call' is not necessarily made to some specific person. It may simply indicate anguish, or alarm, which in some yet to be explained way is picked up by people who have no connection with the individual who is suffering. But in most cases, it is a friend or a relative who picks it up. In 1848 Canon Warburton, a student at Oxford at the time, came up to London to stay with his brother, and found a note saying his brother, who had to go to a dance in the West End, would not be home until after 1 am.

> Instead of going to bed, I dozed in an armchair, but started up wide awake exactly at one, ejaculating 'By Jove! he's down!' and seeing him coming out of a drawing-room into a brightly illuminated landing, just saving himself by his elbows and hands. (The house was one which I had never seen, nor did I know where it was.) Thinking very little of the matter, I fell a-doze again for half an hour and was awakened by my brother suddenly coming in and saying, 'Oh, there you are! I have just had as narrow an escape of breaking my neck as I ever had in my life. Coming out of the ballroom, I caught my foot, and tumbled full length down the stairs.'

In a letter to the SPR Canon Warburton said that although he had not noted down particulars of the scene in the dream, he remembers verifying what he had seen with his brother's description at the time. 'It may have been "only a dream", but I always thought it must have been something more.'

In at least one case, the 'caller' was to be embarrassed when he learned that a fright he had experienced had been picked up by a relation several miles away. Robert Yelverton Tyrrell was widely regarded as among the most eminent classical scholars of the late 19th century, holding the Chair first of Latin, then of Greek, at Trinity College, Dublin. His sister, Mrs Bramly, wrote to the Society for Psychical Research relating a dream she had had about him two or three years earlier.

It was simply a *vivid* dream; I by no means saw an exact enactment of what was going on. I dreamed (being at home in my own house in Killiney, my brother being in his in Dublin) that I saw my brother covered with blood, and that I threw my arms around him and implored him not to die, and that I *felt* the blood touch me, and saw it drop on me.

She did not believe it was true, but she told her husband about it in the morning and, feeling vaguely uneasy, went to Dublin and called on her brother to invite him to come and play tennis.

He replied 'that he should not be able to play tennis for many a day', and then told me he had had an accident the evening before; he was in the garden with his children, and one of them got up on the roof of a small tool-house, which had a glass window on the roof; the child was frightened, and my brother went up the ladder to lift him down; he put one foot on the window and reached forward for the child, when the glass broke and my brother's leg went through, cutting a vein in the leg; it bled *profusely* for a couple of hours before a doctor could be found to bandage it up.

Mr Bramly attested that his wife had told him of her dream before leaving for Dublin that morning; and Professor Tyrrell confirmed 'the details were accurate' – though with manifest distaste: 'I should wish it to be understood that I look on the dream and the accident as a mere coincidence.' The accident had been slight, though he had to admit there *had* been 'a considerable effusion of blood'.

'Unfinished business' dreams

There are innumerable accounts of dreams in which the dead have returned to impart information to the living; information which has sometimes proved of great value. Flournoy's assumption – that the content, rather than the form in which it is presented, is significant – is salutary; the vision of the dead may simply be the subconscious mind's way of underlining the importance of the message, which in many cases has been that a wrong done earlier to the living should be set right.

The best known of the cases is immortalised in the story of Maria Marten and 'the murder in the red barn'. Young Maria, who lived in the county of Suffolk, eloped in 1827 with a farmer, William Corder. Corder continued to write to her parents, but after some months they began to wonder why they had not heard from their daughter. One night, her mother dreamed that Maria had been murdered, and her corpse buried in a red barn which stood on the Corders' land. The next night she had the same dream; and the next. Convinced that her growing suspicions had been justified, she managed to get the floor of the barn examined; and as a result, the body of her daughter was found. Corder was charged with the crime, found guilty and hanged.

There is one even more remarkable case of a dream which accurately described a murder – though in this case the murderers were brought to justice independently of the dream. It was investigated by a Fellow of Pembroke College, Cambridge, Clement Carlyon, and reported in detail in his autobiography *Early Years and Late Reflections* (1856). On the evening of 8 February 1840 Nevell Norway was murdered on the way from Bodmin to his home in Wadebridge in Cornwall. His brother Edmund at the time was in command of a merchant vessel, the *Orient*, on a voyage from the Philippines to Spain. That evening they had just reached St Helena; at 8 o'clock Edmund went below and wrote a letter to his brother. He then went to his berth, fell asleep – as he was to record for Carlyon –

and dreamt I saw two men attack my brother and murder him. One caught the horse by the bridle, and snapped a pistol twice, but I heard no report: he then struck him a blow, and he fell off the horse. They struck him several blows, and dragged him by the shoulders across the road and left him. In my dream there was a house on the left-hand side of the road. At four o'clock I was called, and went on deck to take charge of the ship. I told the second officer, Mr Henry Wren, that I had had a dreadful dream – namely, that my brother Nevell was murdered by two men on the road from St Columb to Wadebridge, but that I felt sure it could not be there, as the house there would have been on the right-hand side of the road; so that it must have been somewhere else. He replied, 'Don't think anything about it; you west-country people are so superstitious! You will make yourself miserable the remainder of the voyage.'

William Lightfoot and his brother James were arrested and charged with the murder, and William confessed to it.

'I went to Bodmin last Saturday week, the 8th instant [February 8, 1840], and in returning I met my brother James at the head of Dunmeer Hill. It was dim like. We came on the turnpike-road all the way till we came to the house near the spot where the murder was committed. We did not go into the house, but hid ourselves in a field. My brother knocked Mr Norway down; he snapped a pistol at him twice, and it did not go off. He then knocked him down with the pistol. I was there along with him. Mr Norway was struck while on horseback. It was on the turnpike-road, between Pencarrow Mill and the directing-post towards Wadebridge. I cannot say at what time of the night it was. We left the body in the water, on the left side of the road coming to Wadebridge. We took some money in a purse, but I did not know how much. My brother drew the body across the road to the watering.'

Apart from the minor detail that the house in the dream was on the left-hand side of the road, when in reality it was on the right, the resemblance was nearly exact; 'the dream must be considered remarkable,' Carlyon commented, 'from its unquestionable authenticity, and its perfect coincidence in time and circumstances with a most horrible murder.' Reviewing the case twenty years later, Robert Dale Owen pointed out that although it was quite natural that Edmund Norway should have dreamed of his brother, 'it was hardly natural that every minute particular of that night's misdeeds perpetrated in England should be seen at the time in a vision of the night, by a seaman off the island of St Helena;' and he listed the resemblances:

Mr Edmund Norway dreamed that his brother Nevell was attacked by two men and murdered.

Mr Nevell Norway was attacked the same night, by William Lightfoot and his brother James, and was murdered by them.

Mr Edmund Norway dreamed that 'it was on the road from St Columb to Wadebridge.'

'It was on the turnpike-road between Pencarrow Mill and the directing post towards Wadebridge.'

Mr Edmund Norway dreamed that 'one of the men caught the horse by the bridle, and snapped a pistol twice, but he heard no report; he then struck him a blow and he fell off his horse.'

James Lightfoot 'snapped a pistol at Mr Norway twice, and it did not go off; he then knocked him down with the pistol.' 'Mr Norway was struck while on horseback.'

Mr Edmund Norway dreamed that the murderers 'struck his brother several blows, and dragged him by the shoulders across the road and left him.'

James Lightfoot 'drew the body across the road to the watering.' The murderers 'left the body in the water, on the left side of the road coming to Wadebridge.'

A more complete set of correspondences, Owen thought, was hard to imagine; in particular, the incident of the pistol twice missing fire.

The most engaging story of an 'unfinished business' dream is the case of the Chaffin Will. James Chaffin had left his farm in North Carolina to his third son, leaving out his wife and the other brothers. In 1925, four years after he died, he appeared in a dream to his eldest son James, telling him there was another will, which would be found in the pocket of an old overcoat. The will was not, in fact, in the overcoat, when James went to look; but there was a note 'Read the 27th Chapter of Genesis in my daddy's old Bible.' As the Bible was in his mother's house, James brought along a neighbour to act as witness. After a protracted search, the Bible was found,

> so dilapidated that when we took it out it fell into three pieces. Mr Blackwelder picked up the portion containing the Book of Genesis, and there we found two leaves folded together; the left-hand page folded to the right, and the right-hand page folded to the left, forming a pocket; and in this pocket Mr Blackwelder found the will.

Apparently James Sr, after reading Genesis xxvii – the account of Jacob obtaining Esau's birthright by false pretences – had changed his mind about willing the property to his third son, and had decided to split it up between his children; but for some reason he had not disclosed the fact to them. The date on the newly discovered will, however, showed that it was made after the other one; and as the third son had died and his widow did not contest it, James Jr and his brothers became the beneficiaries. The story was vouched for by a lawyer who had been concerned in the case.

The commonest dreams in this category, though they lack attestation and, as a rule, drama, are those in which the vision of somebody dead or dying appears in a dream to beg forgiveness. 'I had quarrelled with a friend and he had really hurt me', one of Aniela Jaffé's correspondents in Switzerland told her, for the collection she was making for her book on *Apparitions* (1979).

> From then on I avoided him. Two years later I went abroad for about a fortnight. One evening, after a cheerful talk with friends, without the slightest allusion to spooks or ghosts, I dreamt that this old friend of mine had come and asked me to forgive him. When I turned a deaf ear to his plea, he came up to me and said: 'For heaven's sake don't be so obstinate! Something is awaiting me, that's why I want to be at peace.' With these words he took hold of my hand – I felt a cold hand quite definitely. Then I awoke, only to find the dream figure had vanished. But I heard the sound of a door shutting even though I was wide awake.
>
> Imagine my surprise when two days after this experience I received the news that my friend had been killed in an accident. What impressed me most was the fact that my dream and the hour of his

death had coincided. It seemed all the more extraordinary as there
was a distance of at least seven hundred miles between him and me.

Research

Yeats would have some justification for regarding himself as the first
person to set up experiments in connection with ESP in dreams. As a young
man he used to go and stay with an elderly uncle, George Pollexfen, near
Sligo in the west of Ireland. Pollexfen, a bachelor, was looked after by a
servant who, experience had convinced him, had second sight – if he
arrived home with unexpected guests he would find that Mary Battle had
already set the table for them. He was consequently interested in Yeats'
occult notions and practices; and the two of them used to experiment on
their walks. Yeats, on the sea shore, would imagine some symbol:
Pollexfen, walking among the sandhills, 'would notice what passed before
his mind's eye, and in a short time he would practically never fail of the
appropriate vision.'

Before long, they found that Mary Battle was picking up their
communications in her sleep, if they continued experimenting after she had
gone to bed.

> One night, started by what symbol I forget, we had seen an allegorical
> marriage of Heaven and Earth. When Mary Battle brought in the
> breakfast the next morning, I said, 'Well, Mary, did you dream
> anything last night?' and she replied (I am quoting from an old
> notebook) 'indeed she had'. She had dreamed that her bishop, the
> Catholic bishop of Sligo, had gone away 'without telling anybody'
> and had married 'a very high-up lady, and she not too young, either'.

On another occasion, when Pollexfen had had a vision of a man with his
head cut in two, Mary Battle had woken to find her face 'all over blood'.
Musing on the way in which she received their thoughts 'though coarsened
and turned to caricature', in her sleep, Yeats found himself wondering
whether the thoughts of a scholar or a hermit, 'though they speak no
word', also pass into the general mind.

More elaborate research was carried out towards the end of the 19th
century by Giovanni Battista Ermacora, one of a number of distinguished
Italian scientists who had made their reputations while adhering to

Comte's positivism, but who were so shaken by what they witnessed while investigating mediums – in particular, Eusapia Palladino – that they shed their scepticism, and began to conduct psychical research in earnest. The most celebrated of them, Cesare Lombroso, eventually became a convert to spiritualism. Others, among them Ermacora, strove to remain detached, devoting their time to exploring the phenomena of mediumship and trying to fit them into science's conventional framework.

One of Ermacora's subjects was Signorina Maria Mancini. He found it easy to work with her because her spirit 'control', a young girl who called herself 'Elvira', could hold conversations with him when Maria was in a state of trance, either through 'automatic writing' – Maria would hold the pen, and the words would pour onto the paper – or by 'direct voice,' a kind of ventriloquism in reverse, with Maria as the dummy through whom 'Elvira' conversed in her own voice.

When in 1892, Angelina, a young cousin of Maria's, came to stay, Ermacora found that she, too, knew about 'Elvira', though nobody had told her – nor, as she was only four, would she have understood if somebody had. This gave him an idea. If she had picked up 'Elvira' telepathically, might not 'Elvira' be induced to co-operate in some trials of telepathy between the cousins? He put it to 'Elvira'. She agreed to try, but told him that she could only pass messages while Angelina was asleep. The communication would have to be established in Angelina's dreams.

The procedure which Ermacora followed was to put Maria into a hypnotic trance, in the course of which he could pass instructions to 'Elvira' about what to plant in Angelina's dreams. After some false starts, one of his ideas – to get Angelina to dream of 'Elvira' with a light in one hand, and a portrait of Angelina's mother in the other – worked sufficiently well for him to satisfy himself that he was on the right lines. The child saw 'that little girl', as she thought of 'Elvira', with a light and a portrait, though she did not recognise the mother.

As the tests went on, Ermacora became more adept in producing dream ideas, and 'Elvira' entered into the spirit of the game by suggesting improvements. When he asked for a dream of Maria and himself in a two-oared gondola, going to the Lido, she suggested through direct voice that there should also be horses at the destination and 'the sea with its waves going "Vuuh!"' Angelina duly dreamed of a two-oared boat, gardens, 'lots of horses, and the sea said "Vuuh!"' – the sound that Ermacora had heard from 'Elvira'.

Could Maria be transmitting the information verbally to Angelina? Although Ermacora was satisfied that Maria remembered nothing of what went on in her trances, he decided to check. One day he proposed to 'Elvira' that she should try to get Angelina to dream that she was at the window of her room, looking towards the river.

A lamb would be grazing on the bank. A boat loaded with apples would pass, conducted by one boatman. He would stop close to the iron bridge, and get out to drink at the inn. While the boat was unguarded the lamb would jump in and begin to eat the apples, which would make 'Elvira' laugh very much.

Ermacora satisfied himself that there would be no communication between the two. As soon as Angelina woke up, she was asked to relate her dream which, Ermacora noted proudly, corresponded 'almost exactly' to the programme he had presented to 'Elvira'. The only differences were that Angelina thought the lamb was 'a light coloured dog' (it turned out that she had never seen a lamb) and she did not know where the boatman had gone.

The tests grew more complicated, the control more elaborate; but still, in spite of some failures, Angelina continued for more than six months to produce dreams to order, even when she and her cousin were sleeping in different houses. On one occasion, when Angelina was to be sea-sick in a dream, she woke up under the impression that she actually had been sick. On another, when in her dream she found herself reading, she woke up under the impression she had learned to read.

In his summing-up, Ermacora stressed two points. The results of his work suggested that a distinction must be made between Maria and the 'telepathic agent'. 'Elvira', in other words, must be regarded as a separate personality. But this did not, he insisted, entail belief that the separate personality was a spirit. 'In order not to be misunderstood, I may point out that recognition of the existence of the telepathic agent as a separate personality does not involve any hypothesis as to its nature.' The agent might be a psychical offshoot of Maria's personality; or it might enjoy an independent existence. On this issue, he felt, there was insufficient evidence to reach a decision. But 'taking the word *personality* in the sense which modern psychologists give to it – that is, a succession of states of consciousness; discontinuous, perhaps, but held together by memory and the consciousness of the Ego – then "Elvira" is certainly a personality.'

In his earlier research, into electricity, Ermacora had already established an enviable reputation. His research with Maria, meticulously conducted, remains an impressive source of evidence for extra-sensory communication in dreams. The records of the tests make it clear that he was not being duped by his subjects; and he was careful to invite other researchers (among them William James) to witness what he was doing. His report appeared in 1895, when he also founded a review of psychic studies, along the lines pioneered by the Society for Psychical Research after its foundation in 1882; but his plans for further work were cut off, three years later, by his death.

The Maimonides Dream Laboratory

Impressive though Ermacora's results were to anybody who accepted mediumship and regarded him as a trustworthy researcher, they stood no chance of convincing orthodox scientists, most of whom regarded psychical research of any kind with disfavour, and mediumship with scorn. In order to demonstrate ESP in dreams it became clear that laboratory tests were needed, and this presented obvious difficulties. Telepathy does not occur often, or regularly, in dreams; and there is no known way of inducing it. Volunteers sleeping in laboratories could not be expected to display extra-sensory perception in their dreams sufficiently often to make such investigations worth while.

In 1952 Eugene Aserinsky, a student at the University of Chicago who was studying sleep in young children, noted their occasional rapid eye movements; and he wondered whether they might be related to neurological changes, something that would be relatively easy to test with the help of electroencephalogram recordings, if electrodes were taped beside the children's eyes. The movement occurred in periods of relatively light sleep, it was found – not in itself of much significance; but when fresh experiments were conducted with adults, and they were woken up during these periods, they reported dreams far more often than when they were woken up at other times.

William Dement, then a student at the University of Chicago, embarked on a further investigation in connection with his PhD thesis. He found, among other things, that the length of time of REMs, as the rapid eye movements came to be known, seemed to be roughly proportionate to the length of the dream, as recalled when the sleeper was woken up. The myth that dreams are 'all over in a flash' was consequently demolished. Even more important, dreams became a more acceptable subject for scientific study. They remained subjective, in that the memory of the dreamers had to be relied upon in the absence of any objective way to detect the content of a dream. In strict behaviourist terms, indeed, no reliance could be put on them. But Dement could argue that although knowledge about dreams must depend in the last resort on the dreamers' subjective accounts, they 'become relatively objective if such reports can be significantly related to some physiological phenomena, which in turn can be measured by physical techniques' – an interesting example of the extent to which behaviourist psychology inhibited research at the time, making such excuses necessary.

REMs also aroused the interest of the psycho-analyst Montague Ullman, practising in New York, who had long been interested both in dreams and in parapsychology. There had been laboratory tests by the hundred for ESP with a 'sender' looking at cards of pictures in one room and the subjects writing, or drawing, whatever came into their heads, in another. It would be relatively simple, Ullman realised, to adapt the method to test for ESP in dreams; and in 1960 his 'Dream Lab.' began operations at the Maimonides Hospital in Brooklyn, New York.

The very first trial demonstrated the method's potential, though not quite as planned. The project was being funded by Eileen Garrett, the most remarkable medium of the time, through the Parapsychology Foundation which she had set up; and she was the subject of the first experiment. Three pictures were taken from *Life* magazine, placed in sealed envelopes, and given to Mrs Garrett's secretary, who lived several miles away. At a given signal, she was to concentrate on them. Mrs Garrett duly went to sleep at the lab – and after three hours, there was still no sign of the tell-tale REMs. No telephone call was made to the secretary, therefore, and the sealed envelopes remained unopened. When Mrs Garrett eventually woke up, however, she was able to recall a dream. She had seen horses running in a way reminding her of *Ben Hur*, which she had seen a few days earlier. When the envelopes were opened, one of them was a picture of the chariot race in the film.

Ullman and his colleagues, Karlis Osis and Douglas Dean, were experienced enough parapsychologists to know that one-off examples of this kind, however striking, would not impress psychologists. What was needed, they assumed, was a succession of trials with volunteer subjects to provide statistical validation of dream ESP.

Two rooms were used, isolated from each other. In one, volunteer subjects prepared to sleep, with electrodes attached to them to pick up their REMs whenever they occurred during the night. In the other, the 'sender' opened randomised target pictures or diagrams periodically during the night, and concentrated upon them. Whenever REMs occurred, the sleeper was woken up and asked to describe the contents of the dream; the idea being that even if from time to time a dream coincided by chance with the target, if the tests went on for long enough, and the 'hits' were sufficiently frequent, a case could be made for extra-sensory perception.

In the first series of trials, with twelve volunteers, precautions were taken to prevent any sensory cues reaching them; and outside judges were asked independently to gauge whether any dreams and targets matched. The results, Ullman felt able to claim in his report in *Archives of General Psychiatry* in 1966, 'appear to be sufficiently encouraging to warrant further investigation'; and the trials continued, with refinements to disarm criticism. For example, half the 'target' pictures were not in fact used *as* targets; they were employed as a check. In this way it was possible to find out whether the number of matching 'pairs' selected by the judges was running at a significantly higher rate than the number of 'pairs' found which were there as 'controls', not part of the trials; and this proved to be the case.

The net result of fifteen trials was by any standards remarkable. With one exception, where the outcome was at the level of chance expectation, they revealed that the number of 'hits' had exceeded the 'misses', the odds against chance being responsible being in the region of 100,000 to one. The old bugbear, 'chance coincidence', could not plausibly be brought against the findings. If such results had been obtained in any conventional research project, they would certainly have commanded respect. But the fact that they could be held to be evidence for ESP was enough to damn them in orthodox academic circles. A blind eye was turned on them by psychologists who, if they had done experiments with such statistically significant results, would have had visions of a Nobel Prize; and their antipathy was catered for by sceptics, led by Professor C.E.M. Hansel of the University of Swansea in his *ESP and Parapsychology: A Scientific Re-evaluation* (1980).

Hansel had earlier made it clear that he was not prepared to accept the evidence from trials for ESP, however impressive it might look. If the statistical data from experiments should rule out chance as the explanation, he had claimed, 'the results can only be accounted for by some kind of trick.' Unable to find any serious flaws in the Maimonides evidence, Hansel fell back on the allegation that the volunteers might have picked up information about the targets by other than extra-sensory means. In view of the descriptions in the reports of the elaborate precautions taken to prevent such leakage, the implication could only be that 'some kind of trick' had been employed.

Other critics went even further in their attacks on the credibility of the trials and the trustworthiness of the investigators. As Irvin L. Child of Yale University was able to show in an article in the *American Psychologist* in 1985, they unscrupulously travestied the accounts which had been presented in the scientific papers, and later in *Dream Telepathy* (1973), which Ullman wrote with Stanley Krippner and Alan Vaughan. The reaction provided further proof, if such were needed, that laboratory research of the Maimonides kind to establish the existence of ESP, however meticulously conducted, cannot hope to carry conviction unless and until scientists are prepared to accept ESP. Up to the present, although opinion polls have suggested that a majority of scientists are prepared to concede the *possibility* of ESP, the scientific establishment – the university élite – has set its collective face against acceptance; and its preconceptions are catered for by writers on the academic fringe who have no scruples about distorting the accounts of the experiments, and where necessary imputing fraud to account for their success.

Yet even if the Maimonides results had escaped such treatment, they were not of a kind which would carry total conviction, as in some attempts to repeat them the results were negative. That some should be negative did not dismay parapsychologists. Even at Maimonides, after all, some trials had given near-chance results (which, incidentally, was a powerful argument against the allegations of fraud; had there been fraud, the perpetrators would surely have used it to produce more impressive evidence). Nevertheless experience has shown that the results of trials presenting the case for ESP statistically, even if they show that the odds against chance being the explanation are millions to one, make less of an impression than personal experiences of telepathic or precognitive dreams, or graphically illustrated accounts of other people's experiences. Some of the most striking examples of target-hitting at Maimonides, and in similar types of trial, have been those where the *precise* target has been correctly identified. But where statistical significance has been the main aim, such precision is largely wasted. If a dream is of a ball, and the target is an 'O', that can be considered reasonable for the purpose simply of matching 'pairs'. But it only rates as highly, for this purpose, as a ball in a dream which turns out to have been painted in precisely the same colours, and in the same pattern, as the ball in the target picture. 'Unscientific' though it is considered to be, the public is more likely to be impressed by a few anecdotal examples of direct 'hits' than by bleak statistics.

4

Dreaming the Future

The dreams that arouse the greatest interest – to those who have to listen to them, as well as the dreamers themselves – are those which appear to foreshadow some future event. Prevision, or precognition as it is now more usually called, used to be regarded as one of the commoner manifestations of second sight in those parts of the world where second sight was endemic, as in the Western Isles of Scotland. But by the early 19th century, when the existence of 'seers' was being called in question, belief in prevision was being singled out for ridicule by sceptics of the David Hume persuasion as a particularly absurd superstition, for reasons which Robert McNish gave in 1830 in his *The Philosophy of Sleep* – an early attempt to provide a rational explanation for the disturbingly irrational behaviour of the human mind in sleep.

McNish recalled that he had once dreamt of the death of a near relation. Waking up in 'inconceivable terror' – McNish's own description – he had immediately written to the man's family. His letter had crossed one from them telling him that the relation, though he appeared to have been in perfect health, *had* died – on the morning of the dream. This, McNish explained, was pure chance. To dream the future was impossible. There had been a time when such glimpses of the future occurred, he was careful to add, because God was intervening on behalf of his people. But this was no longer necessary. The world was now, 'in all cases, governed by the fundamental laws originally made by God for its regulation;' and these laws excluded the possibility of communication except through the recognised sense channels.

McNish, in other words, had found himself in the difficult position of trying to fuse the new positivism with traditional Scots Protestantism; a feat achievable only by claiming that God, though all-powerful, had laid down the laws of nature and would have no need to suspend them except in dire emergency (prayers were still permissible for divine intervention to end a drought, or cure the sick). But with scientists gaining in confidence in the course of the century, they ceased to worry about God's role. Only known facts and observable phenomena mattered, Auguste Comte claimed; and the laws of nature were securely based on them.

This still left a nagging worry. Dreams were observable phenomena, at least to the dreamer; and they continued to present examples of what appeared to be glimpses of the future which could not be accounted for by conscious foreknowledge. The contortions to which Comte's positivist disciples were driven in order to explain away this anomaly was to be illustrated in 1861 by Alfred Maury, who had come to be highly regarded for the skill with which in earlier works he had demolished the case for real, as distinct from fake, magic. In *Le Sommeil et les rêves* he described how one day, when he was feeling off-colour, he had retired to bed.

I dreamed of the Terror; I was present at scenes of massacre, I appeared in front of the revolutionary tribunal, I saw Robespierre, Marat, Fouquier-Tinville, all the ugliest faces of that terrible era; I spoke with them; at last after many events which I remember only vaguely, I was judged, condemned to death, taken by car to an immense concourse on the site of the Revolution; I mount the scaffold; the executioner binds me to the fatal plank; he makes it see-saw; the blade falls; I feel my head separate from my body, I wake up in a state of intense anguish, and I feel on my neck the bedrail which had suddenly detached itself, and had fallen on my cervical vertebrae, in the manner of a guillotine blade.

Maury's mother, who was at the invalid's bedside, confirmed that it had all happened in an instant. To Maury, this could only mean that 'at the moment I was struck, the memory of that redoubtable instrument, whose effect my bedrail reproduced so well, had sparked off all the images of that era symbolised by the guillotine.'

As it happened, an alternative explanation was also being advanced by positivists at the time, when confronted by mysteries of this kind. In experiments with mesmerised subjects in the 1840s the Scots doctor James Braid had found that some of them appeared to become clairvoyant; this he attributed to 'hyperaesthesia' while in the trance state to which he gave the name of hypnosis. This notion was taken up by the physiologist William Benjamin Carpenter; in cases such as Maury's, the explanation would have been that the bedrail must have given some indication – a 'creak', say, picked up by the dreamer – that it was about to fall. In France, however, positivists were still reluctant to accept that the mind when asleep enjoyed such powers. Maury's contention that dreams could be all over in a flash was preferred.

It was the measure of the positivists' nervousness about the continuing reports of precognition in dreams that an even more bizarre explanation emerged: 'identifying paramnesia'. The realisation that the two hemispheres of the brain were to some extent performing different functions led to the theory being presented to account for *déjà vu* experiences. The 'I have been here before' feeling, the theory ran, was the result of faulty intercommunication between the hemispheres. One of them picked up, say, a vista, seen for the first time. The other, picking it up a fraction of a second later, might reach the mistaken conclusion that the vista had been seen before. The same hypothesis was put forward to account for those dreams which were only recollected when some scene, or event, brought them back to mind. This was not really recollection, the positivists argued. One of the brain's hemispheres must have slipped fractionally behind the other, leaving the impression that the scene or event had been witnessed earlier in a dream.

These ideas – hyperaesthesia; that dreams are all over in a flash; and that they may not really have been dreams at all – were reinforced by a more commonsense notion: that the vast majority of dreams which appear to foretell the future can readily be accounted for by coincidence. Alfred Lehmann, the psychologist who at the turn of the century was one of the most unsparing critics of the findings of the psychical researchers, was reluctantly compelled to concede that he knew of some dreams in which information was passed to the dreamer which he could not possibly have obtained by natural means, and which subsequently was verified. The explanation, Lehmann argued, could only be that this happened by 'mere accident' – by chance; and this has remained the fall-back for rationalists who cannot accept the possibility of precognition.

'How many times,' Christopher Evans asked his readers in *Landscapes of the Night*, 'have you heard about somebody who has dreamed of a plane crash the day before he was due to go on a flight, has cancelled the trip and been rewarded for his caution because the plane did crash?' Many times, Evans felt sure – and often the story would have been true. But what one needs to do 'is to ask, what is the frequency of non-paranormal dreams of this kind?' when the trip is cancelled but the plane does not crash. Statistics of such occasions are not available; but if they were ...

'Dunne dreams'

Evans was evading a question presented by Edmund Gurney nearly a century before. What proportion of 'striking correspondences' would be required to remove a dream from the 'chance coincidence' to the 'precognition' category? The issue cannot be judged on a simple quantitative basis – even if it were possible to find the frequency of such dreams which do not 'come true' and compare it with those which do. The number of correspondences in any dream in which the future appears to be foretold, and particularly their precision, has to be taken into consideration; much may depend on the quality of the details. Chance, coupled with nervousness about flying, could certainly account for the great majority of dreams about a plane crashing the night before a plane crashes. But it is harder to sustain if the actual make of the aircraft is foreseen; harder still, if what occurs in the dream turns out to correspond in detail to the crash itself.

This point was first brought home to the public in 1927 by J.W.Dunne's *An Experiment with Time*. It was very different from the ordinary run of books on and around this subject, in that for the most part the glimpses his dreams had given to him of the future were insignificant. They had not led him to buried treasure or told him what horses to back. Yet it was precisely because the correspondences were trivial that they were striking. Nobody, his readers could feel sure, would have bothered to invent them. Even in the most dramatic of his dreams, it was not the drama so much as the detail that was impressive. In 1902 Dunne had been in an army camp in the Orange Free State in South Africa, where newspapers rarely arrived.

There, one night, I had an unusually vivid and rather unpleasant dream.

I seemed to be standing on high ground – the upper slopes of some spur of a hill or mountain. The ground was of a curious white formation. Here and there in this were little fissures, and from these jets of vapour were spouting upward. In my dream I recognised the place as an island of which I had dreamed before – an island which was in imminent peril from a volcano. And, when I saw the vapour

spouting from the ground, I gasped: 'It's the island! Good Lord, the
whole thing is going to *blow up*!' For I had memories of reading about
Krakatoa, where the sea, making its way into the heart of a volcano
through a submarine crevice, flushed into steam, and blew the whole
mountain to pieces. Forthwith I was seized with a frantic desire to
save the four thousand (I knew the number) unsuspecting inhabitants.
Obviously there was only one way of doing this, and that was to take
them off in ships. There followed a most distressing nightmare, in
which I was at a neighbouring island, trying to get the incredulous
French authorities to despatch vessels of every and any description to
remove the inhabitants of the threatened island. I was sent from one
official to another; and finally woke myself by my own dream
exertions, clinging to the heads of a team of horses drawing the
carriage of one 'Monsieur le Maire', who was going out to dine and
wanted me to return when his office would be open next day. All
through the dream the *number* of the people in danger obsessed my
mind. I repeated it to everyone I met, and, at the moment of waking,
I was shouting to the 'Maire', 'Listen! Four thousand people will be
killed unless – '

When the next batch of newspapers arrived, a *Daily Telegraph* was among
them, and in the centre sheet – at that time, the main news page – was

VOLCANO DISASTER

IN

MARTINIQUE

TOWN SWEPT AWAY

An avalanche of Flame

Probable Loss of over 40,000 Lives

British Steamer Burnt

One of the most terrible disasters in the annals of the world has
befallen the once prosperous town of St Pierre, the commercial
capital of the French island of Martinique in the West Indies. At eight
o'clock on Thursday morning the volcano Mount Pelée which had
been quiescent for a century, etc.,

A further section of the story had the heading

MOUNTAIN EXPLODES

which was the description an eyewitness on a ship about a mile away had given. The meticulous Dunne, however, was concerned to point out where the dream had actually been wrong. The number in the headline was not 4,000, as in the dream, but 40,000 – though so firmly had the first figure established itself in his mind that he did not notice the difference in the headline until he came to copy it out, years later. In fact, neither figure was correct.

So my wonderful 'clairvoyant' vision had been wrong in its most insistent particular! But it was clear that its wrongness was likely to prove a matter just as important as its rightness. For *whence*, in the dream, had I got that idea of 4000? Clearly it must have come into my mind *because of the newspaper paragraph*. This suggested the extremely unpleasant notion that the whole thing was what doctors call 'Identifying Paramnesia'; that I had never really had any such dream at all; but that on reading the newspaper report, a false idea had sprung up in my mind to the effect that I had previously dreamed a dream combining all the details given in that paragraph.

To Dunne's relief, his next experience, two years later, 'completely squashed' the theory.

I dreamed that I was standing on a footway of some kind, consisting of transverse planks flanked on my left side by some sort of railing, beyond which was a deep gulf filled with dark fog. Overhead, I had an impression of an awning. But this last was not clearly seen, for the fog partly hid everything except three or four yards of the planking ahead of me with its attendant portion of railing and gulf. Suddenly I noticed, projecting upwards from somewhere far down in the gulf, an immensely long, thin, shadowy thing like a gigantic lath. It reached above the plankway, and was slanted so that it would, had the upper end been visible through the fog, have impinged upon the awning. As I stared at it, it began to wave up and down brushing the ceiling.

For a moment he was puzzled, and then he realised that what he was watching was the jet from a fire-engine hose, as seen on newsreel film through smoke.

As I perceived this, the dream became perfectly abominable. The wooden plankway became crowded with people, dimly visible through the smoke. They were dropping in heaps; and all the air was filled with horrible choking, gasping ejaculations. Then the smoke which had grown black and thick, rolled heavily over everything, hiding the entire scene. But a dreadful, suffocating moaning continued – and I was entirely thankful when I awoke.

He would take no chances this time, Dunne decided. When he woke up he wrote down every detail he could remember before the arrival of the morning papers. They contained nothing of relevance. But the evening papers described a big fire in a Paris factory, which dealt in some material that gave off vile fumes when it burned.

A large number of workgirls had been cut off by the flames, and had made their way out on to a *balcony*. There, for the moment they had been comparatively safe, but the ladders available had been too short to admit of any rescue. While longer ones were being obtained, the fire engines had directed streams of water on to the balcony to keep that refuge from catching alight. And then there happened a thing which must, I imagine, have been unique in the history of fire. From the broken windows behind the balcony the smoke from the burning rubber or other material came rolling out in such dense volumes that, although the unfortunate girls were standing actually in the open air, every one of them was suffocated before the new ladders could arrive.

Ordinarily, though, Dunne's glimpses in his dreams of something he would shortly encounter in his waking life were striking, from his point of view, chiefly because chance provided an extremely far-fetched explanation. One night he dreamt of an umbrella, folded, 'standing unsupported, *upside down, handle on the pavement*, just outside the Piccadilly Hotel'. The next day he happened to pass along Piccadilly in a bus, and just before it reached the hotel he saw, walking along the pavement, an old lady carrying an umbrella of the kind he had seen in the dream, and 'she had it *upside down.* She was holding it by the ferrule end, and was pounding along towards the hotel with the *handle on the pavement.*'

Precisely because his dreams were so often of this kind – intimations of nothing except his mind's ability to move forward in time – Dunne decided that it was misleading to think of them as occult, or psychic, in the accepted sense. The need, he argued, was for a new theory of time, and our relationship with it, which would allow us in dreams to roam forward as well as backward; and he presented abstruse mathematical arguments in support of his contention. The verdict of people qualified to follow them, and who have studied them in detail, has been that in so far as the theories are comprehensible they are untenable. Yet *An Experiment With Time* has been influential – more influential, certainly, than the results of conventional research.

One reason for this was that in the early part of the book, where Dunne was simply recounting his dreams, he sounded transparently honest and down-to-earth – which, according to J.B. Priestley, was what he also was in the flesh: 'he looked and behaved like the old regular officer type crossed with a mathematician and engineer.' Even more important was Dunne's suggestion that anybody who cared to experiment had only to place pad and pencil by the bedside, and write down everything recalled of a dream, or dreams, first thing in the morning. When, years later, Priestley asked viewers of his BBC television programme on Time to send him accounts of any experiences they might have had which challenged the conventional view of past, present and future, replies poured in. He found that many of the most striking and best attested cases came from people who had read *An Experiment With Time*, and had followed Dunne's advice. Without it, Priestley decided, 'I suspect that at least a third of the best precognitive dreams I have been sent would never have come my way.'

For those commentators who cannot accept precognition, Dunne has remained an embarrassment. In *Dreams and Dreaming* (1965) Norman MacKenzie mentions him only in passing (along with other 'supernatural explanations' – Dunne would have been appalled to find himself in such company). And Christopher Evans, although as a teenager he had been impressed by *An Experiment With Time*, claimed that when he read it again he found 'only one or two of his "precognitive" dreams to be remotely interesting, and most of them to be thin to the point of insubstantiality' – a sadly misleading comment, in view of the fact that it was the dreams' thinness and insubstantiality, more than any dramatic content, which Dunne was emphasising.

Evans, though, would not have disputed that it is largely thanks to Dunne – and to J.B. Priestley, with his 'Time' plays on the Dunne theme – that 'dreaming the future' is now acceptable (to judge from opinion polls) to a majority of the public in spite of the fact that its implications are for many people disturbing. And although Dunne himself made no serious attempt to reinforce his account of his own experiences from the historical record, had he done so he would have found ample confirmation of the reality of precognition in dreams, even if not of his theories.

Trivia

Surveying the hundreds of reports of precognitive dreams he received, Priestley noted that they tended to run to extremes. Nearly half of them concerned disaster or death; nearly half were of trivialities; only about one in ten was in between the terrible and the trivial. A great range of familiar and, it might be thought, obvious dream material was hardly represented at all: very few romantic episodes or sexual encounters; hardly any relating to important developments in work, such as promotion. 'I can only conclude, then, that precognitive dreaming does not offer us any reflection of people's main interests.'

Priestley could not have known it, but this feature of reports of precognitive dreams fits in well with the thesis Jan Ehrenwald was later to advance, that ESP comes through to us in two main ways, flaw-directed and need-directed – the trivial being for the most part flaw-directed, the information slipping through the brain's filter for no discernible reason; the disasters being allowed through on account of their seeming importance.

Nevertheless it is the trivial dreams which, paradoxically, often make the most impressive case for the reality of precognition. With 'disaster' dreams, it is often easy to surmise either that the information has been fed into the subconscious mind by hyperacuity – we have sensed, without being conscious of it, that something is the matter with friends or relations which will lead to their death; or that chance is responsible – calamities, after all, can be a daily occurrence. But hyperacuity of the senses cannot account for innumerable trivial precognitive dreams, and for various reasons chance coincidence is often hard to accept.

In some cases, as in Dunne's, precognition is hard to reject because the glimpses of the future have occurred to the dreamer so often. In *Second Sight in Daily Life* (1951) W.H.H. Sabine described his experiences, similar in many ways to Dunne's in that often it was as if the dream was a slightly botched prediction of the event. On one occasion, for example, on a train going down to the country, he told his wife of an odd dream he had had the night before. They were walking in the country and asked a man the way.

> He pointed out what he said was the right way, though somehow I had the feeling it was not. The remarkable thing came next, when I saw the man going away from me with his clothes off. However, somehow I could see only his back.

When they arrived, their host seemed worried. His sister Janet, he explained, had gone to the local police. The fact was, he explained,

> There's a man about who's been exposing himself. Last Sunday he suddenly stepped out from the trees in front of Janet, let down one garment and pulled up another. Bit of a shock, of course. So the police are now in hiding, ready to pounce, and Janet's walking up there with the dogs in case he does it again.

Apart from getting the 'flashing' back to front, the dream on its own would provide indifferent evidence for precognition; but it was one of many, some of them more impressive in their detail, though usually with discrepancies from the actual event. In 1940 Sabine dreamed he was shown a map by an Indian fakir: 'the map was very clear, but very simple. It consisted of a pale reddish brown background on which, in a darker shade of the same hue, was depicted a large river, together with a tributary of lesser size. The river and its tributary were shown to the left of the background.' The following day he went to a lecture on psychical phenomena at the French Institute, not knowing what to expect. The lecturer, describing a precognitive dream relating to the Napoleonic wars, asked the audience if a map would make the dream clearer. 'The word "map" made me sit up in some excitement,' Sabine recalled. 'I marvelled indeed when the Professor proceeded to draw on the blackboard a map representing a river and its tributaries, and moreover drew it on the left side of the board.'

Some people are impressed, as Sabine was, by the succession of dreams

providing trivial pointers to the future; others have had only one
experience of the kind, but have found it impressive because of the wealth
of detail it provided. Rudyard Kipling felt certain that the great majority
of dreams which appeared to foretell the future were simply lucky hits. But
one of his dreams, he felt bound to admit in *Something of Myself* (1937), had
'passed beyond the bounds of ordinance'.

> I dreamt that I stood, in my best clothes, which I do not wear as a rule,
> one in a line of similarly habited men, in some vast hall, floored with
> rough-jointed stone slabs. Opposite me, the width of the hall, was
> another line of persons and the impression of a crowd behind them.
> On my left some ceremony was taking place that I wanted to see, but
> could not unless I stepped out of my line because the fat stomach of
> my neighbour on my left barred my vision. At the ceremony's close,
> both lines of spectators broke up and moved forward and met, and the
> great space filled with people. Then a man came up behind me,
> slipped his hand beneath my arm, and said: 'I want a word with you.'
> I forget the rest: but it had been a perfectly clear dream, and it stuck
> in my memory.

About six weeks later, he had to attend a ceremony at Westminster
Abbey, in his capacity as a member of the War Graves Commission, at
which the Prince of Wales was to dedicate a plaque to the dead.

> We Commissioners lined up, facing across the width of the Abbey
> Nave, more members of the Ministry and a big body of the public
> behind them, all in black clothes. I could see nothing of the ceremony
> because the stomach of the man on my left barred my vision. Then,
> my eye was caught by the cracks of the stone flooring, and I said to
> myself; 'But here is where I have been!' We broke up, both lines
> flowed forward and met, and the Nave filled with a crowd, through
> which a man came up and slipped his hand upon my arm saying: 'I
> want a word with you, please.' It was about some utterly trivial
> matter that I have forgotten.

At the time, Kipling said and wrote nothing about his experience; for
the sake, as he put it, 'of the "weaker brethren" – and sisters'. They might

have been tempted by his example to go 'down to Endor'. 'But how, and why,' he asked, 'have I been shown an unreleased roll of my life-film?'

In Kipling's case, what was impressive to him was the way the continuity of the 'life-film' in the dream was repeated in reality. A similar example was to be given by Ann Bridge, one of the most popular of British novelists in the years between the wars, in her *Moments of Knowing* (1970). In private life called Mrs O'Malley, she had been invited for the first time to stay with the Maxwell-Scotts at Abbotsford, the house near the border with England which Sir Walter Scott had built for himself, and in which he died. Compelled as a child to read some of his novels, she had found them unendurable, 'long-winded, boring, and somehow bogus', and had transferred her dislike of the books to the author.

It was a long and detailed dream in which her hostess came in to her room to talk to her before she got up, dressed, and went downstairs, intending to go out into the garden.

At the foot of the stairs was a large hall, at one side of which a door stood open; as I stepped into the hall, a little dog ran through this door, barking sharply – startled, I gave a little scream, and a man's voice called through the door, rather irritably – 'Who is *that*?' I went over and entered the room, saying 'It's Mrs O'Malley – the dog startled me.' A tall, thin, grey-haired man rose from behind a laden desk, and introduced himself as my host; beside him stood a shorter and stouter man, in a suit of tweed of a peculiar dark brownish red, already familiar to me as crotal (a natural dye made from lichen) – he was introduced to me as the factor, as the Scots call a land-agent.

Ann Bridge then dreamed she went out into the garden, which she had not seen before. When she woke up, she dressed and went downstairs.

I had almost reached the hall at the bottom when from an open door on my right, a little dog rushed out, barking. I gave a tiny scream, and from the open door a man's voice said irritably, almost angrily, 'Who is *that*?' Just as in my dream, a tall grey-haired man, Sir Walter Maxwell-Scott, stood up behind his desk and introduced himself. I looked eagerly to see if the man in the crotal tweed suit was there too – yes, sure enough, he was, and was duly presented as the factor. (I think his name was Curle.) We talked for a little while, and then I

went back into the hall and out through the front door; there was that
very peculiar walled space, with the ovals of carving set out in the
solid thickness of the greenery, just as I had dreamt it barely an hour
before.

More often, though, it is one particular episode in a dream, repeated in
reality soon afterwards, which makes the impression; especially if it is not
just what happens, but the precision with which the dream has captured the
scene – even, sometimes, the actual appearance of the people who are
encountered. Charles Dickens was clearly taken aback by the sequel to one
of his dreams which he related to his biographer John Forster.

On Thursday night in last week, being at the office here, I dreamed
that I saw a lady in a red shawl with her back towards me (whom I
supposed to be E). On her turning round I found that I didn't know
her and she said 'I am Miss Napier.' All the time I was dressing next
morning, I thought – What a preposterous thing to have so very
distinct a dream about nothing; and why Miss Napier? for I never
heard of any Miss Napier. That same Friday night, I read. After the
reading, came into my retiring room, Mary Boyle and her brother
and *the* Lady in the red shawl whom they present as 'Miss Napier!'
These are all the circumstances, exactly told.

To the dreamer, and to those who have heard an account of the dream
before the sequel makes it memorable, the most convincing evidence for
precognition often comes on those occasions when it seems as if some
practical joker has been responsible.

Mrs Atlay, a bishop's wife, wrote out an experience of hers for Horace
Hutchinson to use in his *Dreams and Their Meaning* (1891).

I dreamt that the bishop being from home, we were unable to have
family prayers as usual in the chapel, but that I read them in the large
hall of the palace, out of which, on one side, a door opens into the
dining-room. In my dream, prayers being ended, I left the hall,
opened the dining-room door and there saw, to my horror, standing
between the table and the side-board, an enormous pig. The dream
was very vivid and amused me much.

When she went down to the hall to read prayers, the servants had not yet assembled there; so she told her children and their governess about the dream, which amused them, too.

> The servants came in and I read prayers, after which the party dispersed. I opened the dining-room door, where to my amazement, stood the pig in the very spot in which I had seen him in my dream.

Reluctant to accuse a bishop's wife of fabrication, doubters had contented themselves with suggestions that she might have heard the pig making its entry into the palace in her sleep. Impossible, Mrs Atlay assured Hutchinson. Her bedroom was on the other side of the house. In any case, she had ascertained that the pig had only got loose while she was reading prayers. The gardener cleaning its sty had neglected to secure the gate.

Another case from the same period, published in the SPR's *Proceedings*, was contributed by a Scotswoman whose belief that her dreams came true had amused her friends. When she offered one morning to relate a dream to a house party, on the chance it might turn out to come true, the reaction was predictable; but as she was their hostess, she related it nevertheless. In the dream

> I thought there were several people in our drawing-room, among others Mr J., and I left them for a few minutes to see if supper was ready. When I came back to the drawing-room I found the carpet, which was a new one, all covered with black spots. I was very angry, and when Mr J. said it was ink stains, I retorted, 'Don't say so, I know it has been burnt, and I counted five patches.'

As it was a Sunday, the members of the house party went to church; and on their return 'Mr J.' joined them, something he had never done before.

> I went into the dining-room to see if the things were ready, and then going back into the drawing-room I found a spot near the door and asked who had been in with dirty feet; being a new carpet, I was particular. Mr J., as in my dream, said it was surely ink; and then pointed to some more spots when I called out, 'Oh, my dream! My new carpet! Burnt!'

What had happened, she found, was that the housemaid, finding she had allowed the fire to go out, had carried in live coals from another room on a shovel. It had tilted as she was carrying it, spilling some of them, and 'burning *five* holes'. Her daughter testified in a note to the SPR that her mother's version was correct.

In his *Imagination in Dreams* (1894) Frederick Greenwood recalled a macabre example of precognition in one of his own dreams.

One night I dreamt that, making a call on some matter of business, I was shown into a fine great drawing-room and asked to wait. Accordingly, I went over to the fire-place in the usual English way, proposing to wait there. And there, after the same fashion, I lounged with my arm upon the mantel-piece; but only for a few moments. For feeling that my fingers had rested on something cold, I looked, and saw that they lay on a dead hand: a woman's hand newly cut from the wrist.

Although he woke in horror, he put the dream out of his mind; but that day, when he had to make some unimportant business call, he was asked to wait in a room adorned with various knick-knacks.

Glancing by chance toward the mantel-piece (the dream of the previous night still forgotten), what should I see upon it but the hand of a mummy, broken from the wrist. It was a very little hand, and on it was a ring that would have been a 'gem ring' if the dull red stone in it had been genuinely precious. Wherefore I concluded that it was a woman's hand.

Coincidence? 'Visions of severed hands on mantelpieces are not common and, with or without previous dreaming of it, few men have actually seen one, even when taken from a mummy case, in that precise situation.'

J.B. Priestley came across a precognitive dream which, he felt, all but ruled out coincidence. A BBC engineer when a student dreamed that a sparrow-hawk perched on his right shoulder, so that he actually felt its claws. Two hours later, when he was in a downstairs sitting-room of the 'digs' in which he was living at the time, his landlord came in with some junk to be thrown on the fire, including a stuffed sparrow-hawk. One of his fellow students picked it up, came up behind him, 'and dug its claws into the shoulder of my jacket with sufficient force to enable it to remain standing on my shoulder.' He could naturally feel its claws. It was only then that he recalled the dream – though he had in fact recorded it in his notebook, along with other dream material.

Chance coincidence reaches an even greater degree of implausibility in one of the accounts reported to Montague Ullman.

> Early on a Sunday morning on Father's Day, I woke both myself and my husband by laughing out loud. The dream consisted of one scene and no dialogue. My sister, ten years my junior, stood before me in a bulky coat, put her hands in the coat pockets and extended her arms towards me. I could see each hand was filled with bottle caps.

She told her husband, and later her father, what she had dreamed. When the rest of the family arrived for Father's Day Dinner,

> My sister, who was pregnant, was wearing a very full, lightweight summer coat. As I was hanging it up she called to me to bring her cigarettes from the coat pocket. I returned to her with the coat, and while I still held it, she reached into the pockets and came out with – not cigarettes, but two handfuls of bottle-caps.

When her sister saw the bottle-caps, she exclaimed, 'Look what the boys put in my pockets!' 'As you can see,' the dreamer told Ullman, 'the only difference was that in the dream, she was wearing her coat.'

In *Mind-Reach* (1977), which the physicist Russell Targ wrote with Harold Puthoff about their work with Stanford Research Institute, Targ describes how the night before the two of them were going to attend a conference in Tarrytown, New York, he dreamed that one of the speakers, who was wearing a ruffled shirt and a red carnation with his tuxedo, actually sang his speech. The next day, seeing a man dressed as in the dream, Targ jovially asked him whether he was going to sing to them. He was – as band leader and singer, later in the evening.

Quite often there has been the same kind of differences in a reported dream, and the event which followed, as Dunne found in his dreams – differences which on occasion seem only to lend curious support to the view that the dream was precognitive. In *The Mask of Time* (1978) Jean

Forman records a short but vivid dream of a teacher, Mrs Marjorie
Longstaffe, and its sequel.

> I saw my husband (looking rather dwarfed in stature) standing on the
> lid of the piano, reaching up his hand to a table-lamp which was
> standing on the left corner of the piano top. (In reality there is not a
> lamp there.) His hand unfastened, with a quick turn, the light bulb,
> which he threw down on to the floor. It fell on to the corner of the
> hearthrug, just missing the tiles of the fireplace. At this point I entered
> the door – called out to him – and awakened.

She immediately told her husband of the dream, as it was an odd one,
before dressing and going downstairs.

> As I opened the sitting-room door I saw our tabby cat, Jody, in
> exactly the same place as I had seen my husband in my dream – on the
> piano lid, stretching up his paw and overturning a small glass vase
> which I had inadvertently left there, after taking the faded crocuses
> from it on the previous evening. The little vase spun down on to the
> edge of the hearthrug in exactly the same place as the discarded bulb
> had fallen in my dream. It, too, rolled over, unbroken. By instinct, I
> called out to the cat, just as I had done to my husband in the dream.

In reply to the Koestler Foundation's appeal, Mrs R.A. Drake of Hayling
Island in Hampshire has recalled that one day she and a group of friends
were discussing whether they dreamed in colour. She was able to assure
them that she did, by citing a dream she had the previous night. In it, she
was in a divan bed in a room in a semi-basement – she could see the feet
and lower legs of people walking past the windows, and on each side of the
windows there was a curtain, one orange and one purple. The colour
combination had been sufficiently unusual for her to recall it vividly; and
she remembered it when 'about three months later I woke up in the very
same room, with its orange/purple curtains.' Mrs Drake had not met the
friend with whom she was then staying, until after she had the dream.

Sometimes it is as if the practical joker lays on the dream to confound a
sceptic. One of Medard Boss's trainee psychotherapists told him that when,
in the course of his training, he had been confronted with the idea of dream
clairvoyance, it had disturbed him, being against his rationalist beliefs.

Discussing it with his wife, they agreed that only some striking personal experience would convince them. The following morning she related a dream.

> I could see Vicar S. arriving with two boxes. The boxes looked odd to me. I did not dare to open them. Suddenly Anneli A. turned up. The boxes were opened. Anneli A. explained their contents to me. They were children's dresses. In one box there were modern American dresses and in the other there were older and coloured clothes. I felt that the dresses came from Anneli A. and I was surprised. At the same time it seemed that Anneli A. was somehow related to the vicar, perhaps she was his daughter.

They tried to interpret the dream along conventional analytic lines, but without success. They knew the vicar, but had just been told he was away. 'Anneli A.' was a distant relation of his, and the daughter of another vicar; but they had lost touch with her for years. Baffled, he said (as a joke) 'Perhaps it means something which is going to happen in the future!'

> An hour later a parcel of two boxes arrived by post. In the one we found white and modern American dresses and in the other, older and coloured dresses for our children. These dresses came from Anneli A. She had sent them to us because she could not use them any longer. The arrival of these parcels was just as unheralded and strange as the appearance of Anneli A. in the dream and the subsequent waking experience was so striking, that neither of us had the slightest doubt about the clairvoyant character of this affair.

The effect of a precognitive dream on one celebrated freethinker, William Hone, was apparently decisive. Hone had made his reputation as a caustic critic both of conventional Christian beliefs and of those who sought to impose them; and in three trials he had trounced the Attorney General, when he was brought to court for publishing material which the Tory government of the time – just after the end of the Napoleonic wars – considered blasphemous and a danger to the morale of the nation: a parody of the Ten Commandments ('Thou shalt not call starving to death murder'). But according to his anonymous biographer, Hone later had a dream in which he went into a room

where he was an entire stranger, and saw himself seated at a table, and
on going towards the window his attention was somehow or other
attracted to the window-shutter, and particularly to a knot in the
wood, which was of singular appearance; and on waking the whole
scene, and especially the knot in the shutter, left a most vivid
impression on his mind.

Some time later, in a house which Hone did not know, he was

shown into a chamber where he had never been before, which
instantly struck him as being the identical chamber of his dream. He
turned directly to the window, where the same knot in the shutter
caught his eye. This incident, to his investigating spirit, induced a
train of reflection which overthrew his cherished theories of
materialism, and resulted in conviction that there were spiritual
agencies as susceptible of proof as any facts of physical science; and
this appears to have been one of the links in that mysterious chain of
events by which, according to the inscrutable purposes of the Divine
will, man is sometimes compelled to bow to an unseen and divine
power, and ultimately to believe.

Déjà vu

One variety of dream in the trivial category happens to have an impressive
record in persuading people of the reality of precognition; the kind which
is recalled in the *déjà vu*, 'I have been here before' feeling. A questionnaire
which Christopher Evans persuaded a range of British journals to publish
in the 1960s – *The Sunday Times*, the *TV Times*, *Destiny* and *Honey* – and
which brought in a flood of replies from what he took to be a reasonably
representative sample of the nation, revealed that 80 per cent of the sample
had had the experience; and very often it is related to a dream – the person
who has it recalls having the dream, either a remembered one or one which
until that moment had been forgotten – because the situation appears to be
a repeat performance of the dream.

The stock positivist explanation of *déjà vu* (as Dunne had noted) used to
be identifying paramnesia – one hemisphere of the brain, a fraction of a
second behind the other, invents the memory of the dream to account for
the feeling of having been there before. But, describing an account given

to him by Canon Garnier (from whom he had learnt Latin as a boy), Camille Flammarion noted in his *Death and its Mystery* (1920) that the experience of the 'worthy priest' effectively disposed of this notion. In a dream in 1846, Garnier had been travelling along a road down the side of a mountain when he suddenly stopped, without knowing why, at a point where two roads intersected.

About thirty feet from the spot where I was standing, opposite me, in a well-levelled court, there rose, close to the road, a charming little house, white as chalk and bathed in sunshine. The only window, which faced the road, was open; behind the window sat a woman well but simply dressed. Red predominated among the bright colours of her clothes. On her head was a white cap of some very light material with openwork embroidery, of a form that was unknown to me. This woman seemed about thirty years old.

  Standing before her was a young girl of ten or twelve years, whom I took to be her own. She was attentively watching her mother, who was knitting and showing her how it was done: she was barefoot, her hair down her back, and was dressed somewhat like the mother. By the side of the young girl were three children, rolling on the ground: a small boy who might have been four or five years old was on his knees, showing something to his two little brothers, smaller than he, to amuse them; these were flat on their backs before the eldest, and all three were absorbed in their admiration. The two women had given me a rapid glance when they saw me standing there and looking at them, but they had not stirred. Evidently they often saw travellers passing.

He also saw a dog lying beside them, and through a door, three workmen, wearing the linen aprons and pointed hats of the Abruzzi, were drinking and playing cards. A colt went towards their table, and was cuffed for its curiosity.

Three years later Canon Garnier went to Italy for the first time. In the Apennines there was a stop to change horses.

During this stop, I look out of the carriage door and sweat comes out on me; my heart beats like a tambourine, and I mechanically put my hand to my face, as if to remove a veil which troubles me and prevents me from seeing: I rub my nose, my eyes, like a sleeper who awakens suddenly after a dream. I really think I am dreaming, and yet my eyes are wide open; I assure myself that I am not mad nor yet the victim of a most singular illusion. Before my eyes is the little country scene which I saw long ago in my dream. Nothing has changed!

The first thought that comes to me, after I get back my wits, is this: I have already seen this. I do not know where, but I am quite sure of it – that is certain. For all that, I have never been here, as this is the first time I have been in Italy. How does it happen?

Sure enough, there are the two roads that cross, the little wall which holds the earth up at the side of the court, the trees, the white house, the open window; the mother knitting and her daughter watching her, the three little fellows amusing themselves with the dog, the three workmen, drinking and playing, the colt who goes to take a lesson and receives a cuff, the two horses, the sheep. Nothing is changed: the people are exactly those I saw, as I saw them, doing the same thing in the same attitudes, with the same gestures, etc. How is that possible? But the fact is certain and for fifty years I have wondered. Mystery! First, I saw it in a dream; secondly, I saw it in actual reality, three years after.

An even more detailed refutation of the 'paramnesia' theory was related to the Italian psychical researcher Ernesto Bozzano, and used in his collection of cases of precognition. It came from a renowned fencing master, the Chevalier Giovanni de Figeroa of Palermo, describing a dream he had had in 1910, so vivid that he actually woke up his wife to tell her about it in detail. He was somewhere in the country; in front of him was a house and beside it, a hut and a cart with a harness on it.

Then a peasant, whose face has remained sharp and clear in my memory, clad in dark-coloured trousers, his head covered with a soft hat, approached me and invited me to follow him, which I did. He led me behind the building, and through a low and narrow door we entered a little stable, four or five metres square, or more, full of dirt and manure. In this little stable there was a short stone stairway which turned inward above the entrance door. A mule was fastened to a movable trough and, with his hind quarters, obstructed the passage by which one reached the first steps of the stairs. The peasant having assured me that the animal was gentle, I made him move and climbed the stairway, at the top of which I found myself in a little chamber, or attic, with a wooden floor; and I noticed hanging from the ceiling, winter watermelons, green tomatoes, onions and green corn.

In this same room, which served as an anteroom, was a group of two women and a little girl. One of these two women was old and the other young; I supposed that the latter was the mother of the child. The features of these three persons also remained engraved on my memory. Through the door which opened into the adjoining chamber I noticed a double bed, very high, such as I had never seen.

Two months later he went to Naples to help a friend in a duel, which led to his being involved in a duel himself. With his seconds he went to Merano, to a place he had not been before, and did not even know existed. Suddenly he realised that a field, beside which their car had stopped, was familiar. 'I know this spot,' he told one of his seconds. 'This is not the first time I have come here; at the side of the path there ought to be a house; at the right, there is a wooden hut.' Everything turned out to be as he had seen it in his dream, including the cart with the harness on it.

An instant later a peasant in black trousers, with soft black hat, exactly like him I had seen two months before in my dream, came to invite me to follow him into the house and, instead of following him, I preceded him to the door of the stable, *which I already knew*, and, on entering, saw the mule fastened to the trough; then I looked at the peasant, to ask him if the beast was harmless, for his hindquarters prevented me from climbing the little stone stairway, and he assured me, as in the dream, that there was no danger. Having climbed the stairs, I found myself in the attic, where I recognised the watermelons up under the ceiling, the green tomatoes, the onions, the green corn, and, in the little room, in an angle at the right, the old woman, the young one, and the child, as I had seen them in my dream.

In the neighbouring chamber, which I had to enter in order to remove my things, I recognised the bed that had so much astonished me in my dream because of its height, and I laid my vest and hat on it.

In addition to his seconds, de Figeroa named a number of friends to whom he had told his dream and would vouch for having heard it. The fact that he told about the dream before its realisation, Bozzano claimed, 'excludes the hypothesis that the impression of the already seen could be reduced to a trick of the memory!'

What remains impressive about many of these cases is that it is the backdrop – the scenery – which provides the reminder of the dream, because unless the dream had set the scene correctly it would probably not have been recalled, as it was in a case which was first published in a letter in the *Spectator* in 1881. Thomas Warren Trevor was staying with his friend Canon Johnson in Wales. He dreamt that he was one of a shooting party, and one of them shot a woodcock; 'when I awoke I was impressed with a very vivid recollection of my dream, and its *locality*, which, as it appeared to me I had never seen before.'

Returning with his friend from a walk the following afternoon, they encountered the local squire's gamekeeper, who walked on ahead with his friend. Suddenly Trevor, who had never previously been in the neighbourhood, realised that the place was familiar.

I stopped to collect my thoughts and reconcile the inconsistency. In a moment it flashed upon me that this was the scene of my last night's dream. I had a strange feeling of expectation; the identity of the scene became every moment clearer and clearer; my eyes fell on the exact spot where the woodcock of my dream had risen; I was certain the event of my dream would be inevitably re-enacted. I felt I must speak, and that there was not a moment to lose. I shouted to my friend, 'Look out! I dreamt I shot a woodcock here last night.' My friend turned and replied, 'Did you?'

The words were hardly out of his mouth and the gun off the keeper's shoulder (I was still intently gazing on the very foot of ground), when up gets a woodcock – *the* woodcock of my dream, and falls to the keeper's gun – a capital snap shot. We were all not a little astonished, the keeper, moreover, remarking that he thought all the woodcocks had left the country some weeks before.

Possibly because they are so familiar that they are not thought of as out-of-the-ordinary, relatively few accounts of *déjà vu* experiences have been sent in to the Foundation; but the consultant metallurgical engineer Dr E.G. West recalls that once, when he was called in for an important interview, he realised on entering the Board Room that he had had the interview before, in a dream a few weeks earlier. In the dream, a director of the company had entered the room behind him, and spoken to him in an accent markedly different from the accents of the rest of the Board; and so it turned out in reality.

Cases where *déjà vu* can be put to good use, except to confirm precognition, appear to be unusual; but in a sense Dr West was later to be a beneficiary. Applying for another post, he had been trying to anticipate how the interview would turn out. A few days before it was due to be held, he had another dream in which he was being interviewed, and the chairman of the Board was a man he had once known. This made it easier for Dr West to prepare answers to likely questions, in the hope that when the time came he would find he had been to the interview before, in his dream. So it turned out – even down to the layout of the laboratory in which the interview was held. His answers, and a statement he had prepared, 'made the interview so satisfactory that again I obtained the post.'

Sometimes precognition in such dreams is supplemented by retrocognition: glimpses of the past which cannot be accounted for by the dreamer's memory. Frederick Grisewood, well known and greatly admired as one of the BBC's broadcasters in radio's golden days before television captured the mass audience, gave an example in *Country Life* in 1947. When he was about twelve years old he had a succession of dreams about a country house, in which he was living apparently in Stuart times, with a fine estate and a trooper, Jan, with whom he would go riding on the downs. The dreams continued for about a fortnight, then stopped, and he never dreamed of the house again.

Seven years or so later he was staying with some friends who showed him round a part of the Sussex countryside he had not been in previously, and took him to call on a friend of theirs. As the car drew up in front of the house

I sat up and gasped. It was unquestionably my dream house. There could be no mistake about it. The surroundings were different. Much of the woodland had been cleared. But the house was exactly as I remembered it in my dream. It is impossible to describe my feelings. I was seething with excitement.

The common put-down at the time, Grisewood knew, was to say that, in a case like this, one Jacobean house can look very like another. But his memory of his dreams was so complete that he was able to point out changes which had been made. 'I see that tapestry has gone,' he observed to his hostess. 'How on earth did you know there was any tapestry there?' she asked; it had indeed hung there, but had been removed long before Grisewood was born. He told her of his dreams: 'Let's go round,' she said, 'and you can tell exactly what it was like then.' When they came to 'his' bedroom:

'You've bricked my window up,' he protested. 'There was a lovely window here, and I used to look out on to the garden through it. It was just here.' He tapped the plaster as he spoke and it sounded hollow.

'I'll get my husband to open it up and pull away the ivy from outside,' she said. 'We must have your window again!'

A believer in reincarnation would be likely to claim this as evidence for a past life; whatever the explanation, it is hard to dispute that Grisewood in his dreams had access to information about the house and its past that cannot have reached him through ordinary sensory channels.

The comedian Roy Hudd has had a similar experience. As a child, he had many dreams about a certain house and its neighbourhood; and they continued on into his adult life. One day, in a district of London he had never visited before, he realised that it was the scene of his dream; and he took his wife to the house, where from outside he described to her what his dreams had showed to him of the interior – in particular some mirrors. It turned out to have been the home of the comedian, Dan Leno. Hudd's dreams, they subsequently found, had given him an accurate representation of the rooms as they had been when Dan Leno was living there – he had installed the mirrors so that he could practise his acts while watching himself as if from the viewpoint of the audience.

Inevitably, *déjà vu* episodes which 'break' a dream make much more of an impact on the dreamer than on his listeners unless, like Grisewood, he is able to exploit the knowledge gained from his dream to startle them. What is chiefly interesting about them – a little worrying, too – is that unlike the normal run of precognitive dreams they 'break', quite often, long after the dream.

'During the year 1900, at the age of about eleven, I had a wonderful dream,' the Russian-born aeronautical engineer, Igor Sikorsky (who constructed and flew the first four-engined aircraft and, after emigrating to the United States, founded the Aero Engineering Corporation which took his name, and built helicopters and flying boats), recalled in his autobiography, *The Story of the Winged 'S'* (1939).

> I saw myself walking along a narrow, luxuriously decorated passageway. On both sides were walnut doors, similar to the stateroom doors of a steamer. The floor was covered with an attractive carpet. A spherical electric light from the ceiling produced a pleasant bluish illumination.

He felt a slight vibration, of the kind experienced in a ship; but he knew it was no ordinary ship – it was flying. He had been assured that such a thing was impossible; but the dream left a powerful impression on him which only gradually faded.

In 1931 his firm delivered 'The Flying "S"', better known to the public as the American Clipper. He had often flown in it while it was being tested, but not since it had been fitted out to attract Pan American Airlines passengers. Invited to join the acceptance flight, he stayed in the cockpit until the pilot reduced power to begin the descent, then he decided to go back to have a look at the passenger accommodation. When the passage light was switched on for him,

> I realised, at that very moment, that I had already seen all this a long time ago, the passageway, the bluish light, the walnut trimmings on the walls and doors, and the feeling of smooth motion, and I tried to recall when and how I could have received such an impression, until I finally remembered the details of my dream of some thirty years before.

The autobiography, Sikorsky explained, was designed to tell the story of 'how a dream of early youth finally became a reality'.

J.B. Priestley had one dream of the distant future, though not so distant, and less romantic. In *Rain Upon Gadshill* (1939) he described how as a schoolboy he had had a dream in which an uncle whom he rarely saw

> suddenly appeared in a doorway and glared at me angrily. I woke up shivering with fright, and the dream impressed itself on my memory.

Then, years afterwards, during the war I was home on leave and, waiting for the second house of a neighbouring music hall to open, I was having a drink at a rather crowded bar. I felt somebody staring at me, and looking down the bar saw this same uncle, glaring just as he had in that old dream. We had not met for years, and he was not sure that this fellow in uniform was his nephew, but he came across to reproach me angrily about something that was actually no fault of mine. But his manner – for he had had a few drinks and was inclined to lose his head – secretly frightened me.

Was it a coincidence? Possibly, Priestley thought, but he had had so many such experiences – particularly of the *déjà vu* sort, in which he had seen for the first time a landscape or a house or a scene in a play, and been haunted by the feeling that he had seen them before – for the explanation to satisfy him. 'All coincidence? That is what the scientists, the psychologists who think they are scientists, and the orthodox philosophers all tell us, and they ought to know. But I do not believe them.'

Déjà vu episodes, whether they are recognised as coming from a dream, or remain unexplained, can be extremely worrying. We will presumably never know why *déjà vu* had so powerful an effect on Shelley that he was unable to finish his project *Catalogue of the Phenomena of Dreams, as Connecting Sleeping and Waking*. After describing how dream landscapes had sometimes haunted him, he recalled that the most remarkable event of this nature, for him, had happened five years before, in 1810, at Oxford.

I was walking with a friend, in the neighbourhood of that city, engaged in earnest and interesting conversation. We suddenly turned the corner of a lane, and the view, which its high banks and hedges had concealed, presented itself. The view consisted of a windmill, standing in one among many plashy meadows enclosed with stone walls; the irregular and broken ground, between the wall and the road on which we stood; a long low hill behind the windmill, and a grey covering of uniform cloud spread over the evening sky. It was that season when the last leaf had just fallen from the scant and stunted ash. The scene surely was a common scene; the season and the hour little calculated to kindle lawless thought; and it was a tame uninteresting assemblage of objects, such as would drive the imagination for refuge in serious and sober talk to the evening fireside and the dessert of winter fruits and wine. The effect which it produced on me was not such as could have been expected. I suddenly remembered to have seen that exact scene in a dream of long –

Here he was 'obliged to leave off, overcome by thrilling horror,' Mary Shelley wrote. She was to recall his coming to her from writing it, 'pale and agitated, to seek refuge in conversation from the fearful emotions it excited.'

Predestination?

From these examples the question arises: do they imply predestination? To the German philosopher Artur Schopenhauer, they did. That dreams so often foreshadow future events, trivial as well as serious, he argued, was highly significant; and he cited one of his own in the trivial category, because it so clearly illustrated *the rigorous necessity of what happens, even of what is most accidental*.

One morning I was writing with great care a long and most important business letter in English. When I reached the end of the third page, I took the ink-well, instead of the sand-box, and poured it over the paper; the ink ran off the desk to the floor. The servant came in at my ring, brought a pail of water, and began to wash the floor to get off the spots. While she was doing this she said: 'I dreamed last night that I took some ink spots off here by rubbing the boards.' 'That's not true!' I answered her. – 'It is true, and I have already told it to the other servant, who sleeps with me.'

Just then the other servant, who was about seventeen years old, chanced to come in, to call the one who was washing the boards. I went toward her and asked her: 'What did she dream last night?' – Answer: 'I don't know.' Then I said: 'But she told you about it when she woke up.' Whereupon the young girl replied: 'Oh, yes! she dreamed that she washed an ink spot off the floor here.'

To Schopenhauer, the dream was remarkable because it was about an involuntary action occurring against his will, the consequence of a small mistake; yet 'so necessary, and so inevitably determined that its effect existed, several hours in advance, as a dream in the consciousness of

another. Here appears in the clearest manner the truth of my proposition:
everything that happens, happens of necessity.'

What Schopenhauer had neglected to consider was what *would* have
happened if the servant had told him of her dream before he poured the ink
over the letter, giving him the chance to take some precaution to prevent
it. Certainly the servant's dream was an interesting testimonial to the
existence of *some* element of predestination, but in no way proved that
everything that happens, 'happens of necessity'.

The case for predestination is at its strongest in two types of
precognitive dreams: those in which the action in the dream is fulfilled a
long time in the future; and those in which an attempt is made to avert
destiny's threatened course, but without success.

In 1774, Newton and Cunningham, two young friends of the poet Anna
Seward of Lichfield, were invited to one of her salons to meet John André,
a newly commissioned officer, who was on a farewell visit to her as he was
leaving to join his regiment in Canada. While they were waiting for him
to arrive, Cunningham described a vivid dream he had had the night
before, which he could not get out of his mind. André's biographer,
Winthrop Sargent, put his account of it into direct speech.

'Listen, this is very odd – you never heard anything like this one. I fell
asleep and suddenly I found myself in a strange forest – a place I had
never seen before. Suddenly I heard a horseman approaching at full
speed. As horse and rider dashed up to a spot near where I seemed to
be standing, I saw three men jump out of a thicket where they had
evidently been in hiding. They stopped the horse, seized the bridle and
then forced the rider to dismount. Once on the ground they made him
submit to a rough search through his clothes and boots. When they
finished with this they hustled him away as a prisoner.

'Do you know, Newton, I felt so sorry for that fellow in my dream
that I woke up at that point. I never knew what they did with him.
By and by I managed to drop off again. I was soon back in my
dreaming, but this time I was not in a forest but standing with a large
crowd massed in front of a gallows. There a man was being hanged.
I seemed to be near enough for a good look at his face – and here's the
amazing thing – I recognized the very same man who was stopped,
searched and arrested in that first dream. Don't you think that was
extraordinary?'

Newton agreed that it was, but something even more extraordinary was to follow when André arrived. Cunningham stared at him, Newton noticed, as if he were a ghost. 'I'll tell you why,' Cunningham explained later.

'André is the very man I saw in my dream that I was telling you about before they came in – the man whom I saw captured in the first dream and then hanged in the second. He was unmistakable.'

At the time that was an absurdity to be laughed off, but six years later, when Major André was taken and then executed as a spy, the dream was remembered.

Some melancholy accounts of dreams accurately predicting unwelcome events far in the future have come in to the Koestler Foundation. In one of them a girl of about 13 had a succession of nightmares; in the room she shared with her sister, she would see her sister's decaying corpse on a trestle table. The dreams continued for about a year, culminating in one in which her sister, dressed in a nurse's uniform, plunged out of their top-floor flat window.

Two years later her sister, by that time in Queen Alexandra's Royal Army Nursing Corps, was posted to Cyprus, where she celebrated her 21st birthday. The following day a telegram arrived to say that she had been killed in an accident; it subsequently transpired that she had died from injuries sustained in a fall from the balcony of her flat.

Recalling that the dreams J.W. Dunne related in *An Experiment With Time* had drawn 'from the future as well as the past', Graham Greene has wondered, unnervingly, in *Ways of Escape* whether a novelist may be doing the same,

since so much of his work comes from the same source as dreams? It is a disquieting idea. Was Zola, when he wrote of the imprisoned miners dying of poisoned air, drawing something from a 'memory' of his own death, smothered with fumes from his coke stove? Perhaps it's just as well for an author not to reread the books he has written. There may be too many hints from an unhappy future. Why in 1938 did I write of D. listening to a radio talk on the Problem of Indo-China? (Was there any such problem then, serious enough to reach the English radio?) Six years were to pass before the French war in

Vietnam began and eight more before the problem of Indo–China became vivid to me as I stood, scared motionless, beside the canal filled with Viet Minh bodies near the cathedral of Phat Diem.

One of the most disturbing experiences in this 'predestined' category, in our own time, was to be the subject of the Michael Redgrave film, *The Night My Number Came Up* (1954). In 1940 Air Marshal Sir Victor Goddard was about to fly from Shanghai to Tokyo when he overheard, at a party, a man describing a dream he had had the previous night in which Goddard had been killed in a plane crash. The man then described his dream in detail. The plane had been a Dakota; it carried three civilians, two men and a girl; and after a difficult flight through snow it had crashed on a rocky, shingly shore.

Goddard knew he would be flying on a Dakota, but he also knew that only military were to be taken; there could not be three civilians with him. Or, rather, he *thought* he knew. In the course of the following day three civilians, two men and a girl, were added to the plane's complement. They took off early the following morning and that afternoon, through snow, the pilot saw a beach on which it would be possible to do a crash landing. As the Dakota was running low on fuel, he decided to chance it and did a wheels-up landing on the beach. All had turned out as the dream had foretold – except that Goddard lived.

Inevitably it is the dramatic examples of what appears to be relentless fate that are published; but sometimes trivial cases are remembered and reported by the people who have experienced them. Aniela Jaffé has given some in her *Apparitions* (1979).

In the summer of 1913, I dreamt that my brother was in a great crowd at Zurich Main Station and that I had arrived too late to meet him. When he actually announced his visit, I said to myself: 'Well, that's not going to happen.' To make sure, I arrived at the station an hour before the train was due. I waited, then a notice went up: 'Forty minutes late'. I walked about the station for a while, but always hurried back to the platform. But what happened? About twenty minutes later I experienced exactly what had occurred in my dream. The engine had broken down, but the train was only twenty, and not forty minutes late.

Another example, from a trainee sales girl, related how her instructor had arranged to take her class to visit a food factory, and she was looking forward to the excursion. In a dream the night before,

> I saw myself quite distinctly on the way to the station, but as I gaily turned the last corner, to my horror I saw the train moving out of the station with all the other girls, who called and waved to me, and then, of course, disappeared without me. When I woke up I laughed about the dream and thought to myself: Well, this won't happen to me, for never in my young life had I missed a train.

She thought no more about the dream. After lunch she checked her watch by the radio time signal, and set out in good time for the station.

> But what did I see? Exactly at the same spot as in my dream I saw the train rolling away, while all the girls called to me in exactly the same words. I was thunderstruck for the moment, and could not have looked very bright; for it seemed to me quite impossible that I should have taken twenty minutes to walk from my boarding-house to the station – a distance of about five hundred yards which should not have taken more than five minutes. But both my watch and the station clock said 12.50. I went sadly back to work and had to confess to our superior that I had simply missed the train ... To this very day I do not know how those twenty minutes passed.

The issue whether or not it is possible to exploit precognition to dodge fate aroused Louisa Rhine's interest. In an attempt to provide an answer, she examined the records of well over a thousand cases of precognition sent in to her and her husband between 1930 and 1955. Of these, in 433 cases the foreseen events were of a kind which the people involved would have wanted to prevent, but nearly two-thirds of them made no attempt to do so. In other cases, the attempt failed. A New York girl, for example, who dreamed that a beautiful diamond ring she wore was badly damaged, as if by burning, did her best to be careful to protect it; but it came off when she threw some tissues into the kitchen incinerator, and was found there, in the condition she had seen it in her dream, when the ashes were raked out.

In other cases, people who had premonitions took steps to prevent the circumstances in which the event which they wished to avoid could happen

– say, by not taking the route where they had 'seen' an accident. In one example, however, fate circumvented the precautions. An Oregon woman who awoke with the impression that her three-year-old son was going to be involved in an automobile accident took him to her mother's, where she assumed he would be safe. While she was there, the fear suddenly lifted; and so great was the relief that she burst into tears.

> But just then came a hard ring at the doorbell. A policeman with an excited crowd behind him was holding the little boy, limp in his arms. The child had been hit by a runaway car when, as she was told, he had been sitting quietly under a tree in the yard. The car had jumped the curb.

It is clear that many people are still worried by 'seeing the future' in dreams, for fear that this does imply that the future is predetermined. Letters to the Foundation have reflected this concern; in some, the writers say that they have never disclosed the dreams they recall to anybody before. One woman, giving interesting examples from her own experience, notes that she finds the prospect of further such dreams 'terrifying'. There is, in fact, a mass of evidence supporting the assumption that the future is prearranged – but only up to a point.

One of Dunne's dreams illustrates this, though he did not realise it. In his dream a horse appeared to have gone mad. It escaped from a field and chased him. The next day, while he was out fishing with his brother, a horse began to behave as in the dream. It, too, escaped from its field, and came towards them; 'we both picked up stones, ran thirty yards or so back from the bank, and faced about.' As it happened, the horse galloped off in another direction; but Dunne's comment – 'there is no dodging Fate' – looks as inappropriate in retrospect as Schopenhauer's. By alerting him to the possibility that the horse might come after him, the dream had given him the opportunity to dodge Fate by retreating to a safer position and arming himself with a stone.

From the historical evidence, and from the material her correspondents have sent to her, Jaffé concludes that 'the factor of Fate – a guidance vastly superior to the conscious will of man – emerges with great clarity. Man is neither free nor capable of exercising his ego-will against the power of his own destiny.' But, she adds, the experiences 'also show that there is a human freedom, when it is conceived in quite a different sense, namely as a moral problem or a question of consciousness. One can almost say that man's freedom consists of being able either to struggle against Fate or to accept it.' When men and women have been given advance information in dreams of what Fate has in store for them, they have often shown that they can thwart it.

The thwarting of Fate

Inevitably, the destiny-dodging dreams which have attracted most attention have been those which have resulted in lives being saved. John Fox, in his *Book of Martyrs* (1554), described how a member of the Protestant congregation in London in Queen Mary's time dreamed that the Queen's messenger had arrived to arrest the deacon, and had found the list of the members of the congregation, about three hundred in all. He woke up in a fright; and when he fell asleep again, had the same dream. The deacon, when he heard it, was inclined to dismiss the warning as pandering to superstition; but he was persuaded to hide the list. The next day he was arrested; but as the Queen's messenger did not find the list, the congregation were saved from being burnt at the stake.

Recounting the story, Aubrey added another of his own.

When Doctor Hamey (one of the physicians' college in London) being a young man, went to travel towards Padoa, he went to Dover, (with several others) and showed his pass, as the rest did, to the Governor there. The Governor told him, that he must not go, but must keep him prisoner. The Doctor desired to know for what reason? how he had transgrest? well, it was his will to have it so. The pacquet-boat hoisted sail in the evening (which was very clear), and the Doctor's companions in it. There ensued a terrible storm, and the pacquet-boat and all the passengers were drowned: the next day the sad news was brought to Dover. The Doctor was unknown to the Governor, both by name and face; but the night before, the Governor had the perfect vision, in a dream, of Doctor Hamey, who came to pass over to Calais; and that he had a warning to stop him. This the Governor told the Doctor the next day. The Doctor was a pious, good man, and has several times related this story to some of my acquaintances.

If Izaak Walton's *Life* (1651) is to be trusted, Nicolas Wotton, a British Ambassador in France in Mary's reign who was later to become Dean of Canterbury, dreamed that his nephew Thomas had been involved in a conspiracy which, if he could not be extricated from it in time, would lead to his execution and the ruin of his family. As he was not superstitious, he might have ignored the warning had he not had the same dream the next night. He therefore wrote to Queen Mary, asking her to arrange that Thomas should be brought before the Lords in Council for interrogation on 'such feigned questions as might give a colour for his commitment into a favourable prison; declaring that he would acquaint Her Majesty with the true reason for his request, when he should next become so happy as to see and speak to Her Majesty.' Thomas was later to admit that he had had 'more than an intimation' of the conspiracy which Sir Thomas Wyatt, the Duke of Suffolk and others had entered into, to try to prevent the Queen's marriage to the Catholic King Philip of Spain, for which they were arrested and executed. Thomas might have become involved, he thought, if his uncle 'had not happily dreamed him into a prison'.

In his *Inquiries concerning the intellectual Powers* (1840) John Abercrombie cited similar examples, one of which he asserted was from his own knowledge 'entirely authentic'; and Robert Dale Owen later gave a fuller version, with the names of the people concerned which Abercrombie had omitted. Young Joseph D'Acre of Kirklinton in Cumberland had come north to stay with his uncle and aunt, Major and Mrs Griffith, in Edinburgh. One afternoon he told them that he and some friends proposed to go on a fishing expedition the following day, and they raised no objections.

During the ensuing night, however, Mrs Griffith started from a troubled dream, exclaiming, in accents of terror, 'The boat is sinking! Oh, save them!' Her husband ascribed it to apprehension on her part; but she declared that she had no uneasiness whatever about the fishing-party, and indeed had not thought about it. So she again composed herself to sleep. When, however, a similar dream was thrice repeated in the course of the night, (the last time presenting the image of the boat lost and the whole party drowned), becoming at last seriously alarmed, she threw on her wrapping-gown, and without waiting for morning, proceeded to her nephew's room. With some

difficulty she persuaded him to relinquish the design, and to send his
servant to Leith with an excuse.

The morning was fine, and the party embarked; 'but about three o'clock
a storm suddenly arose, the boat foundered, and all on board were lost.'

From 1882 on, the *Journal* and *Proceedings* of the SPR contained a number
of accounts from people who felt that they had been saved by dream
warnings. One shipowner had the unusual experience of benefiting twice.
At the time of the first dream, William E. Brighten was working as a
solicitor's articled clerk in Norwich; but he had somehow managed to buy
an old paddle steamer, and with a friend, also an articled clerk, decided to
go off on a week's holiday, dispensing with a crew. They reached Great
Yarmouth, where they moored beside a barge and settled down for the
night.

I must have slept some hours before my dream commenced. I thought
my eyes opened, and that the top of the cabin had become
transparent, and I could see two dark figures floating in the air above
the funnel. They appeared to be in earnest converse, pointing towards
the mouth of the river and then at the rope by which the boat was
moored; at last they turned to each other, and after some gestures
they seemed to have resolved upon a plan of action, and each floated
in the air, one to the stem and the other to the stern, holding out a
forefinger, and at the same moment each forefinger touched a rope
and instantly burned it like a red-hot iron.

Released, the boat started off downstream, eventually reaching the sea
and beginning to sink.

At last the waters appeared to reach my mouth and I was drowning,
choking. With a wild effort I bounded from the couch, burst the
doors outwards, shivering them to pieces, and found myself (in my
night-clothes) awake outside the ruined doors on a calm, bright,
moonlight night, and instinctively turned to the head rope: to my
horror it had just parted. Turning for the boathook I saw beside me
my friend C. who had been aroused by the crash, and he shouted that
he saw the stern rope go at the same time.

Hanging on to the barge with the help of the boathook, they were able to hold off the tide until they could arouse assistance and tie up again for the rest of the night.

Brighten, Frank Podmore reported to the Society, was a shrewd, unimaginative, practical man. His second experience was to be even more bizarre. By 1876 he owned a 35-ton schooner, with a captain and a crew of three; and visitors were on board. The schooner was securely anchored off Gravesend, and Brighten was asleep in his cabin when a voice rang in his ears, 'Wake, wake, you will be run down.' He dropped off to sleep again, but when the same voice and words roused him, he went up on deck, to find that the schooner was enveloped in thick fog. There seemed nothing he could do, so he returned to his bunk, only to be again roused by the voice.

> I then somewhat more hastily dressed, went on deck, and climbed some way up the rigging to get above the fog, and was soon in a bright, clear atmosphere with the fog like a sea at my feet, when looking round I saw a large vessel bearing down directly upon us. I fell, rather than scrambled, out of the rigging, rushed to the forecastle, shouted to the captain who rushed on deck, explained all in a word or two; he ran to the tiller, unlashed it, put it hard a-port; the swift current acting upon the rudder caused the boat to slew across and upward in the current, when on came the large vessel, passing our side.

Discussing the Brighten evidence, the psychical researcher H.F. Saltmarsh was careful to consider the possibility in his *Foreknowledge* (1938) that an experienced sailor may develop hyperacute faculties which will alert his senses to danger, even if he is asleep. 'Hyperaesthesia' of this kind might have told Brighten, first, that the fog had descended, and then, that a ship was bearing down on his schooner. That his senses should have been attuned to picking up fog is certainly likely: the altered sounds, the lowered temperature, the fog-laden air would all have been contributing. But – the ship? Brighten's five senses would have had to be hyperacute indeed, to tell him that the ship, still at a distance, was on course to ram his schooner. In any case, so far as Brighten was concerned, the essential point was that, thanks to his dreams, he had been able to take avoiding action just in time.

When, at the end of the 19th century, Flammarion appealed for accounts of psychic experiences, including those in dreams, he was inundated with replies. One of them came from a former magistrate and Deputy in the French National Assembly, M. Bérard, in the form of an article which had appeared in the *Revue des Revues* in 1895. During his career, having just presided over a trial for some appalling crime, he had retired to a remote part of the countryside to recuperate; finding himself lost in the course of a long walk, he decided to spend the night at a shabby wayside inn, where there was nobody but the innkeeper and his wife. Accustomed as a magistrate to take precautions, M. Bérard searched his room and found a door concealed behind some hangings, which led to a ladder. He blocked the entry as best he could with a rickety wash-stand, so that the door could not have been opened without making a din, and went to bed.

During the night he woke up with a start, as it appeared somebody was trying to push the door open; but when he shouted 'Who's there?' there was no answer, and he thought he might have been dreaming. Falling asleep he had a nightmare.

I believed that I saw, I *did see*, in my sleep, the chamber where I was, and in the bed some one, either myself or another, which it was I did not know. The secret door opened of itself. The host entered, a long knife in his hand. Behind, on the threshold of the door stood his wife, dirty and in rags, shading the light from the lantern with her black fingers. The host approached the bed with a cat-like step, and plunged his knife into the heart of the sleeper. Then he lifted the corpse by the feet, his wife took the head, and they both descended the narrow ladder. But here occurs a curious detail. The husband held between his teeth the slender ring which supported the lantern, and the two murderers descended the narrow stairs by the dim light of the lantern. I awoke with a start, in terror, and with my forehead bathed in sweat.

M. Bérard thought no more of the dream until three years later, when he read in a newspaper that a lawyer who had been staying in the vicinity of the inn had disappeared. As a wagoner happened to have seen him near the inn, the innkeeper's wife was to be called before the *juge d'instruction* to give evidence. Suspicious, M. Bérard asked his colleague if he might attend. The woman, who did not recognise him, told the *juge d'instruction* that the missing lawyer had come to the inn, but had not stayed the night;

there were only two rooms, and they were both occupied – as the guests had testified.

'And the third chamber, the one over the stable?' I cried, interposing suddenly.

The hostess gave a start, and appeared to recognize me all at once, as if I were a sudden revelation. I continued with audacious effrontery, and as if I was inspired: 'Victor Arnand slept in that third chamber. During the night you came with your husband, you holding the lantern, he a long knife; you climbed up by a ladder from the stable; you opened a secret door which led into that chamber; you yourself remained on the threshold of the door while your husband went to murder his guest, before robbing him of his watch and his pocket book.'

It was my dream of three years before which I narrated; my colleague listened aghast; as for the woman, overpowered by terror, with her eyes staring and her teeth chattering, she stood as if petrified.

'Then,' I continued, 'you took up the corpse, your husband holding it by the feet, you descended the ladder with it. In order that you might have light, your husband carried the ring of the lantern between his teeth.'

And then the woman, terrified, pale, with her legs shaking under her, said: 'You saw it all, then?'

The corpse of the lawyer was found under a heap of manure – leaving M. Bérard to wonder if he would have shared the same fate had he not blocked off the hidden door.

In the United States at this time Richard Hodgson won a reputation second only to Gurney's for his careful checking of the reports which came into his American SPR about psychic experiences. One of them, dated 14 October 1891, came from George Kinsolving; at the time, rector of the Church of the Epiphany in Philadelphia; shortly to become Bishop of Texas. In his dream, he was in some woods when he came across a rattlesnake 'which when killed had two black-looking rattles and a peculiar projection of bone from the tail'. The next day he went for a walk with his brother.

As we started down the side of the mountain I suddenly became vividly conscious of my dream, to such an extent as to startle me, and to put me on the alert. I was walking rapidly, and had gone about thirty steps, when I came on a snake coiled and ready to strike. My foot was in the air, and had I finished my step I would have trodden upon the snake. I threw myself to one side and fell heavily to the ground. I recovered myself at once and killed the snake with the assistance of my brother, and found it to be the same snake in every particular with the one I had had in my mind's eye. The same size, colour, and the peculiar malformation of the tail.

Andrew Lang, referring to the tale, was disposed to be critical because Kinsolving's brother, Arthur, in his account thought that the snake had only one rattle. Otherwise his version fully corroborated George's.

It was quite characteristic of churchmen at the time, and indeed has been since, to be disturbed rather than delighted by such examples of dream protection. 'It is my belief that my dream prevented me from treading on the snake,' Kinsolving commented to Hodgson, 'but I have no theory on the subject, and get considerably mixed up and muddled when I try to think on the line of such abnormal experiences.' He would not expect God, in other words, to communicate through a dream; and guardian angels had come to be regarded as a relic of superstition.

Occasionally rationalists were less inhibited, allowing superstition to break through. 'In a few days we are expecting Miss Anthony to make us a visit. She has had a very remarkable dream,' Elizabeth Stanton noted in her diary towards the end of the last century. Susan Anthony had made her name as the hard-headed leader of the American women's suffrage movement, and the organiser of the International Council of Women; she had been ordered by her doctor to rest, and had been advised to go to Atlantic City. It was there she had her vivid dream – a nightmare, in which she was being burned alive in one of the city's hotels. In the morning she told her niece, who had accompanied her, 'we must pack and go back to Philadelphia.' The next day the hotel in which they had been staying, and ten neighbouring hotels, were destroyed by fire.

Aniela Jaffé's collection of psychic experiences includes two cases of warning dreams which could be regarded as responsible for saving lives. Both came from parents.

My son was doing his military service at Basle. One night he dreamt of his father who was dead. He only saw his face and one raised hand, and heard him say: 'You must not cross the bridge.' In the morning he forgot the dream, but the next night he saw the same apparition and heard the same words. He was then sent to work in the cookhouse, where he over-ate so completely that he awoke with a temperature and had to stay in bed while the others went out on maneuvers. About three hours later news came to the barracks that a bridge had collapsed, burying half a train under it. There was one dead and a number of men were seriously injured; the rest escaped with bruises and scratches. My son was well enough to help in the rescue work; his temperature was normal again. The doctor was puzzled, but my son knew that his father had saved him.

In the second, a father described how one morning in spring he had decided to transplant and tie his raspberry bushes.

I went into the garden with my two children. The younger one went straight to the sandheap while the elder one came with us to the berries. When I looked at the bushes I suddenly felt a terrible oppression settling round my heart which I can hardly describe in words. I set to work but was soon overcome by anxiety. I told my wife how strange I felt. Yet at that very moment a question came into my mind 'What is this anxiety about?' Yes, that's it: I had already done this job on the raspberry bushes in a dream, and something unpleasant had happened which I can't remember. I knew at once that I must keep an eye on the little girl – she was two – and every two or three minutes I looked in her direction. Suddenly, when I looked again she had vanished. I sent my older child to see what she was doing and to make sure that the garden gate was shut. She ran off ... passed the water-barrel, stopped, looked into it, bent down – a heart-rending scream: 'Mummy!' and she pulled the little girl out of the barrel. The little girl was blue in the face and no longer breathing, but I carried her to the doctor anyway, and he was able to save her life.

In his *Riddle of the Future* (1974) Andrew MacKenzie has described the case of a well-known London surgeon who dreamt that the first patient he was going to see in his consulting rooms, after the week-end, had a patch of discoloured flesh on one of her buttocks. As it was the first time he had ever examined a patient in a dream it stuck in his mind; and on the Monday he was curious to see whether the first patient would be coming to him on account of the patch. But she had come for some other reason. 'So much for my dream!' he thought.

His next patient, however, when he examined her turned out to have a tumour, making a discoloured patch, on one of her buttocks; and he was so taken aback that he heard himself say, in her hearing, 'But it's two inches lower!' She had come to him for some different reason, but he was sufficiently impressed by his dream to decide that the tumour must be removed. 'If I had not removed it,' he believed, 'the woman would have died.' Nor had the dream been inaccurate in suggesting that she would be the first patient that morning. It turned out that she had been first on the list; but that a nurse from his hospital had been sent in before her.

Although J. W. Dunne was not himself interested in warning dreams, as such, some of the correspondents who wrote to him about the outcome of their experiments along the lines he recommended, writing full accounts of their dreams immediately on waking, believed that they had been warned. A London man told him in 1929 that he had had a number of indications of precognition in his dreams, most of them of no interest except *as* indications. But on 24 June he had recorded

A street; I am in the middle of it; not a soul in sight: a car emerges from a side-street on my right, curves straight on me; the last I recollect is its front wheel one inch from my right leg.

On 24 August, at about 9.45 in the morning, he was in the middle of the junction of Cannon Street and Queen Victoria Street.

The whole space for some ten seconds was quite empty of either traffic or pedestrians. I remembered my dream, recalled by the same impression of isolation in an empty space.

Suddenly a car rushed in on my left, and turned towards me, and it was almost upon me before I realised that I must get out of the way.

As facts go, this is insignificant; walking daily about the City, one would sooner or later narrowly escape being run over. But such an isolation in the middle of a busy thoroughfare is very rare and, coupled with the subsequent happenings, seems to me worthy of serious consideration.

In an age when traffic accidents are the most frequently encountered form of unexpected deaths, coincidence must be held to account for many dreams about them which appear to come true. But there are other cases like this, of the *déjà vu* variety, in that the dreamer, aware of what is about to happen, takes action to avert danger.

Dr E.G. West, the metallurgist engineer who has found dreams so useful in his career, has experienced one which may have spared him from abruptly terminating it. In the dream

> I saw a very realistic car smash due to a vehicle travelling very quickly down a steep hill with a cross road at the bottom, and later on I recognised the spot whilst driving along one of the cross roads. It was so real that I stopped before reaching the cross, and there indeed saw a car rushing down the hill towards me in such a way that had I driven on, there would have been a smash! but on this occasion the other vehicle was able to turn successfully into the other side road.

A bizarre case of a dream premonition apparently averting a fatal road accident was sent to J.B. Priestley. A woman – he did not name her – living in Ireland dreamed that she was driving her car on a road she knew, near her home, when suddenly a little girl of about three years old appeared in front of the car. 'I did all I could but found it impossible to avoid hitting her'; and the girl was killed.

When she woke up, she realised to her alarm that she was going to have to drive along the road that morning to visit her daughter; and she decided to take particular care at the point she recalled from her dream. However, there was no sign of the child: only a group of women standing at a bus stop.

> Relieved beyond words, I glanced down at my speedometer to check, and on lifting my eyes was completely horrified to see, standing still in the middle of the road, the little girl of my dream correct in every detail, even to the dark curly hair and the bright blue cardigan she was wearing.

It was just possible for her to bring the car to a halt, without hitting the girl, who never moved. The women at the bus queue paid no attention, and the girl remained standing in the road while the driver, very shaken, drove on. Her daughter, when she arrived, looked upset. She had been worried; the night before, she explained, she had had a vivid dream. 'In it, you ran over and killed a lovely little girl, dressed in a bright blue cardigan and with lovely dark curly hair.'

As Priestley was anxious that any examples he used should not be shown up later to be spurious, he took the trouble to ask for attestation. The woman's husband recalled that she had told him about the dream before she drove to her daughter's; and her daughter confirmed that she had dreamed that her mother had killed the little girl. But this, as Priestley realised, presented a problem. If a car nearly runs over a three-year-old, the three-year-old is going to be frightened. If a fatal accident is narrowly avoided, the onlookers are unlikely to show no sign of interest, particularly if a small child is involved. Could it have been a phantasm, Priestley wondered, from the shared dream? But if so, the mystery deepens.

Of the 'destiny thwarted' dreams which came in to Louisa Rhine, the one which most impressed her was from the conductor of a Los Angeles street car. In his dream he was taking the street car across an intersection when another one, going in a different direction, blocked his view of a big red truck which was doing an illegal turn; and they collided.

Three people were in the truck, two men and a woman. The men were sprawled in the street, dead, and the woman was screaming in pain. The conductor thought that he walked over to the woman and she looked at him with the largest blue eyes he had ever seen and shouted at him, 'You could have avoided this.'

He awoke, soaked with perspiration, got up and went to work, forgetting about the nightmare. As he approached the intersection, he suddenly felt sick with fear; but it was only when the conductor of an approaching car waved to him, just as he had done in the dream, that it came back to him.

He at once put on the brakes and shut off the power. A truck, not a big truck completely red, as in the dream, but a panel delivery truck with space for advertising on the side painted over with bright red, shot directly into his path. Had he been moving at all he would surely have hit it.

Three people were in the truck, two men and a woman. As the

truck passed in front of him, the woman leaned out of the window and looked up at him with the same large blue eyes he had seen in the dream.

Racing drivers must often dream of crashing; one of them has had reason to believe that a dream not merely saved him, but enabled him to win the 1967 Indianapolis 500. A.J. Foyt, sleeping fitfully, 'had a sort of vision in which he was leading on the last lap when a smash-up took place in front of him, and he had to brake to beat it.' In the actual race, Foyt gained the lead.

He came through the next-to-last lap and into the last lap and around into the last turn. All the while his mind was working hard and he thought about an accident and he slowed sharply.

'It was as though I had a premonition,' he said later. 'I had dreamed about it, and then I came around the last corner and there it was! If I hadn't already slowed down, there is no way I could have gotten through it.'

As things were, Foyt was able to edge his way through, and win the race.

In some cases where a threat appears to have been averted as the result of a warning in a dream, it is possible to argue that the situation (or whatever is foreshadowed in the dream) might not have happened anyway. Louisa Rhine was careful to make this point, illustrating it with the case of a New York woman who dreamed that she heard a scream, and saw her two-year-old son falling from a window. She ensured that the window was safe, but two days later she put the child's mattress on it for airing, pulled the window down tight on it, and went into another room. Suddenly she recalled her dream, rushed back, and found the child had managed to push the window up. The mattress had actually fallen out. The mother claimed she had grabbed the child just in time to stop him falling after it; but would he, in fact, have fallen?

There is no way of knowing; but from the mother's point of view (not to mention the child's) it does not matter. The warning dream, and the sudden recollection of it, enabled her to take the action which ensured his safety. And the same applies to another dream Louisa Rhine cited. A girl who was staying down in the country was going to New York for the night, and planned to stay alone in the family's town house. The night before, she dreamed that while she was there, she woke up to find a man's hands around her throat. The next day she started for New York, but then changed her mind and returned to the country. 'The following day a call came from the city police that the town house had been robbed the night before, the night she would have been in it.'

Even if she had been there, she would not necessarily have woken up with the burglar's hands on her throat; but this was not the particular point which Louisa Rhine was illustrating. The dream, she suggested, might not have been precognitive: the warning 'could have been the result of telepathic awareness of the robber's intention to commit robbery'. In many cases of 'dreaming the future' a similar possibility arises: what is seen represents what will happen *if* an intention is carried out later. Again, though, this is irrelevant to the issue of whether we should pay more attention to what seem to be psychic promptings in our dreams. The important point was that by heeding the warning the girl had avoided what would almost certainly have been a terrifying experience, and might have ended in her death.

Although it tends to be the life-preserving dreams that are most often recalled, several have also been recorded where they have prevented some other unwelcome consequence. Eleanor Sidgwick was sceptical about precognition; but she had to admit in her survey of the cases sent in to the SPR that one which had appeared earlier in a Munich journal was 'exceptionally well authenticated'.

In 1886 'Frau K.' dreamed of 'the outbreak of a rapidly spreading conflagration, which through its terrifying grandeur had a paralysing effect on me'. The thought immediately occurred to her on waking that it was her securities, kept in a fire-proof safe in a local brewery, which were at risk. When she had the same dream three nights later, she tried to persuade her husband that they were in danger. At first he refused to collect them, but after days of her badgering he at last consented, 'less on account of the dream than for the sake of my comfort'. She then left for the country, where suddenly she had the dream again.

Instead of, as before, being frightened by the exciting scene, there came over me a feeling of relief as of being saved from a great calamity by the timely saving of the papers. On the morning of the 15th I made known my dream experience to those around me. Sadly enough the warning was fulfilled; for the following day, I received written information that the brewery, in which was the above-mentioned safe, had been reduced to ashes by a destructive fire, which had broken out on the 14th of September. As I afterwards heard, the building was burnt to the ground; the fire-proof safe was exposed to flames and heat for 36 hours, so that the proprietor's papers which were preserved in it were completely charred. These dreams, therefore (as has happened to me before) saved me from a great misfortune.

No fewer than five witnesses testified to the accuracy of Frau K.'s account; her husband, three members of her family and the brewery proprietor, who confirmed that the 36 hours of heat which the building had sustained had destroyed all the papers in the safe. As Mrs Sidgwick pointed out, the most interesting points were that the anxiety about the papers, though it arose from the dream, did not actually feature in it – though it might have been in the dream and forgotten. 'The occurrence of the final dream simultaneously with the fire,' she had to admit, was a coincidence 'which certainly adds great weight to the reasons for regarding the whole set of experiences as supernormal.'

Some of the precognitive dreams whose information has been used to good purpose have been in the trivial category – except to the dreamers. When one of three linnets which Goethe's Boswell, Eckermann, kept as pets flew away, and he could not find it, he went to bed inconsolable. But that night he dreamed that he was looking for it, and found it on the roof of a house in the neighbourhood.

I called to it, and it approached, moved its wings as if asking for food, but still it could not venture to fly down. I ran through our garden into my chamber and returned with the cup of soaked rape-seed; I held the favourite food towards it, and it perched upon my hand. Full of joy, I carried it back into my chamber to the other two.

When he awoke he went straight to the place he had seen in the dream, and it was there. 'Everything happened as I had seen it in the dream. I called, it approached, but it hesitated to fly to my hand.' He went back for the food; and it flew to his hand.

When Dame Edith Lyttelton – among other occupations, a British delegate to the League of Nations – asked for cases in a broadcast she made in 1937, one came from the woman manager of a chocolate-packing department in a factory, who had thirty or forty girls to supervise. One night she dreamed of the chocolates getting 'all mixed up'; and the following morning felt impelled to examine the work of one of the packers. The girl, she found, was putting cheap jellies in by mistake with the best gingers; an episode which the girl corroborated, as she remembered the manager telling her that she had been induced to check by a dream.

Of the warning dreams sent in to the Foundation, one account from a woman is unusual and rather disturbing.

One morning I woke up to find I was not in my own bed, in my flat, but in the bed of a male colleague. Although I had never been in his flat before, I knew immediately where I was; but I did not have any of the feelings of surprise, horror or exhilaration which might reasonably be associated with such an event. I should perhaps emphasise that I grasped the situation through tactile rather than visual evidence, as I hadn't yet opened my eyes.

A few seconds later she realised it had been a dream. She was in fact in her own bed.

I was very bewildered by the experience, because, being very much in love with someone else at the time, I had never had any fantasies, speculations or even passing thoughts about him in this light. If I had, I would certainly not consciously have thought about being in bed with him, because in 1956 nice provincial girls didn't think about going to bed with people – certainly I didn't.

Still, he was 'amusing, not bad-looking, five years older than me and single'. He was not taboo. As it happened, both of them were to go in their official capacities to the same university function that evening.

During the course of the evening he invited me to accompany him to the local pub, and, to cut a long story short, I eventually found myself in what might be described as a necking situation. I was terribly surprised by this, but with the morning's experience very much in mind I managed to terminate it then and there. Had I not been forewarned, I am reasonably sure that a combination of complete unpreparedness, gratified vanity and loneliness (I was in my first job and at the other end of the country from home and boy friend) would have led to my finding myself where I had appeared to be that morning.

So far, so light-hearted. But Mrs C – now in her middle fifties, a mother of three children – points out that in 1956, had she not had the dream warning, a range of unsavoury possibilities could have arisen. In the absence – as there would have been – of contraception, pregnancy could have led to a shot-gun marriage which neither of them would have wanted (he had his own girlfriend); or single parenthood, with loss of job and/or adoption for the baby; or an abortion (though she does not mention this, perhaps because she would not have contemplated it). She has never, she claims, told anybody about her experience before; and she insists that although she had often had vivid dreams between sleeping and waking in the morning, it 'was *nothing like these*'.

Unheeded warnings

For every apparent premonitory warning in a dream which has been heeded, there must be scores which have been ignored. In most of them, probably, the dreamers have subsequently felt relieved that they took no action, as no dire consequences followed. But in some notorious instances, dire consequences *have* followed. Whether a warning, had it been given, would have prevented a catastrophe in many cases remains uncertain. But in some, it is hard to dispute that if it had been given and acted upon, the course of events – even, occasionally, the course of history – might have been altered.

On 28 June 1914 Monsignor de Lanyi, Bishop of Grosswardin in Hungary, had a nightmare. As a professor of the Hungarian language in Vienna, he had for a time been tutor to the Archduke Franz Ferdinand. In his dream,

I had gone to my desk in order to look through my letters. Right on top there was a black-bordered letter bearing a black seal with the coat of arms of the Archduke. I immediately recognized his writing. I opened it and on top of the letter I noticed a light blue picture, like those on a picture postcard, on which there appeared a street and a narrow passageway. Their Highnesses were sitting in a motor-car, facing them was a general, and next to the chauffeur there was an officer. On both sides of the street there was a large crowd. Two young fellows suddenly jumped out from the crowd and fired at Their Highnesses. The text of the dream letter itself was, word for word, as follows: 'Dear Dr Lanyi, I herewith inform you that today my wife and I will fall victims to an assassination. We commend ourselves to your pious prayers. Kindest regards from your Archduke Franz, Sarajevo, the 28th of June, 2.45 a.m.

In terror, and in tears, de Lanyi went to his desk, noting the time, and recording the dream.

I even copied some of the Archduke's writing as I had seen it in the dream. My servant entered my study at 5.45 a.m. and noticed how pale I was and that I was telling my beads. He asked me if I felt ill. I said: 'Please call my mother and our guest. I wish to say mass for Their Highnesses for I have had a terrible dream.' I then went to our chapel with them. I passed the day in fear and trembling until at 3.30 p.m. a telegram brought news of the assassination.

Not merely did de Lanyi write his account; he drew a picture of what he had witnessed in the dream, which he showed that day to two witnesses; and he also sent his account the same day to his brother Edward, a Jesuit. A journalist from the *Wiener Reichspost*, hearing about the dream, undertook to check on the story, and found that the Bishop's drawing closely resembled those which were to appear of the scene of the assassination in the newspapers. A well-known editor, Bruno Grabinsky, also obtained confirmation from the Bishop's Jesuit brother. As Medard Boss pointed out, relating the episode, it could be objected that assassination was in the air at the time. But this could not account for the detailed nature of the dream; 'after all, there are an infinite number of ways in which the assassination could have been carried out: for instance on the way to Sarajevo, on the steps of the city hall, four people instead of five, one victim instead of two, etc.'

On 2 October 1975 'an ordinary English housewife', as she described herself, posted a letter to the Prime Minister of Israel, Golda Meir. She had been meditating a few days earlier when she had slipped into a dream, which had disturbed her so much that, after consulting with friends, she had finally decided she ought to transmit its contents.

Dear Mrs Meir,

I am sorry to bother you with this letter, but I feel that you are the only one who can assess if it is important or not for your country.

When I was meditating, an Arab crept into my vision. I was so surprised I 'watched' him because he was acting in a stealthy, underhand way. He was in a cave and had reached this point by a small boat. He carefully crept along the wall of the cave until he came to a turning point and peeped around it. When he found it was all clear he turned and beckoned into the darkness behind him.

Then another Arab in a boat, the same boat that the first man had travelled in, slowly made his way to the edge of the water.

He got out carefully and then, by means of a rope pulling arrangement, sent the boat back into the water. The rope was marked so that the boat would stop at a precise spot.

In the vision, the writer explained, she had the impression that the boat contained an atomic bomb, and she watched it go off: 'the whole hill exploded!' She had never been in Israel, but in the next development of her dream she seemed to be with Israeli soldiers in a place where there was a huge inland lake on the east, and the Mediterranean on the west.

I 'knew' this was where the Arabs had entered in their small boat.

When I was up on the parapet with the patrolling soldiers I heard 'the Heights of Golan'.

You will know, or be able to find out, if such an area exists. If it does I feel you should guard it well.

I have simply been used as a 'link' to get this information through from a higher level of vibration. I have told you of everything I received. I hope it will be of some use to you.

From an ordinary English housewife,
Mrs Tanya Forest (a pseudonym)

By the time the letter arrived, about two weeks later, the war had begun. On 6 October Egyptian forces had crossed the Suez canal in dinghies and established themselves on the east bank, and Syrian troops had broken through the Israeli lines on the Golan heights.

Evaluating the case in the SPR *Journal* from the standpoint of parapsychology, the Israeli psychical researcher Gilad Livneh pointed out that there could be no doubt that the letter had been written and posted before the attack, and it was extremely unlikely that the writer could have had inside information of a kind which would have prompted her to write it. Some, even if not all, of the details were remarkably accurate. Chance coincidence could not be ruled out, Livneh cautiously admitted, but 'the specific perception of an Arab attack on Israel, the proximity in time between the percipient's experience and the unexpectedness of the war, strongly suggest precognition as a plausible explanation.'

According to Livneh, when the letter arrived on 25 October Golda Meir was 'stunned'. She asked her secretary, 'Had you received this letter on 2 October, what would you have done?' 'I would have thrown it away,' the secretary replied, adding, 'But I would not put you on the spot, and won't ask you what would you have done.' Whatever Golda Meir would have done, it can scarcely be doubted that had the letter arrived the day after it had been posted, and had the Israeli commanders been told that information received pointed to an imminent attack, the leading forces could have been dealt with much more expeditiously than they were. For, as it happened, the attack came at a time when Military Intelligence had been assuring the government that the probability of a renewed war was 'lower than low'.

Sometimes no action has been taken after warning dreams because the dreamers have not grasped the significance of what they have witnessed until too late. Baron von Hellembach, the Hungarian writer whose scientific and philosophical works were greatly esteemed a century ago, was mortified to feel that he could have intervened had he realised what a dream of his portended. He had told M. Hauer, Director of Mines and head of the Department of Chemistry at the Vienna Geological Institution, that he had been doing some research into crystallography, and would like to discuss it with him – Hauer being an internationally recognised expert.

I had always put off my visit, but finally I decided to make it the following morning. That very night I dreamed I saw a man, pale and trembling, supported by the arms, by two men. I paid no attention to this dream, and I went to the geological institution; but as the laboratory was in a different place from where it had been in former years, I mistook the door, and, finding the right door locked, I looked through a window and saw the exact scene shown in my dream; they were supporting Hauer, who had just poisoned himself with cyanide of potassium; they were carrying him into the vestibule, just as I had dreamed.

The Belgian author and playwright Maurice Maeterlinck, winner of the Nobel Prize for Literature in 1911, had a rather similar, though less disturbing, experience, which he described in *La Vie de l'Espace* in 1928. In his dream,

being in Belgium and thinking to reach Ghent by a short cut, I came to a town that I did not recognize. A young man standing at the door of a church kindly told me that I was in Bruges. I wanted to go into the church but, I do not know why, he strictly forbade me to enter. We chatted and he told me that he was the son of one of my childhood friends. Since I had rarely met this friend during the last twenty years, I had never seen his son. Next, a sort of bus shot out of the church and the young man got into it. The bus started with a kangaroo-like bound, took a right-angled corner at a crazy speed and overturned. The majority of the passengers were hurt and I noticed my friend's son among them.

About a month later, Maeterlinck met his childhood friend.

He told me that his son, whom I had known as a tiny tot, had been the victim of a car accident three weeks ago; his car, which he was driving himself, had overturned on a corner. In addition to a head wound and severe bruises, the radius and ulna of his right arm had been fractured. He had not yet recovered completely, but he would come out of it all right. At the time I did not establish any correlation between the accident and that dream, which I had completely forgotten. It was not until I had returned home that a vague recollection began to stir in my brain. I opened my notebook and, after I had written to my friend, I learnt that the event had taken place two days after my dream.

A correspondent from Dyfed in Wales has recalled in a letter to the Foundation that she once dreamt she was staying in a Channel port, went out for the evening, and couldn't find her way back to the hotel where she was staying. Unable to remember its name, or even the name of the street it was in, she 'spent nearly all the night frantically going up and down side-streets and all over the town, trying to find it, getting increasingly desperate, exhausted and worried because I had left someone staying there who I knew would be very worried about my not returning.'

Some weeks later her son came home, and told her he had been to France for a week-end with a friend, the friend's girl-friend, and their baby; and the two men had not enjoyed themselves.

He started telling me exactly what had happened in my dream. I told him not to tell me any more as I knew all about it, and told him. It was exactly as I had dreamt. In the evening he and his friend had gone out for a drink, leaving his girl-friend and the baby in the hotel. They couldn't remember the name of the hotel or the street, and had spent half the night looking for it, very tired and worried.

The writer had never had a dream of the kind before; 'and the most puzzling thing is that I had the dream two or three weeks before the occurrence.'

Many a premonition must have been withheld by the dreamers for fear that they would be laughed at, particularly if the warning proved to be unfounded. This was what deterred John Williams, the manager of some tin mines in Cornwall.

About the second or third day of May, 1812, I dreamed that I was in the lobby of the House of Commons (a place well known to me). A small man dressed in a blue coat and white waistcoat, entered, and immediately I saw a person whom I had observed on my first entrance, dressed in a snuff-coloured coat with metal buttons, take a pistol from under his coat, and present it at the little man above-mentioned. The pistol was discharged, and the ball entered under the left breast of the person at whom it was directed. I saw the blood issue from the place where the ball had struck him, his countenance instantly altered, and he fell to the ground. Upon inquiry who the sufferer might be, I was informed that he was the chancellor. I understood him to be Mr Perceval, who was Chancellor of the Exchequer.

(Perceval was in fact also Prime Minister.) When Williams awoke he told his wife what he had seen; it was 'only a dream', she said, and advised him to go to sleep again, which he did – only to have the same dream. Again, when he told his wife, she urged him to dismiss it from his mind.

Upon my falling asleep the third time, the same dream without any alteration was repeated, and I awoke, as on the former occasions, in great agitation. So much alarmed and impressed was I with the circumstances above related, that I felt much doubt about whether it was not my duty to take a journey to London and communicate upon the subject with the party principally concerned. Upon this point I consulted with some friends whom I met on business at the Godolphin mine on the following day. After having stated to them the particulars of the dream itself and what were my feelings in relation to it, they dissuaded me from my purpose, saying I might expose myself to contempt and vexation, or be taken up as a fanatic. Upon this I said no more.

Spencer Perceval was assassinated in the lobby of the House of Commons on 11 May.

Some business soon after called me to London, and in one of the print-shops I saw a drawing for sale representing the place and the circumstances which attended Mr Perceval's death. I purchased it, and upon a careful examination I found it to coincide in all respects with the scene which had passed through my imagination as a dream. The colours of the dresses, the buttons of the assassin's coat, the white waistcoat of Mr Perceval, the spot of blood upon it, the countenances and attitudes of the parties present were exactly what I had dreamed.

Williams did not write out his account until twenty years later – when it was desirable, he felt, to set the record straight, because various versions had been circulating. But he had told many people at the time, who testified that they knew of his dream and his dilemma, before the news came through of the assassination.

One of Louisa Rhine's sadder case histories was from a woman who, in a nightmare, had seen a plane crash on the roof of a lakeside cottage which she recognised as one not far from where she was staying. So certain was she that her dream would come true that she began to feel she should send a warning to the local fire brigade. She had the strong impression that if she did not, the fire engine would take the wrong route to the crash and arrive too late. But she did not make the call.

Preparing dinner that night for her husband, she cried out to him when she heard a plane overhead that it was going to crash. 'Try to stop the firemen before they take the canal road. They have to take the basin road, and they don't know it!' Listening to the sound of the plane's engines, he assured her it was all right. It was not; a few seconds later it crashed. The firemen did take the canal road, and they were too late to save the pilot, who was burned to death. 'I was a wreck for weeks,' she told Louisa Rhine, 'wondering how I could have prevented it.'

Sometimes it is the people who have been warned who have been too embarrassed to take avoiding action, either because they do not credit dream warnings, or because they do not care to be laughed at for pandering to superstition. In 1844 the United States Navy launched a warship, the *Princeton*, with an unprecedentedly powerful cannon, the 'Peacemaker'; and to celebrate, President Tyler was invited to take a cruise, along with senators, congressmen and their wives, so that they could be treated to a demonstration of fire power. Tyler, a widower, asked the girl he proposed to marry, Julia Gardiner, to come on the trip, along with her father, a former New York State senator. The night before the cruise, she had a nightmare in which she was standing on the deck of a ship she had never seen before when two white horses came towards her, ridden by skeletons; one of the riders, when he turned towards her, displayed her father's face. She declined the invitation, and begged her father not to go: but he laughed at her fears.

The wife of the Secretary of the Navy, Thomas Gilmer, also had a dream about death that night. She, too, pleaded with her husband not to go on the cruise – even after they had gone on board the *Princeton*. He declined to disembark.

Nathaniel Tallmadge, Governor of Wisconsin, was among the guests. After the 'Peacemaker' had been fired three times he suddenly felt frightened and, instead of staying by the cannon, went down to the cabin where the wives were assembled. As he reached it there was a violent explosion: the cannon, in firing the fourth round, had burst, killing Gilmer and Julia's father.

In several cases where a dream has presaged danger or death the dreamer, or the person to be warned, has not been given a sufficiently clear picture to prevent the event happening. Calpurnia's dream on the night before Caesar was assassinated seems to have been in this category; as was the dream of Abraham Lincoln, a few days before he was assassinated. He had gone to bed weary, he told his friend Ward Lamon:

I soon began to dream. There seemed to be death-like stillness about me. Then I heard subdued sobs, as if a number of people were weeping. I thought I left my bed and wandered downstairs. There the silence was broken by the same pitiful sobbing, but the mourners were invisible. I went from room to room; no living person was in sight, but the same mournful sounds of distress met me as I passed along. It was light in all the rooms; every object was familiar to me; but where were all the people who were grieving as if their hearts would break? I was puzzled and alarmed. What could be the meaning of this? Determined to find the cause of a state of things so mysterious and so shocking, I kept on until I arrived at the East Room, which I entered. There I met with a sickening surprise. Before me was a catafalque, on which rested a corpse wrapped in funeral vestments. Around it were stationed soldiers who were acting as guards; and there was a throng of people, some gazing mournfully upon the corpse, whose face was covered, others weeping pitifully. 'Who is dead in the White House?' I demanded of one of the soldiers. 'The President,' was his answer; 'he was killed by an assassin!' Then came a loud burst of grief from the crowd, which awoke me from my dream. I slept no more that night; and although it was only a dream, I have been strangely annoyed by it ever since.

Mrs Lincoln told the President that although she did not believe in such things, she wished he had not told her about the dream. 'Let us say no more about it,' he replied.

In one of the cases investigated in the early years of the SPR a warning, had it been a little more explicit, might have prevented a murder. It was to be written out in detail for the investigator, Frank Podmore, by the dreamer, Frederick Lane. Lane had been understudy to William Terriss – then one of the leading West End actors.

On the early morning of the 16th December 1897 I dreamt that I saw the late Mr Terriss lying in a state of delirium or unconsciousness on the stairs leading up to the dressing rooms in the Adelphi Theatre. He was surrounded by people engaged at the theatre, amongst whom were Miss Millward and one of the flatmen who attend the curtain, both of whom I actually saw a few hours later at the death scene. His chest was bare and clothes torn aside. Everybody who was around him was trying to do something for his good.

The dream, Lane explained, was 'like a tableau on which the curtain would rise and fall'. He then dreamt that 'we did not open at the Adelphi that evening.'

Lane had to go to the theatre that day for a rehearsal, and he told some of his fellow-actors about his dream. In the evening, Terriss and another member of the cast, J.H. Graves, were entering the theatre through a door in Maiden Lane when an actor who had an imagined grievance against Terriss, and had become deranged, ran across the road and stabbed him. Graves managed to seize the man and call a constable, whom he accompanied to Bow Street; when he returned, he told the judge at the subsequent trial, he 'found Mr Terriss lying at the foot of the stairs, a few paces from the door', in a state of delirium – just as Lane had seen in his dream. Podmore checked the story by interviewing some of the cast, who confirmed Lane's account. There was no indication that Lane felt embarrassed that he had not warned Terriss, or anybody else. He appears to have told the dream to the cast simply as a curiosity.

In other cases, it is hard to see what could have been done even if both the dreamer and the individual marked in the dream as at risk were prepared to take the warning seriously.

In 1937 Professor W.H. Tenhaeff of the University of Utrecht – holder of the first Chair of Parapsychology to be set up in Europe – was told by a medical colleague about a patient who had unusual dreams. When they were introduced, the woman said she would keep Tenhaeff informed about them; and a few days later, on 27 November, she described a dream in which everything was so clear she could not put it out of her mind.

I saw a railway crossing and a long road and pasture. Behind the gate to the left stood a truck. A car comes along at a terrible speed trying to cross at the last moment but as it crosses, a tire bursts and the car crashes at full speed against the gate and the truck behind it. The driver of the car was killed immediately. I saw his face when he was lying there, it was Prince Bernhard.

Two days after the letter reached Tenhaeff, he heard on the radio that Prince Bernhard had been involved in an accident. It turned out to have occurred on a stretch of road beside a railway, close to a gate into a meadow. Lorries nearby were loading sand, and the Prince's car had struck one of them. There was no level crossing, no burst tyre; and although the Prince had been laid out on the road, he survived. As 'Dunne dreams' go, this was close enough to the reality. But even if the Prince had heard about the dream, the chances of his recognising the fated scene would surely have been poor.

The number of cases where a dream has pointed clearly and specifically to some course of action which has not been taken, with fatal results, appears to be small; though there was 'a very celebrated one', according to Cicero, who related it in his essay on divination.

Two Arcadians who were intimate friends were travelling together, and arriving at Megara, one of them took up his quarters at an inn, the other at a friend's house. After supper, when they had both gone to bed, the Arcadian who was staying at his friend's house saw an apparition of his fellow-traveller at the inn, who prayed to him to come to his assistance immediately as the innkeeper was going to murder him. Alarmed at his intimation, he started from his sleep; but on recollection, thinking it nothing but an idle dream, he lay down again. Presently, however, the apparition appeared to him again in his sleep, and entreated him, though he would not come to his assistance while yet alive, at least not to leave his death unavenged. He told him further that the innkeeper had first murdered him and then cast him into a dungcart, where he lay covered with filth; and begged him to go early to the gate of the town, before any cart could leave.

Shaken, the dreamer roused himself, went to the gate, and there met the driver of a dungcart. What, he wanted to know, was in the cart?

The driver, upon this question, ran away in fright. The dead body was then discovered and the innkeeper, the evidence being clear against him, brought to punishment.

Cases where clear-cut dream premonitions have been ignored with unfortunate, though less lethal, results, are common enough. Maeterlinck recorded one, rather similar to Schopenhauer's.

I dreamt that a bottle containing peroxide of hydrogen was on a small three-legged table in a corner of the dressing-room. One of the legs stood on a beige-coloured carpet, the other two on the floor of Provençal tiles. In passing, a clumsy movement of my knee jogged the little table, the bottle fell over, rolled and dropped on to the tiles, where it broke. The peroxide of hydrogen spread over the carpet, which began to smoke as if it had caught fire. Motionless and dumbfounded, I watched the destruction of my carpet without trying to do anything to save it.

When he woke up, Maeterlinck jotted down the dream out of interest, but did not consider it to be important. In any case, when he looked he found there was no bottle on the little table, and that its leg was standing on a red, not beige, rug.

Three days later, when my dream was completely forgotten, I bought a pint of sulphuric acid which I needed for my accumulators and put it on the little table. A few hours later I bumped into it; the pint bottle rolled over, fell and broke. The rug was quite damp and began to smoke copiously, and it was only then that I suddenly remembered the dream I had had three days before this happened. Two errors of detail will be noticed: the beige carpet which was actually in the adjoining bedroom, and which took the place of the red rug, and the pint of sulphuric acid which was substituted for the peroxide of hydrogen. The second error is rather curious, for peroxide of hydrogen flooding the carpet would not have caused smoke or fumes. Chemical reality had won the upper hand over dream fantasy.

That failure to heed a dream warning can be embarrassing as well as expensive has been confirmed by champion jockey Willie Shoemaker. Ralph Lowe, the owner of the horse Shoemaker was to ride in the 1957

Kentucky Derby, dreamed that at the end of the race the jockey was 'standing up and misjudging the finish'. He told Shoemaker about the dream before the race. It would not happen, Shoemaker assured him. But it did.

One of the cases sent to the Foundation has a curious resemblance to the dream of Archdeacon Bevan. Unlike in his case, the warning went unheeded, though with only mildly embarrassing results. In or around 1975 a civic service was to be held at St Barnabas's Church in Bath, and the headmaster of the nearby Southdown School, F. Bennett, was asked to read one of the lessons. The day before, he read the passage through a number of times.

> That night I had a dream. I was at the service and I mounted the lectern for my reading, and looked down at the Bible which had been opened for me. I took a second look with some alarm. I could not find where to begin reading. The verses of the passage, instead of being clearly defined as they are in the Bible, were confused and ran into one another. As I glanced down the page, neither could I see where the passage ended.
>
> However, after a few seconds I found the place and began. But the confusion did not end there. As I read, I found the words were quite strange, quite different from those I had prepared although the meaning was much the same. With some relief I identified the place where I had to stop and finished the reading.

The next morning he told his wife and family of the dream over breakfast 'with a certain amount of merriment'. They went to the church and took their seats. The churchwarden came up, asked if everything was all right, and said he would open the Bible at the right page. When the time came, Bennett went to the lectern.

> There followed a long pause (my wife, afterwards, told me she 'knew' what had happened). I looked down and, as in the dream, I could not find where to begin the reading. The verses in this edition of the Bible had been run together, and it was difficult to identify the first verse of the passage to be read. Neither could I readily see where the passage ended. As in the dream, the words were different, but the meaning was the same.

Bennett had prepared the reading from the Authorised Version; the book on the lectern was the New English Bible.

In another of the Foundation's cases, a dream warning which went unheeded came true – but without any unwelcome consequences. When Mary Collis of Honiton in Devon was to take her exam at the London Academy of Music, she dreamed that she had learned the wrong set piece; but both her mother and her teacher laughed when she told them, and said that this was impossible. After she had played it, her examiner told her it *was* the wrong piece – but she had played it so beautifully, he would say nothing about it. As a result, she won her coveted bronze medal.

Warning dreams, then, often present problems. Is the message to be relied upon? If so, can it be acted upon, and how? The significant fact, though, is that such warnings are occasionally given; and experience has shown it is worth taking them seriously when it is at all possible to do so. That such warnings can reach us through the agency of dreams means that they are potentially a valuable – and in some instances, invaluable – human asset.

Gamblers' delight

What remains puzzling is the relative paucity of accounts of really useful precognitive dreams in the life-enhancing sense, as distinct from the life-preserving: dreams like one which was reported to and investigated by Maurizio Macario, a former deputy in the Sardinian parliament whose *Du Sommeil, des rêves et du somnambulisme* was published in 1857. Angèle Bobin, a baker's daughter, grew up in the small town of Charité-sur-Loire in the Department of Nièvre. Of ravishing grace and beauty, she had several aspirants for her hand in marriage, including one greatly favoured by her parents on account of his wealth. She resisted because, she insisted, she could not love him. Her parents, however, continued to nag her to accept him until, exasperated, she went to the church, prostrated herself before the statue of the Virgin, and prayed fervently to be given guidance in the choice of her future husband.

Her prayer was answered the following night. She dreamed that she saw in front of her a young man in travelling clothes, wearing a large straw hat; and an inner voice told her this was to be her husband. Full of her dream, and confident she was under the Virgin's protection, she confronted her

parents and told them firmly but respectfully that she had finally decided
not to marry the man of their choice.

'Some time later, finding herself at a ball in the town, what was her
surprise when she met the young traveller who had appeared in her dream!
At the sight her heart beat tumultuously in her breast, and a blush suffused
her cheeks.' Strangely enough, the young man on seeing her experienced
the same emotion. Soon after, they were married.

Intrigued by the tale, Macario followed it up and found the young man,
Emile de la Bedollière, an editor on the journal *Le Siècle*. When asked
whether he would confirm the account – it was eventually to appear in
Macario's book – he wrote to say that it was 'of the most complete
exactitude'.

Rare though such cases are, there is one exception: dreams which have
enabled the dreamers, and sometimes their friends, to lay bets and win
money. Sceptics rightly point out that whenever there is a big race there
are stories of dream winners; dream losers may be far more common, but
are not remembered. Where simply a name or a number is dreamed, too,
chance can reasonably be held accountable if it turns out to be a winner.
But again, in some cases the detail strengthens the case for precognition.
Flammarion cited as an example the experience the French surgeon Baron
Larrey – 'as distinguished as a man of the world as he was honest as a
scholar' – had related to him.

All in one night he dreamed *four* numbers for the lottery and the next
morning, as he was in haste to begin his calls, he asked Madame
Larrey to make the bets on them herself. But what was his annoyance,
when he returned home to find that the numbers had appeared – and
that his commission had been forgotten!

It is impossible to attribute this coincidence to chance; the player
had 2,555,189 chances against him.

One number, yes; perhaps even two; but *four*! Today we know that
the future can be seen.

In her *Moments of Knowing* (1970) Ann Bridge recalled some dreams
which the diplomat Douglas Jerram described to her husband, who took
them down. When he was Ambassador to Stockholm, Jerram had been on
friendly terms with the then King of Sweden.

Race meetings in Sweden generally took place on Sundays; and on a certain Saturday night Jerram had a very vivid dream that he was at one – he was anxious to place his bets but was impeded by the crowd from getting anywhere near the Tote. At this point he turned round and found the old King jammed next to him in the crowd. Together they climbed over some iron railings and managed to get to the box where bets were made. Jerram knew nothing about the horses, but the King said, 'You just put your money on Mandalay; he is an outsider, but I am sure he will win.'

The next day, Jerram went to the races, where as usual he sat in the box reserved for diplomats.

Looking over the shoulder of the man in front of him he was shocked to see on the latter's newspaper, in banner headlines – 'Death of the King'.

Jerram realised that he must leave at once, but he hurriedly ascertained that there was a horse running, at longish odds, called not Mandalay but Manderley. He pushed all the money he had brought with him – nearly £100 – into the hands of a close friend with urgent instructions at all costs to put the lot on Manderley. Then he left the racecourse to call on his Swedish colleagues to condole, and to concert arrangements for a memorial service in the English church.

Manderley won, and Jerram made nearly £1,000.

Dreams have sometimes enabled gamblers to win at the tables. Once, in his sleep, Osbert Sitwell recalled in *Left Hand, Right Hand*, a voice said to him 'Back the number fifteen when the casino clock is at the hour.' He put all the money he had brought with him on number fifteen, 'and I won!' He had also had other dreams of future events, 'not so pleasant', but he did not relate them.

Even more striking is the account which the celebrated American attorney Loomis C. Johnson provided for Megroz's 1939 collection. While in St Louis during the First World War, Johnson had been in the habit of playing poker with his fellow lawyers on Saturday evenings. One Wednesday night, he dreamt that he was at the party the following Saturday.

The weekly poker game was in full swing, and I had been losing all evening. Finally on one deal I picked up my hand and found it to contain three kings, a knave and an ace. Naturally I opened the 'pot'. And, still in my dream, the betting was brisk. Finally came the draw. I discarded the ace (being superstitious concerning 'knaves') and asked for one card. When, in my dream, I picked up the card that had been given me, I found it to be an ace but – as things sometimes happen in dreams, without causing surprise – even as I looked at the card it gradually changed complexion and finally became a 'jack', thus giving me a 'full house' – three kings and a pair of knaves. Yes, even in my dream I won the 'pot', and it was rather a good one.

It was so vivid a dream that he made notes about it, to show to his friends. Towards the end of Saturday's game, which had proceeded as in his dream, he picked up the dream hand; and the betting went as in the dream.

I had been looking for it, that I must confess, but I did not see how the ace could turn into a knave.

Nevertheless when the time came for the draw, I discarded the ace and asked for one card. Under American poker rules when a card on the draw is faced – that is, falls on the table face upwards without being touched by the drawer – it is a dead card. The drawer then proceeds in regular order, and at the end the player whose card was faced receives another in place of the dead card.

When I asked for one, it was faced in being dealt to me, and it was an ace. The draw went on and finally I received my card to replace the faced card, and it was a knave. Thus was my dream fulfilled.

He then showed his friends the notes he had made of the dream. 'It is hardly necessary to add,' he told Megroz, 'that for a long time thereafter, before anyone would bet against me on a hand, I had to give an assurance on my honour that I had not been dreaming!' This was a case, Megroz felt, where the details 'put "coincidence" virtually out of the question.'

An account sent to the SPR in 1898 by Donald Murray, then on the *Sydney Morning Herald*, described a dream which had foretold the winner of the Melbourne Cup in 1870. That was nearly three years before, but Murray had followed up the story, and found considerable attestation. The

Melbourne Cup, he admitted, often produced dream winners; according to the *Herald*'s sports editor, people actually ate large pork dinners the night before in the hope of finding the winner in the course of a restless night. But this dream had unusual features.

A week before the race, the Hotham Stakes was won by Nimblefoot; and this prompted a story in the *Bendigo Independent*. Nimblefoot's owner, Walter Craig of Ballarat, had apparently told friends that he had dreamed he saw a horse, 'ridden by a jockey wearing his well-known colours, but with crêpe on his left sleeve', coming in first for the Melbourne Cup. The *Independent's* story was prompted by the fact that Craig had died – and when Nimblefoot won the Hotham Stakes, the jockey was wearing the colours and the crêpe.

'Whether Nimblefoot will win the Melbourne Cup is another matter,' the *Independent* concluded. 'Should that be the case, it will be somewhat startling.' It was: Nimblefoot won at 100 to 7, to the satisfaction of friends of the owner, some of whom had secured a 'double' on the strength of his account of his dream. The stories of the vast sums that had been made, Murray admitted, could no longer be checked; but there could be little doubt that the story of the dream was true. It had certainly appeared in the *Independent* before the big race, as this could be checked in the newspaper's files.

There is another sequence of dream winners which cannot be explained away by the fallibility of human memory; it is too well documented and attested. And in this case, although the results did little to line the dreamer's pockets, they were to have a decisive effect on his future life.

The son and heir to Lord Kilbracken, an Irish peer, John Godley had served in the Fleet Air Arm during the war, and took advantage of the government's Further Education and Training Scheme to return to Balliol College, Oxford. Two months later he had a dream in which he was reading an evening paper, in which the winners of that day's races were printed in full. When he woke up, he could remember two of them – Bindal and Juladin. At breakfast

to my excitement and amazement, I found that they were both of them engaged that afternoon.

I told several of my friends, some twelve or fifteen undergraduates, and they in turn passed on the story. Pound notes were thrust into my hands. I called my bookmaker and made my own wager: fifty shillings

to win Bindal, fifty shillings to win Juladin, and a fifty shillings win
double, which was as much as I could possibly afford out of my grant.
I also put just under five pounds on each horse for my friends. There
was now nothing more to do but wait for the first result – Bindal's.
Soon after three, I walked up to Carfax and bought a paper with
studied nonchalance. He had won; the odds were five to four.

This gave Godley confidence that Juladin would win, too. He could
have found out as soon as the race had been run, but he feared the spell
would be broken if he did not follow his dream.

This meant waiting another hour, and, when at last the time came, I
bought my *Evening Standard* with real confidence. It wasn't misplaced;
Juladin had made it at five to two.

I had won altogether just over thirty-four pounds. My friends,
between them, had won about the same. There was considerable
celebration in Oxford that night.

Godley had known the horses by name, even if he had not known they
were runners. His next dream winner he had never heard of, Tubermore.
In fact there was no such horse – but there was a Tuberose, running the
following day. At the time, Godley was at home with his family; and his
brother remarked how odd it was that neither the owner, the trainer nor
the jockey knew it was going to win, 'but *we do.*' Tuberose, an outsider,
duly won at a hundred to six.

Three months later, Godley dreamt that he called his bookmaker to ask
the result of the last race. He replied, 'Certainly, Sir: Monumentor, at five
to four.' Again there was no such horse; but Mentores was running in the
last race at Worcester that day, and was favourite at five to four. Godley
laid his bet. Again, he felt he must be careful to replay his dream. Instead
of getting an evening paper, he waited to ring his bookmaker. Their
conversation went precisely as it had done in his dream, except that the
odds were slightly better, six to four.

A pause followed of nearly a year before the next dream, in which he
actually 'saw' two races. He did not hear the name of the winner of the
first, but recognised the Gaekwar of Baroda's colours and his jockey,
Edgar Britt. In the second, he heard the crowd shouting 'The Bogie' and
'The favourite wins,' before he woke up – to find that the Gaekwar of

Baroda had a horse running that day, to be ridden by Edgar Britt; and that in the next race, the favourite was The Brogue.

This was near enough, he thought. This time he did not content himself with telling his friends. He wrote out a description of his dream, had it witnessed, sealed, and stamped with an official time stamp. He also rang the *New York Times* office in London, hoping to get some money for the story if the double came off. The reporter suggested he should try the *Daily Mirror* instead.

At that moment, without knowing it, this unknown American reporter altered the whole course of my life. I thought for about two minutes; it was three-forty-three. And then I decided: Damn the publicity! I'll sell it to the *Mirror*! By three-fifty I had told my tale in brief, and in return for their promise to buy the story if both horses won, had given them their names. Both of them, of course, *did* win, and my 'nap' selections had scored six out of six.

Four months later, nemesis. Godley dreamt a loser. As he pointed out, though, this dream was in a different category from the rest; he already fancied the horse's chances, and had put a bet on it.

It was a year before he had another race dream; and this time, though he knew the horse's name, Timocrat, he had not known it was running that day. Timocrat won at four to one. Four weeks passed and he dreamed that he was reading the next day's paper. The names of two horses stayed in his mind when he awoke: Pretence and Monk's Mistake. Pretence, he found, was not running that day; and as things turned out Monk's Mistake, which was due to run, was scratched. But both horses were runners the day after.

Up to that point, Godley's bets had been relatively modest from lack of funds. All told, he had won less than a hundred pounds. Now he decided to risk every penny he had, 'and a bit more besides'. Pretence won: Monk's Mistake would have won, but lived down to its name at the last fence, taking off too early, catching the fence top and stumbling. Godley won £44 on the day; had it not been for the stumble, he would have won £1,240.

With that the dream-winner series ended. Godley was to tell the story in a book, *Tell Me the Next One*, and again, briefly, in his autobiographical *Living Like a Lord*. There can hardly be any doubt as to its accuracy, considering how many of his friends knew of the dream winners before they ran, and the written attestations. The fact that there were small discrepancies in names and bookies' odds, too, only follows the Dunne pattern. And the losers could be accounted for: Claro, by the fact he had already bet on it; Monk's Mistake, because it had been scratched on the day after his dream. Had it won on the next day he could have made the equivalent of more than £10,000 in 1980s sterling. In any case, six winners out of eight in the space of three years again makes coincidence sound shaky as an alternative to precognition.

For Godley, the important outcome of his dream-winner series was not the cash – or the cachet among his friends, some of whom made considerably more than he did – but the result of his telephone call to the *Daily Mirror*. The *Mirror* splashed it, and paid him 25 guineas.

More was to follow, however. At the time I had a further six months before taking my degree. I wanted to write, but having no professional experience, the prospects were too chancy; it is practically impossible for a would-be writer to go direct to a national paper, and I did not fancy working for an unknown paper in the provinces. On my tutor's advice, therefore, I was taking, *faute de mieux*, the whole series of examinations for the Foreign Service, which, if I passed them, I would join as a Third Secretary after graduating in December.

He not merely passed; he came out top of more than a hundred candidates in this, the most prestigious of civil service exams. At the same time, however, he had an offer from the *Mirror* of an eight-week trial period on the editorial staff. He seized the chance.

The trial went well, and I stayed eighteen months with them; from the *Mirror* I moved to the *Sunday Express*, and I have been writing in one form or another, ever since. There can be no possible doubt that this was all a direct result of Baroda Squadron winning the four o'clock at Lingfield.

Another remarkable series of dream winners has been related by Thelma Moss, a medical psychologist at the Neuropsychiatric Institute at the University of California, Los Angeles, in her survey of evidence for paranormal phenomena, *The Probability of the Impossible* (1974). Ten years earlier a psychologist friend of hers, Mrs Sammie Hudson, had begun to have very vivid dreams, which for her was unusual. Eventually she related one of them to her husband during breakfast, saying that she had seen a horse race and heard the announcement of the winner's name. Her husband checked the races for that day, and found that a horse of that name was running on the opposite coast of the United States; it duly won.

For the next four months, two or three nights each week, Mrs Hudson dreamed of horse races, in which the announcer loudly and clearly announced the name of the winner as it crossed the finishing line. Her husband located the tracks at which the announced horses would be running, and bet on them. Eventually they won enough money to buy a luxury automobile.

As soon as they had bought it, the dreams stopped; though some years later Mrs Hudson took advantage of some further dreams, in which she won jackpots at Las Vegas, to go there. They picked up seven hundred dollars as a result.

In folklore there is a tradition that psychic powers vanish if used to obtain wealth. They need to be exploited with discretion where money is involved. On this basis, the Hudsons must consider themselves lucky; Godley, more typically, unlucky. The author and journalist, Christopher Booker, has a cautionary tale.

I had a vivid dream one night that I was looking at the column of figures printed next to the runners in a newspaper racecard, showing the performance of the horses in previous races. I am in no sense a racing man, but one series of figures stuck indelibly in my mind. While getting up the next morning I learned from the radio that it was Derby Day. I ran my eye down the list of runners in *The Times* and found that one horse had exactly the same numbers against its name that had appeared in my dream. It was called Shirley Heights. I mentioned this curious fact to someone, and had the feeling that I should 'put down a marker' on my dream by placing a small bet on Shirley Heights to win. I had a strong sense that I shouldn't bet too much – just a pound, as if to demonstrate the efficacy of the dream rather than attempt to make a large profit. Shirley Heights won, and I collected £8.

But then, the pay-off. In 1985 he had another vivid dream, this time of a set of numbers which he remembered when he woke up. Again it turned out to be Derby Day; and when he consulted a newspaper he found that they coincided with those next to one of the runners.

> I was so carried away by this coincidence that I decided to have another bet – only this time I put rather more on the horse, £10. I was very much aware that I was not just demonstrating the dream but hoping to make a profit. The horse came nowhere. When I looked at the numbers for the winning horse they were different from my dream in just one digit. I have learned my lesson!

Of the gambling dreams received by the Foundation, none has been striking enough to rebut seriously the 'coincidence' case, but for some precognition is marginally the more likely explanation. Don Blakeson, Associate of the Royal College of Music, has twice been the beneficiary. In 1959, while serving in the army in the 'Blues' he dreamed he was living in some future time, and was 'turning over the pages of a rather dog-eared leather-bound tome on the history of horse-racing'. One of the illustrations struck him: a full-page colour print of a horse whose jockey wore Sir Humphrey de Trafford's colours. Blakeson recognised the jockey, Harry Carr. The print bore the caption: 'PARTHIA, Derby Winner, 1959'. Parthia duly won the next day. On the second occasion, ten years later, he dreamed that he saw a tombstone inscribed simply 'P. Waldron'. In the racing programme the next day 'I saw that the jockey P. Waldron (who is, I am delighted to say, still riding to this day) was booked for only one ride.' The horse duly won.

Dream winners tend to appear immediately before the race; but Lord Kilbracken has had one longer-term success, years after his undergraduate experience. Some months before the 1958 Grand National he dreamt that it would be won by the third favourite, What Man. On an assignment abroad, he was out of touch with racing; but he found Mr What had been entered. As it was an outsider, the facts did not seem close enough to warrant a bet; only when the odds fell to 18–1, making Mr What third favourite, did he stake £25 on it to win. The outcome: a profit of £450.

Research

Laboratory research designed to test for precognition in dreams presents

much greater difficulties than tests for dream telepathy or clairvoyance –
for obvious reasons. The event or object foreseen in the dream may take
place days or even years afterwards; and whereas the link between
something which has played a minor role in the dream and its counterpart
in a target picture is likely to be noticed if it occurs the next morning, the
same linkage may easily be missed if there is a protracted gap between the
two.

Nevertheless one set of trials at Maimonides in 1969, with the young
psychic Malcolm Bessent who came over from England to be tested, had
impressive results; and the following year a protocol was devised which, it
was hoped, would provide reasonably satisfactory controls. The
experiment called upon him to sleep in the lab for sixteen nights. On the
first night, he would try to dream precognitively about the pictures which
would be in the target sequence, selected by a randomising process the
following night. On the second, he would try to dream about *that* night's
target sequence – and so on. The targets and the dreams were then sent to
three outside judges, who were asked to rate likenesses on a scale from one
to one hundred.

On the last of the nights that he was to attempt dream precognition,
Bessent reported a dream about Dr Robert Morris (who has since been
appointed first professor of Parapsychology at the University of Edinburgh). In the dream Morris, who had been doing research with birds, had
taken Bessent out to a sanctuary: 'I remember seeing various kinds of
doves,' Bessent recalled, 'and Canadian geese. There were many many
different kinds.' The target was a selection of slides showing a variety of
birds, in the water, on land and flying. To Ullman, this was 'a stunning
direct hit'. There were five 'direct hits' on the eight nights when Bessent
tried to dream precognitively, and a couple of near-misses – only one total
failure. On the other nights, when he was not attempting precognition,
there were no direct hits. Taken together, Ullman felt justified in claiming,
the two Bessent studies 'lent experimental corroboration to the precognitive hypothesis'.

5

Lucid Dreaming

There is one other type of dream about which relatively little is known, as serious exploration has only recently begun. Awareness in the course of a dream that it *is* 'only a dream' is quite a common experience, and probably always has been (it was mentioned by Aristotle); but 'lucid dreaming', in the sense of deliberately exploiting the capability, appears to have been rare – though apparently it is used by Tibetan Yogi. They are encouraged to learn from experience, according to Evans-Wentz, in *The Tibetan Book of the Dead* (1927), 'that the character of any dream can be changed or transformed by willing that it shall be.'

In the West, the first person to explore lucid dreaming was the Marquis Hervey de Saint-Denys, who happened to have found as a child that he was able to exert a measure of control over his dreams, and who published his *Les Rêves et les moyens de les diriger* (1867) when he was 45. In it he described the way in which he had learned how to dictate the course his dreams took, up to a point. Hervey did not take much stock of the possibilities of exploiting this ability, but he did learn how to banish nightmares by telling himself it was only a dream.

The Marquis's book attracted little attention; Frederic Myers does not appear to have known about it when, in 1887, he expressed regret 'that we are too indolent in regard to our dreams; that we neglect precious occasions of experiment for want of a little resolute direction of the will.' We should consider what we would like to test in our dreaming, he urged; 'when going to sleep we should impress upon our minds that we are going to try an experiment – that we are going to carry into our dreams enough of our waking self to tell us that they *are* dreams, and to prompt us to psychological inquiry.' But, Myers admitted, he had only rarely succeeded in influencing the course of his dreams; and his posthumous *Human Personality* in 1903 did not return to the issue.

Freud mentioned the subject, and cited Hervey, in *The Interpretation of*

Dreams; but only in passing. 'If the content of a dream goes too far in overstepping the censorship, we think "After all, it's only a dream!" – and go on sleeping.' It was not until shortly before the First World War that a research paper appeared, 'A Study of Dreams' by Frederic van Eeden, a Dutch psychiatrist, which endeavoured to bring 'lucid dreams' (as he was the first to call them) within the confines of serious research.

Van Eeden first experienced lucidity – a term which, at the time, was ordinarily used as a synonym for second sight – in 1897, when he had dreamed that he was floating through a landscape in the early spring and watching the trees as they went past. 'Then I made the reflection, during sleep, that my fancy would never be able to invent or make an image as intricate as the perspective movement of little twigs seen in floating by.' He began to experiment, and found that he could dream that his body in bed was in one position, when in fact it was in another, and that he could make the transition gradually from being asleep in his dream body to waking up in his real one – a 'most wonderful' experience. This led him on to the concept of a dream body capable of separating itself from the real one – a forerunner of the similar impression which was soon to be reported by people having 'out-of-the-body' experiences. Over a period of fourteen years, van Eeden had made notes of 352 lucid dreams; they seemed to him to be the most interesting of all the different types of dream, 'worthy of the most careful observation and study'.

The fact that his article on the subject appeared in the *Proceedings* of the SPR was an indication that it was unlikely to receive careful attention from orthodox psychologists, for whom the notion of lucidity had an occultist taint. But it was taken up by Mary Arnold-Forster in her *Studies in Dreams* (1921), because she had come to believe that 'more than we yet realise, the control of our dreams lies within our power.' Personal experience over many years had convinced her that the waking mind could direct the activities of the mind during sleep: 'I believe that we can stop at will the recurrence of "bad" dreams, or dreams that we dislike or dread, and that we can, to a considerable extent, alter the very nature of our dreams by using in our sleep the same faculty of rational selection and rejection that we use with regard to our thoughts and to our wandering fancies by day.'

The technique, she explained, resembled hypnosis. If suggestion under hypnosis was capable of exercising such remarkable powers over the mind, 'it should not be impossible to conceive of a process by which our normal consciousness is able to control to some degree the working of our

THE POWER OF DREAMS

subconscious or dream mind in sleep.' She could only offer her own experiences as a guide; but it had been the knowledge that she, and many others, had known when dreaming that it *was* 'only a dream' that gave her the idea for the first step.

This was the era when Emile Coué's claims for the power of auto-suggestion, along with his incantation 'Every day, in every way, I get better and better,' was internationally celebrated. Mary Arnold-Forster varied the formula to 'Remember this is a dream. You are to dream no longer,' repeating it to herself during the day and on going to bed. For her, it worked. For a while, it simply woke her up when she was having a 'bad' dream, but later it enabled her to remain asleep, and to continue the dream with the 'bad' part banished. In one dream which she described, where she found herself in danger from a conspiracy, such was the degree of intelligence that auto-suggestion had provided her, that her dream control, rather than banish the conspirators, allowed their machinations to continue so that their secret could be unmasked. 'The arch-conspirator, a white-faced man in a bowler hat, had tracked me down to the building where I was concealed, and which by this time was surrounded; but all fear had departed, the comfortable feeling of great heroism, only fully enjoyed by those who feel themselves to be safe, was mine.'

This method could be of particular value to young children, Mary Arnold-Forster believed. If they realised their own ability to control their dreams, the fear of nightmares and the nightmares themselves could be banished.

Mary Arnold-Forster's work made no more of an impact than van Eeden's. The followers of Freud and Jung continued to be mainly concerned with interpretations of dream material; and orthodox psychologists, still uneasy about handling subjective phenomena, preferred to deal with sleep rather than with dreams. From time to time works appeared in which the writers – Ouspensky was one – wrestled with the subject; and the accumulating evidence was surveyed in 1968 by Celia Green of the Institute of Psychophysical Research, based in Oxford. But as she was to lament in *The Decline and Fall of Science* eight years later, the only researchers who were prepared to study lucid dreams were parapsychologists. Surely, she urged, the neurophysiological condition of people exercising some rational faculty while asleep was a worthy subject for research?

As it happened, one academic psychologist thought so: Charles Tart, Professor of Psychology at the University of California, Davis. In his

Altered States of Consciousness (1969) he had described some of his own lucid dreams, and reprinted van Eeden's paper. Tart, though, was also a leading parapsychologist. His recommendation would in all probability have produced no action had his book not impressed the young Stephen LaBerge, acquainting him for the first time with the subject.

In his *Lucid Dreams* (1985) LaBerge gives full credit to his forerunners, including van Eeden and Celia Green. Ordinarily an academic psychologist would have been unlikely to have heard of either of them; but prompted by Tart's comments, LaBerge had studied them and had decided to keep a journal in which he recorded his lucid dreams. Soon he had hundreds. Even if he had had thousands, he realised, it still would have made no impression in the academic world; what was needed was a way to demonstrate lucid dreaming physiologically. The method he eventually hit upon was almost ridiculously simple, in retrospect. As there were rapid eye movements in sleep, the eye muscles must be functioning.

> I knew that lucid dreamers could look freely in any direction they wished while in a lucid dream, because I had done this myself. It occurred to me that by moving my (dream) eyes in a recognisable pattern, I might be able to send a signal to the outside world when I was having a lucid dream. I tried this out in the first lucid dream that I recorded: I moved my dream gaze up, down, up, down, up, to the count of five. As far as I knew at the time, this was the first signal deliberately transmitted from the dream world.

Again, he could have claimed to have made this signal scores of times, without impressing psychologists in the dream research area. He needed a dream laboratory; and his good fortune was that Stanford University not only had the one where some pioneer work had been done in sleep and dreaming, but was also prepared to take him on as a PhD candidate. In 1978 he had the first lucid dream ever to be recorded on a polygraph, and witnessed by one of his collaborators on the venture.

By 1980 a number of other volunteers had shown themselves able to signal lucidity, and LaBerge had presented his results in his PhD dissertation. Understandably elated, he and his colleague Lynn Nagel decided to report their findings to a wider audience. What followed was predictable. One of the referees to whom *Science* sent the report recommended acceptance; the other damned it, because he did not believe in the possibility of lucid dreaming. *Nature* did not even bother to send it to referees; the topic, LaBerge was informed, was 'not of sufficient general interest' (the relation of *Nature* to science, though it is still often referred to as the premier science journal, resembles that of the Royal Academy Summer Exhibition's to art). Still, the paper did eventually appear, in *Perceptual and Motor Skills*, in the summer of 1981.

There was a curious sequel. In 1980 the journal *Nursing Mirror* had carried an article on lucid dreams by a British parapsychologist, Keith Hearne, who turned out also to have used his research for his PhD to do work along the same lines as LaBerge. On the strength of it Hearne had actually obtained his doctorate two years before LaBerge. But Hearne had wanted to do more research before publishing his findings, and had actually begged psychologists who knew about them not to reveal them. As a result it was to be LaBerge who won the initial credit, when academic resistance to accepting lucid dreaming broke down under the weight of the accumulating evidence.

The implications of LaBerge's findings are – or should be – clear enough for psychologists. But what of the public? Obviously many of us will be interested to see if we can induce lucid dreaming, whether from curiosity or in the hope of putting an end to our bad dreams.

LaBerge emphasises that having occasional lucid dreams is like finding money in the street; cultivating them is like learning a trade to earn an income – 'if this sounds like work, it is.' But he believes that anybody who has good recall of dreams and who is sufficiently motivated can learn to dream lucidly, and that it becomes progressively easier with practice. The most useful aid to lucidity, as Mary Arnold-Forster found, appears to be auto-suggestion. In *Creative Dreaming* (1975), Patricia Garfield described how she used the formula, 'Tonight, I *will* have a dream.' Coué would not have approved. The will, he used to insist, is nothing, the imagination everything – illustrating his assertion by asking people if they could will themselves to salivate and, when they agreed they could not, he would remind them how easy it is to make the mouth water by imagining some particularly favourite dish.

Still, Coué was all for formulae which would stir the imagination; and LaBerge offers MILD – Mnemonic Induction of Lucid Dreams. The intention must be there; dreams must be carefully recalled; the induction process must be urged along with reminders such as 'Next time I'm dreaming, I want to remember to recognise I'm dreaming;' and the most fruitful time to practise is in the awakening period in the morning, when lucid dreams have most often been reported.

And the benefits? At the head of the list, potentially, is the likelihood that lucid dreaming will join meditation and other altered states of consciousness as a way to improve the mind's control over the body. 'Since we generate, while dreaming, body images in the form of our dream bodies, why shouldn't we be able to initiate dream processes during lucid dreams by consciously envisioning our dream bodies as perfectly healthy?' – another echo of Coué, who called upon the waking imagination to do precisely that, by awakening the dormant therapeutic resources of the unconscious mind.

Next, there is the banishment of 'bad' dreams. Here LaBerge followed Mary Arnold-Forster's method. When he dreamt he was threatened by muggers, lucidity came to his rescue; he attacked them, heaping them into a pile and setting fire to them. 'Out of their ashes, I arranged for flowers to grow, and I awoke feeling filled with vibrant energy.' Like her, too, he has taught the method successfully to a child.

Third, problem-solving. LaBerge cites Mendeleev's dream 'table of the elements', and Howe's dream invention of the sewing machine; in both cases the 'incubation' period when a problem was left unsolved was ended by illumination in a dream. In theory, at least, lucid dreaming could assist in reducing the incubation period by enabling the illumination to reach consciousness sooner.

And, most important of all, the possibility is opened up of using lucid dreams to secure and promote good health, by tapping the mind's subliminal resources for advice.

6

Dream Interpretation

From earliest times, far back into prehistory, dreams have played an important part in determining the courses taken by individuals, by communities, and by nations. 'Generally they were instruments of guidance', J.S. Lincoln noted in *The Dream in Primitive Culture* (1935). 'Kings, warriors, statesmen and heroes treated their visions with respect and awe accorded only to manifestations of the divine powers.' But always there was a problem. Dreams were commonly confused, and confusing. The information they provided could be clear, but often it needed to be extracted by somebody presumed to be skilled in interpretation.

In almost all tribal communities, explorers, missionaries and anthropologists have found, one of the chief functions of the shaman is to be a diviner of dreams. 'It is in dreams that the pure sacred life is entered, and direct relations with the gods, spirits and ancestral souls are re-established,' the eminent anthropologist Mircea Eliade observed in his *Shamanism* (1951); one of the pre-requisites for becoming a shaman has been to have such dreams in childhood, and if necessary to learn how to induce them later as part of the training programme. Even when the shaman's role had been hereditary, qualification had finally depended on the ability to communicate with the spirit world in dreams or trances.

In the Old Testament, the prophets took on the shaman's role – as described in what is surely the most celebrated of all legendary dream stories. 'I have dreamed a dream, and there is none that can interpret it,' Pharaoh told Joseph, who had made his reputation as a dream interpreter in Pharaoh's prison. In the dream, seven lean kine ate seven fat kine, and seven thin ears of corn ate seven good ears. Seven years of plenty, Joseph explained, would be followed by seven years of famine. So it turned out; and the prediction meant that sufficient stocks were laid aside in the good years to enable Egypt to survive the bad ones, and even to benefit by selling its surplus to other countries which had not taken the same precautions.

By that time, however, inspired interpretation of this kind, believed to have a divine source, was being corrupted by the need to cater for the whims of rulers. When King Nebuchadnezzar related his dream – a strong tree had grown up to heaven, but an angel had appeared and ordered it to be cut down – his wise men prudently told him they could not interpret it. The prophet Daniel had to tell him nervously that *he*, the king, was the tree. As diviners who transmitted unwelcome information often suffered for it, they began to adapt their interpretations to suit the needs or the wishes of their employer – even if this meant claiming that dreams 'go by opposites'; if he dreamed that he fell, it would be relayed back to him as a sign that he would rise to new heights. Inevitably divination became suspect. 'As to divination in sleep,' Aristotle commented, 'we cannot lightly either dismiss it with contempt or give it confidence.'

It was the interpretations, though, which generated mistrust, rather than the actual information provided in dreams – as in the case of another of the most celebrated dreams of history; Calpurnia's, the night before Julius Caesar was assassinated. Caesar described the dream to Decius (in Shakespeare's version):

> She dreamed tonight she saw my statue,
> Which, like a fountain with a hundred spouts
> Did run pure blood

and said she had begged him to stay at home. Decius – one of the conspirators – insisted she had misinterpreted it: the dream

> Signified, that from you, great Rome shall suck
> Reviving blood.

Another development, accompanying the decay of inspirational divination, was interpretation by rote – oneiromancy. A papyrus in the Cairo museum indicates that it had already begun to take a hold in the Egypt of the Pharaohs, though on an infantile level: if a woman kissed her husband in a dream, it meant trouble; if she gave birth in a dream to a crocodile, she would have many children. But the *Oneirocritica*, written by Artemidorus of Daldus in the second century AD, for all its frequent absurdities was on a different level. Sometimes it reads like a preview of Freud's *Interpretation of Dreams*.

Artemidorus set out to show how the dramatisations and the symbols in dreams could be translated into what was happening, or about to happen, to the dreamers. Sometimes the interpretation was relatively straightforward.

To see oneself hanged or strangled in a dream, even by oneself, is a prediction of imminent anguish or abandoning one's home.

But Artemidorus was a believer in 'opposites'.

Death and marriage are closely related in dreams. That is why he who dreams of being dead will have a good chance of getting married, and that is why the invalid who sees himself celebrating his own wedding receives the warning of his imminent death.

The invalid who dreams of being dead, or put in the earth and buried (which has the same meaning) will get better, for the dead are no longer ill.

The sexual content of dreams clearly fascinated Artemidorus.

If a man dreams that he is masturbating in privacy, he will have either a male or a female slave, because the hands enclosing his penis represent attendants.

Possessing a brother, whether older or younger, is suspicious. The dreamer will be on top of the brother, and can disdain him.

As Freud was to acknowledge, some of Artemidorus's ideas were perceptive. He had studied, and tried to make use of, the available evidence; he did not simply repeat old wives' tales; and he was careful to insist that dream interpretation could not be satisfactory if it went simply by the book – it required a thorough knowledge of the dreamers and their circumstances as well. Yet in retrospect, *Oneirocritica* is less impressive than the commentary on dream divination written by Synesius of Cyrene early in the fourth century AD. A neo-Platonist who had become a convert to Christianity, Synesius had succeeded in rallying his countrymen to throw out invaders from Libya; and eventually on their insistence he became their bishop. His treatise on dreams suggests that their confidence in him was well founded.

It should come as no surprise that dream messages were often obscure, Synesius argued. In so far as their source was divine, they were not intended to provide guidance to anybody and everybody. As with information obtained from oracles, interpretation might be necessary. But when understood, dreams might disclose the whereabouts of missing treasure or suggest a cure for illness. They might even make somebody quite uncultured into a poet – 'that has happened in our time, and does not seem to me very astounding.' Much of Synesius's time had been spent in writing, and in hunting; and in both, dreaming had been invaluable. 'It has frequently helped me to write books,' he recalled. 'Here it cuts something; there it brings in new matter instead.' When his prose had begun to get too flowery, a dream would show him how 'to smooth down the excrescences'; 'Thus it has restored my diction to a state of sobriety, and has castigated my inflated style.'

In his favourite pastime of hunting, too, dreams had often provided him with guidance. Most important of all, in the years he had been compelled to spend as ambassador for his country in Constantinople, his dreams had given him advance warning of plots against him, helped him in his work, and had eventually won him the confidence of the Emperor. 'We, therefore, have set ourselves to speak of divination through dreams, that men should not despise it, but rather cultivate it, seeing that it fulfils a service to life.'

Synesius warned against using devices for divination – a course hateful to the gods. Dreams were the best source; 'if you are worthy, the god far away is present with you.' And fortunately, dreams were personal and private possessions.

Each one of us is perforce his own instrument, so much so that it is not possible to desert our own oracle even if we so desired. Nay, even if we remain at home, she dwells within us; if we go abroad she accompanies us; she is with us on the field of battle; she is at our side in the life of the city; she labours with us in the fields and barters with us in the market place. The laws of a malicious government do not forbid her, nor would they have the power to do so, even if they wished it, for they have no proof against those who invoke her. For how, then? Should we be violating the law by sleeping? A tyrant could never enjoin us not to gaze into dreams, at least not unless he actually banished sleep from his kingdom.

By that time, however, the Church was turning its face against divination. Although it could not stop people interpreting their own dreams, it could punish as a heretic anybody who publicly practised divination in any form. And after the Renaissance, it was Artemidorus who was rediscovered, thanks to his having been translated into Arabic. When Rabelais' Panurge was wondering whether or not he should marry, and dreamed that a pretty young woman had 'flattered me, tickled me, stroked me, groped me', he told Pantagruel that she had jokingly put horns on his head. 'If I have any skill in dream interpretation,' Pantagruel told him, 'your wife will not really, to outward appearances, stick horns on your forehead'; but far from being faithful she would violate her pledge, break her marriage vows, prostitute herself, 'and so make you a cuckold' – a point, Pantagruel explained, which had been 'clearly and manifestly explained and expounded by Artemidorus, just as I have related it.' In England, where the *Oneirocritica* was published in translation in 1518, it was to go through twenty new editions over the next two hundred years.

Inspired divination did not recover its lost status. Whether dreams had any meaning at all became a matter for debate. In the eyes of the Catholic Church they could carry divine messages; but as they were also a channel for the devil, they were not to be trusted. Luther was in no doubt that the lust they conveyed was often diabolically inspired – 'in the night time, and in the midst of man's sleep, may this sin arise and run out in his dreams'; but he felt that they needed studying, in order to get to know Satan's subtle designs, as 'ignorance of the devil's artifice is not fit for Christians.' Soon, however, Lutherans were paying less heed to the devil. By the 17th century, Keith Thomas noted in his *Religion and the Decline of Magic* (1971), 'severe Protestants paid little attention to dreams.' When King James I refused to allow a warning dream, which his wife related, to stop him from going to Scotland his subjects were impressed; and Thomas Hobbes asserted bluntly in his *Leviathan* that 'there can happen in sleep no imagination, and therefore no dream, but what proceeds from the agitation of the inward parts of man's body' – a point of view that was often to be echoed.

Yet there were always individuals who might have been expected to share the prevailing scepticism, but who were impressed by the weight of the evidence for the value of dream interpretation. It was too strong, Joseph Addison argued in the *Spectator* in 1712, to be rejected by anybody who was prepared to accept historical evidence at all: 'whether such dark presages, such visions of the night, appear from any latent power of the soul during this her state of abstraction, or from any communication with the supreme being, or from any operation of subordinate spirits, has been a great dispute among the learned; the matter of *fact* I think is incontestable, and has been looked on as such by the greatest writers, who have never been suspected either of superstition or enthusiasm.'

Although William Hazlitt did not care to pronounce upon the precognitive element in dreams – 'the power of prophesying or foreseeing things in our sleep, as from a higher or more abstracted sphere of thought, need not here be argued upon' – he believed there was 'a sort of profundity in sleep', and that it could be usefully consulted as an oracle. Dreams sometimes gave revelations of what was being kept out of our thoughts: 'we may be aware of a danger that yet we do not choose, while we have the full command of our faculties, to acknowledge to ourselves; the impending event will then appear to us as a dream, and we shall most likely find it verified afterwards.' We could make use of this, he suggested, to detect loves or hates in their incipient stage, before we would ordinarily become aware of them; 'in sleep we reveal the secret to ourselves.'

The possibility of extracting useful information from dreams attracted a number of commentators later in the 19th century – Abercrombie, Brodie, Symonds, and in particular Henry Maudsley. Maudsley credited dreams with what he described as a 'plastic' power; an 'unconscious mental function' which did not operate through simple association of ideas. 'We are dealing with something more than that,' he insisted; 'with an actual constructive agency, whereby ideas are not merely brought together only, but new products are formed out of them.' The basis might be some event of the previous day; but the way in which dreams develop, by 'an entirely involuntary operation', showed that 'mind is capable of those intelligent functions which are the essence of its being, independently of will and consciousness; or at any rate that the potentiality of them lies not in the consciousness, nor in will, but in the plastic quality of the brain.'

Maudsley, in other words, had come to accept the existence not merely of an unconscious mind – a concept still rejected by orthodoxy at the time – but also of a subliminal self, or at least of the mind's power to reason as if independently of the conscious self. And for him, it was dreaming that provided the proof.

> The plastic power of the supreme cerebral centres on which I insist as something deeper than conscious mental function, evinces its spontaneous and independent nature in a striking way by those singularly coherent dreams which everybody has at one time or another, and in which he sometimes puts forth as much intellectual power as he ever displays when awake. Many stories have been told, on good authority, of persons who have in their sleep composed poems, solved hard problems in mathematics, discovered the key of a perplexing difficulty, or done like wonderful things; and while bearing in mind that dream achievements which seem to us very clever at the time prove oftentimes to be nonsense when we awake, it may be granted that one who is fitted by natural abilities and training to do good intellectual work when awake may occasionally chance to do it in sleep, getting the good of a good understanding even in his dreams. These instances illustrate the spontaneous nature of the process of creative activity, with which consciousness and will have no more to do as active agents than with the imaginative creations of the inspired poet; for it is only when the products are formed that they rise into clear consciousness, and only when they are known that they can be willed.

Had this view been acceptable, it would have transformed attitudes to dream interpretation, by showing that there was something worth examining dreams *for*. But as Frederick Greenwood lamented in his 1893 survey, the general opinion by then had become that 'dreams were valueless'. Greenwood himself believed that on the contrary, interpretation could be extremely valuable – but only so long as it was not accomplished by rote; 'it is no less absurd to compare the dreaming of one man with that of another, than to assume in all mankind an equal capacity for composing music.'

Freud and Jung

Ironically, when a few years later dream interpretation began to recover its hold over the public it was through the Artemidorean channel, rather than along the route proposed by Synesius and revived by Maudsley and Greenwood. It was stimulated by Freud's theories, presented in 1899.

'By general consensus *The Interpretation of Dreams* was Freud's major work,' his disciple and biographer Ernest Jones noted, 'the one by which his name will probably be longest remembered.' Although the six hundred copies which were printed took eight years to sell, in the long run it was to do more than any other single work to establish the reality of the unconscious mind.

So far as the reading public was concerned, it eventually established that dreams have a hidden meaning, usually erotic, but capable of being extracted with the help of a knowledge of certain stock symbols; and that dreams also fulfil a wish – not in the usual sense but, as Freud himself put it, 'one dreams so as not to have to wake, because one wants to sleep.'

The wishes that dreams revealed were often those of which the conscious self was unaware, presented in a form which might become clear under analysis, but which was ingeniously censored so as neither to alarm the dreamers sufficiently to wake them up nor, when they awoke, to confront them with unpleasant truths of a kind they would not be able to face – murderous feelings, say, about parents. The wishes consequently appeared in a variety of disguises: hints, allusions, symbols, even puns. And it was the examples Freud provided of these disguises that were to attract the attention and controversy which was to make his name a household word.

Rooms, he claimed, represent women. The uterus might be represented by a cupboard, or a carriage. 'Sharp weapons, long and stiff objects, such as tree-trunks and sticks, stand for the male genital' – as did airships. Rooms, cupboards and airships were the manifest content; but from the point of view of analysis it was the latent content which mattered. Freud was careful to insist that the symbols, though they might be common to people in certain linguistic or cultural groups, should not be employed in analysis without reference to the dreamer, and to the dream as a whole. He further insisted that he made no claim to have solved all the problems relating to dreams. But the confident manner in which he presented his theories, in particular that dreams were the disguised fulfilment of repressed desires, tended to obscure such qualifications, and to leave the impression that the straightforward content of a dream was of little or no importance.

It was this, rather than the main theories in the book, which riled later writers about dreams – William Archer, for one. It was possible, he complained in his book *On Dreams* (1935), to argue 'from almost any "manifest content" to almost any "latent content" that may suit your purpose'. As an illustration, Archer took the dream in which a doctor had handed in an honest statement of his small income; the next night he dreamt that his statement had aroused suspicion, and he would be prosecuted. Freud had explained this with the help of his theory of dream censorship, by saying the dream was a poorly concealed fulfilment of the dreamer's wishes to be known as enjoying a large income. 'It seems to me that he does the Censor an injustice,' Archer remarked. 'The wish is so well disguised that it needs the insight of monomania to discover it.' To extend the wish-fulfilment theory to every case, he thought, was 'mere gratuitous dogmatism'. And what made it worse, Archer complained, was that if he presented a dream (in his book he related several) which he felt certain was *not* wish-fulfilment, Freud could of course claim that Archer was too inexpert in psycho-analytic methods to recognise the repressed wish. 'Thus psycho-analysis provides itself with a loop-hole of escape from every possible difficulty,' Archer protested. 'Its dialectic is conducted on the somewhat too facile principle of "Heads I win, tails you lose."'

Archer's line of criticism has often been echoed since, notably by Hans Eysenck and Christopher Evans. In *Landscapes of the Night* (1983), Evans drew attention to another irritating example of Freud's ability to have it both ways. In one of the dreams Freud had cited, a woman had had a frustrating time shopping, as the butcher did not have what she wanted, and the market was closed. This was a case of opposites, Freud had explained. 'The meat shop is open' brought to mind the Viennese 'Du hast deine Fleischbank offen' – 'your flies are undone'; to Evans, a 'partly laughable, partly pitiable' diagnosis.

Some of Freud's contributions to the interpretation of dreams, however, remain important; particularly those which illustrate the remarkable ingenuity of the dreaming mind, even to the point of playing upon words. In his memoirs Sir Edward Marsh, a leading civil servant in the years between the wars, described how by coincidence he found himself in 1937 sitting next to Harold Nicolson at a dinner, the night after he had a dream in which Nicolson was concerned – worth telling, Marsh thought, as it involved 'a really curious mental phenomenon'.

I dreamt I was looking at Harold's new book which I knew was called

Small Talk – but to my surprise the title on the book was *The Oarist*. 'What an awful word,' I thought, 'and I had no idea the book was about Rowing.' Then I woke up, and remembered the Homeric word οαριϛτυϛ which means 'familiar conversation' – in fact, '*small talk*'.

Dreams played a vital part in Jung's career, as his *Memories, Dreams, Reflections* makes clear. 'At every crisis point in his eventful life,' Michael Fordham, co-editor with Jung of Jung's *Collected Works*, has recalled, 'a dream or a vision provided essential sources for furthering a solution.' And Laurens Van der Post, one of Jung's closest friends, has described in his biography how Jung came to regard dreams as 'a master compass of his spirit, almost an automatic pilot keeping his life on course'.

Sometimes the manifest content sufficed to provide the guidance; often the dreams needed interpretation, but it could be of a relatively simple kind – as one which came to Jung's help when he was engaged on his first major work, *Psychology of the Unconscious* (1911). He was well aware that Freud, who had regarded Jung as his heir-apparent, would not approve. For a couple of months he was unable to continue writing it, and might not have been able to resume, Van der Post thought, had the dream not come to his help.

As always in the past when he had reached an apparently insoluble crisis in his life, the appropriate dreams came to his aid. He was fond of saying, 'He who looks outwardly, dreams. But he who looks within, awakes.' Because his attention was directed outwardly towards Freud, he dreamt; and through the dreaming was compelled to look within and to awake to his own self, and to a greatly extended view of his role and life. All that is important for understanding the future course of events is that the image which represented Freud in this dream was a peevish Austrian Customs official, old-fashioned and out of date, trying to control as it were the exports and imports of the spirit. There could be no doubt that the image stood for Freud and his spent professional role in Jung's life. This image possessed a certain poetic justice, however ironic, seeing how much importance Freud attached to a mechanism of censorship in dream material, and how one of the main differences between him and Jung was that the dream, for Jung, was no façade, hiding the truth from the dreamer, but an urgent summons of unrealised being and meaning for recognition.

To a friend who said he had been too busy with his writing to pay attention to his dreams, Jung replied, in effect, 'You have got it the wrong way round. Your writing can wait but your dreams cannot, because they come unsolicited from within and point urgently to the way you must go.'

Jung diverged from Freud in his attitude to dreams in a number of directions, but chiefly because he felt Freud's theory was too constricting. Certainly there were dreams which embodied repressed wishes, he wrote in *Modern Man In Search of a Soul* (1933); 'but what is there which the dream cannot, on occasion, embody!' Dreams, he believed, could give expression to 'ineluctable truths, to philosophical pronouncements, illusions, wild fantasies, memories, plans, anticipations, irrational experiences, even telepathic visions, and heaven knows what besides'. This recognition of their diversity made him reluctant to propound any general theory; but according to Mary Ann Mattoon in her *Understanding Dreams* (1984) – the first attempt, she claims, to systematize Jung's theory of dream interpretation – he employed four tests to estimate an interpretation's validity:

1. Does the interpretation 'click' with the dreamer?
2. Does the interpretation 'act' for the dreamer?
3. Is the interpretation confirmed (or not disconfirmed) by subsequent dreams?
4. Do the events anticipated by the interpretation occur in the dreamer's waking life?

Interpretations, in other words, may be correct, but are of no help to patients unless they grasp the significance of their dreams, and take the appropriate action. If they do, subsequent happenings can show whether the interpretation was right for them.

This approach, less dogmatic than Freud's, has established itself among Jungian analysts, but at the cost of a certain loss of confidence in using dreams. They are no longer to be considered to be of such importance, Michael Fordham explains, because unconscious processes are now more familiar. It is not such a shock any more for patients to be faced with the stark contrast between their conscious and their unconscious desires. They can be eased through this formerly traumatic stage in analysis without so much time being spent on dissecting their dreams.

There are many indications, however, that this is not the only reason for the way in which dreams, so fundamental an influence in Jung's life and work, have been downgraded by his followers. Many of them are uneasy about the extra-sensory component – 'dreaming the future', in particular.

Jung himself accepted the existence of precognition and was prepared to exploit it in therapy. On one occasion he dreamt that a new patient arrived; although puzzled by her symptoms, he decided she must have a very unusual father-complex. The next day, when a young Jewish girl arrived for an appointment, he thought 'Good Lord, this is the little girl of my dream!' Although he could find no trace of a father-complex, recollection of the dream prompted him to inquire about her grandfather, a rabbi. It turned out that he had become an apostate, and her neurosis was related to the terror this had aroused in her.

Some of Jung's disciples simply brush this aspect of his work aside. Jung's 'scepticism about prophetic dreams suggests that he entertained the possibility of such unlikely events only because he had found instances of them,' Mattoon observes in the only reference she makes to the subject. 'Moreover, he insisted that each precognitive dream can be verified as such "only when the precognized event has actually happened" usually long after the dream's occurrence; hence, such dreams are of little use in foretelling the future. It is apparent, therefore, that Jung approached dreams with empiricism, rather than with the mysticism of which he is accused.'

There could hardly be a more misleading description of Jung's attitude – or a more revealing indication of why so many of his disciples shy away from his preoccupation with the occult, as they regard it. *Memories, Dreams, Reflections* shows that from adolescence Jung was fascinated by psychic phenomena; his doctoral thesis arose out of his investigation of a spiritualist medium; and periodically he would find himself the focus of forces which, he knew, could not be accounted for in conventional scientific terms. As he stated in a paper read at a meeting of the Society for Psychical Research in 1919, he was firmly convinced of the reality of the 'facts', as he described them. But science, he thought, must confine itself 'to the limits of cognition', because those were its limitations at the time. 'We must admit that our intellectual conceptions are deficient so far as a complete comprehension of the world is concerned,' he concluded. 'But when we make use of intellect, as is the case of science, we have to adapt ourselves to the demands of intellectual criticism, and we must limit ourselves to the scientific hypothesis so long as there is no reliable evidence against its validity.'

Long before he died in 1961, Jung had moved away from this cautious position. He remained an empiricist in the sense that he judged the evidence about cases of apparent precognition on their merits; and he would have agreed that they can only be verified if and when the event actually happened. But his 'scepticism' about prophetic dreams was no more than a very reasonable desire that the evidence should be trustworthy; and he was well versed enough in the subject to know that far from the precognized events usually happening 'long after the dream's occurrence', the collections of precognitive dreams have shown that the great majority of events pretold in dreams occur within hours or days. Impressive long-term prophecies form only a tiny proportion.

This aversion to ESP has meant that little account has been taken by analysts of its possible significance. But a few – mostly Freudian – have recognised it. In this context it is not so much precognition which is important – glimpses of the future can occur which have no bearing on the problems which have led the patient into analysis, even if they turn out to be correct – but the possibility of telepathic communication between analyst and patient.

Freud himself provided only one example. The positivist assumptions of his early years made him initially unwilling to accept anything in the occult category. Later he became ambivalent on the subject of ESP, as he admitted in a paper written in 1921 (though, at the request of some of his followers, not published at the time). There was another reason for his caution, as he disclosed in a paper he actually read that year; he had never himself had any experience of ESP in a dream. It was only with the greatest reluctance, he admitted, that he concerned himself with these occult questions. Still, he felt bound to record the occasion when a patient, arriving for his analytic hour, brought up matters 'which were related in a striking manner to an experience of my own immediately before his hour'.

Some of the ways in which extra-sensory communications can intervene in analysis were surveyed by G. Devereux in his *Psychoanalysis and the Occult* (1953); and cases have been reported since by Eisenbud, Ehrenwald and others. On one occasion Eisenbud had to deal with a patient who was taking up a lot of his time; and he decided he would have to telephone his daughter, who had been coming to him on a visit, to put it off for a while. Another of his patients, the next day, told him she had dreamed of coming to his office and finding a young child there whom she took to be his daughter. 'You indicated that you were busy,' she told Eisenbud. It was as if he was saying to his daughter, 'Go home, I have no time for you.'

Ehrenwald has recalled that in 1972 a patient of his reported that she had dreamed she was back in school, reading a poem, 'but I had lost the page – or I could not remember it. Also the poem was not finished; I tried to figure out the last verse.' On the night of the dream, Ehrenwald had been in New York, attending a dinner at which those present had to make small contributions, such as a verse. He had decided to recite a humorous German poem, but found that he had lost the draft of the translation he had made of the verses; he had to try to reconstruct them. He had managed to do so – but he had not been able to get the last verse right.

Most analysts, though, whatever their persuasion – Freudian, Jungian, pragmatic – still shy away from accepting ESP. It appears to them in the role of an unwelcome intrusion – as Robert Van de Castle, a leading authority on the psychical aspect of dreams, has noted in a paper, 'Sleep and Dreams' (1977). Patients may pick up information which the analyst would prefer to keep to himself or, as in Eisenbud's case, pick up intimations of a problem bothering the analyst. Even those who accept ESP may be reluctant to publish examples – quite apart from not wanting to irritate those of their colleagues who reject ESP; 'if the dream has been produced because the patient has zeroed in on some disowned problem of his, the therapist must be willing to make a public confession of that problem and to share all the intimate, embarrassing details that would be entailed by such a disclosure.'

Ullman and Zimmerman give an example in *Dream Telepathy* (1979). A patient related a dream to her analyst: she had been giving a dinner party to which a mean, ruthless man, an associate of her father's, had been invited, and she found she had forgotten to lay the table. 'I put my silver knives, forks, etc. on the tray. The silver was all a mess. Was there enough? The important man looked down scornfully at my table.' As she had several sets of silver cutlery, the patient did not know why she was worried in the dream. The embarrassed analyst *did* know. The night before, she herself had invited friends around, and had been very worried in case there was not going to be enough silverware.

Analysts, and psychologists in general, find it difficult to accept that ESP is one of the sources of information in dreams, for a reason which Ehrenwald has noted. 'Psi-induction', as he calls it, of this kind, 'conceivably blended with simple suggestion, may well be taken as a serious threat to the validity of any one of the existing rival systems of psychotherapy. More than that; it may raise doubts as to the very possibility of arriving at verifiable scientific statements from data derived from situations of the type of the clinical interview of the analyst/ analysand relationship.' Scientists may be tempted to relish psychotherapy's plight. But they should remember their own problems, Ehrenwald reminded them, arising out of the similar doubts which quantum physics have thrown up about the nature of reality.

Halse Rivers

Potentially the most valuable contribution since Freud's to the development of dream interpretation is the work of a man whose reputation has not survived, except perhaps among anthropologists: W.H.R. Rivers' *Conflict and Dream*, published posthumously in 1923. Halse Rivers' notable career in anthropology in the islands of the south Pacific had been interrupted by the outbreak of war in 1914; and in the course of it, working as a medical psychologist in the Royal Army Medical Corps, he became the leading authority on shell-shock and other consequences of trench warfare. In this capacity he acknowledged his debt to Freud. At the time he had been a student, he recalled, 'the psychology of dreams was not deemed worthy of inclusion in a course of academic psychology.' The revolution that had subsequently taken place, he thought, was entirely due to Freud; and among the many aspects of Freud's influence, 'none is more prominent than that concerned with dreams and their interpretation'.

Nevertheless Rivers was critical of Freud's dream-interpretation theories. His wartime duties began to bring him into daily contact with officers and men suffering from psychoneuroses (shell-shock was the euphemism which still had to be employed to ensure that they were sent to a hospital rather than jailed or shot for cowardice); and he decided to study the *Interpretation of Dreams* more carefully. It 'left a most unsatisfactory impression on my mind. The interpretation seemed to me forced and arbitrary, and the general method of so unscientific a kind that it might be used to prove anything.'

In particular, Rivers ridiculed Freud's idea that some elements in dreams can be interpreted by their opposites – 'such a method would have reduced any other science to an absurdity'; and he challenged Freud's view that the latent content appears in disguises so that the repressed desires which it reveals should not shock us when we awake, by revealing to us the lecherous or murderous designs which we harbour in our unconscious minds.

The disguises, Rivers argued, arise out of the fact that dreaming is a primitive, even infantile, form of mental activity. Our dreams represent a regression to childhood ways of feeling. Children, for example, who want to get rid of somebody they dislike may say they want to kill them – unaware of what the actual deed would entail. When we commit murder in our dreams, Rivers argued, we are behaving like children. Not that we necessarily want to get the *person* out of the way; it may be the conflict which he personifies. Rivers accepted that the dream work has to account for dramatisations and symbolism, mixed up with simple memories of recent events, all jumbled together. What dreams do, he argued, is confront us with the difficulties we are up against in our waking lives, but in dream terms. And often, in so doing, they provide us with the clues – if we have the knowledge and understanding to pick them up – which will enable us to solve our problems and resolve our conflicts.

Rivers cited the example of nightmares. At Craiglockhart mental hospital, where he was working in 1917, shell-shocked soldiers would arrive who re-lived, night after night, the horrific experiences which had led to their being taken out of the line and sent to hospital. No wishful thinking there, obviously! But as they recovered, he found, their nightmares took on a less intense, less alarming form; and the symptoms – sweating, shivering, screaming – died away. Children are nightmare-prone, this led Rivers to suggest, because the process of growing up presents them with emotional problems of a kind they are intellectually unprepared to cope with. The recurrent nightmare is an indication that a problem remains unsolved. The gradual lessening of its terrors indicates that a solution is being found.

Dreams, Rivers decided, represent an evolutionary expedient. It had long puzzled ethnologists that sleep, which, on the face of it, leaves animals in danger from predators, should be common to so many species. But suppose it is not simply a form of physical relaxation? 'The reaction of the animal to danger,' Rivers pointed out, 'would be greatly assisted if there were present in sleep some kind of mechanism by which the animal began to adapt its behaviour to danger while still asleep.'

But why, if dreaming was useful in evolutionary terms, had its benefit been lost? Precisely because dreams had remained so primitive a way of putting information across, Rivers surmised. As they lack a coherent structure, and on waking are so childish or bizarre, dreams seem irrelevant to our lives, and we quickly forget them. He felt sure that we could learn to appreciate them, and to make use of the information they contain – as he had found he could do himself. His dreams, like most people's, were a mishmash of material from past and recent memory, mixed up with symbols and dramatised, as a child dramatises, but tucked into them was useful information.

Rivers cited an example. In a dream he was playing billiards with an eminent psychiatrist. After Rivers played a stroke, the two white balls were left touching a cup and saucer on the table. 'You should have made a two and a three of it,' the psychiatrist remarked; and the dream ended.

The manifest content was easy to account for by the previous day's happenings. At dinner that evening Rivers had been examining some unusual coffee cups; and earlier in the day he had sent the psychiatrist, with whom he had often played billiards in the past, a copy of an article. But why 'a two and a three'? Gradually it dawned on Rivers that this was the solution to a problem which had been worrying him. Deeply humane, he cared constantly for the welfare of patients who came to Craiglockhart Hospital. (One of them, Siegfried Sassoon, was to recall with profound gratitude his debt to Rivers, 'that great and good man', in one of the volumes of his autobiography, *Sherston's Progress*.) A young officer, Rivers knew, was making himself an intolerable nuisance, in a room with two others, one of whom was clearly suffering from the newcomer's inability to settle down. But there had been no free beds in any of the other three-bed rooms. Rivers recalled that an event the previous day could leave a *two-*bedded room free, 'and I now saw this would enable me to move both the companions of the noisy patient, instead of only one, and put them together in the newly available room.' In the subsequent reshuffle, the disturbing patient could be accommodated with patients better able to deal with him.

That dreams could reveal a 'soaring of life to a higher plane' was to Freud absurd; it could be believed 'only by mystics and pietists'. Although Rivers was far from being a mystic or a pietist, he was convinced that dreams could give such a lift, and that they could solve, or help to solve, 'such practical problems as are presented by the course of daily life and, though in fantastic form, may express conclusions better than those reached by the waking consciousness.' If this hypothesis is correct, 'we have here a definite contribution to the evidence upon which it may some day be possible to formulate a scheme of the constructive function of the dream.'

Unluckily Rivers, still in his fifties, had died before *Conflict and Dream*, a collection of his lectures, could be revised. The Freudian analysts, fighting their corner, were not likely to take kindly to anybody so critical of their master's ideas; and the rival behaviourists have paid little attention to dreams, except to scoff at the Freudians' use of them.

The massive manifesto *Learning Theory and Behaviour Therapy*, published in 1960 at a time when behaviourism was dominant in academic psychology, mentioned dreams only once. In the introductory chapter Hans Eysenck, Professor of Psychology at London University and behaviourism's champion in Europe, provided a table contrasting its theory and practice with psychotherapy. In psychotherapy, he explained, interpretation of dreams was an important element; in behavioural theory 'interpretation, even if not completely subjective and erroneous, is irrelevant.'

A few attempts have been made since to provide a stable, coherent basis for interpretation, notably by Calvin S. Hall, in *The Meaning of Dreams* (1966). From his research Hall came up with some useful ideas; in particular that it is often desirable to obtain a series of dreams for the purpose of interpretation, as single dreams are unlikely to provide all the necessary clues. Like Rivers and Maudsley, he became convinced that dreams not only presented a faithful record of our inner problems and conflicts, but also reflect our efforts to resolve them. But Hall did not pursue this positive aspect of dreams, beyond indicating the help they can give the quest for self-knowledge; and he rejected the possibility of extra-sensory communication or precognition.

So far as the public is concerned, Freud's way of interpreting dreams – or the filleted popular version – is still easily the best known. More surprisingly, *The Interpretation of Dreams* is still regarded as a major scientific contribution. That his disciples should have held this view is not surprising: J.S. Lincoln expressed their feelings when he claimed in *The Dream in Primitive Cultures* (1935) that the facts about dreams 'as uncovered by Freud by the application of a scientific method, are as free from projected preconceptions as those uncovered through the method of any science.'

Even so devoted a Jungian as Mary Ann Mattoon agrees that Freud was 'the first person to undertake the development of a scientific method for dream interpretation.'

To call Freud's work on dreams 'scientific' is an abuse of this much abused term. What Freud did was to conjure up a hypothesis, based on his experience with a small and far from representative sample of people. It was interesting, up to a point illuminating, and undeniably influential; but in several respects it was unreliable, particularly in its contempt for the manifest content of dreams and its rejection of their potential value in tapping the gold reserve in the subliminal mind – allowed for in Myers' contemporaneous theory. Myers, and before him Edmund Gurney, were in fact more scientific in their approach to dreams: collecting case histories, checking them carefully, and letting the evidence for their potential speak for itself, without trying to force it into a mould.

Healing dreams

Two other types of interpretation remain to be considered: one being the use of dreams to promote health.

In his research into dream divination in early civilisations and classical antiquity, for his *Understanding of Dreams*, Raymond de Becker found that 'endoscopy', as he called it, was universally employed. Anybody who feared the onset of an illness, or who found that conventional treatment did not work, could try 'incubation' to induce the appropriate dreams. Incubation had originally been used as a way of obtaining guidance of all kinds from the gods by going to sleep in some secluded place, and hoping one or more of them would appear in a dream. In time, certain places built up a reputation as particularly in the gods' favour; temples would be built there, and sleeping quarters provided. The gods did not necessarily confine themselves to giving therapeutic recommendations; but some of the temples were to become identified with healing, under the aegis of Aesculapius. And although the precise nature of the methods used in them to induce dreams remains obscure – a form of hypnotism, apparently, was employed – it is clear that endoscopy was highly regarded even by the hard-headed physicians who wrote the Hippocratic treatises: 'accurate knowledge of the signs which occur in dreams,' one of them claimed, 'will be found very valuable for all purposes.'

When the patient was awake, the writer explained, his attention was focused on the information reaching him through his five senses; 'but when the body is at rest, the psyche is stirred, and rouses, to become its own master.' Much of the material in dreams arose out of daytime happenings and thoughts, and this was healthy, so long as it did not reveal conflict. But if it did, some disorder was indicated; and the more serious the conflict, the more serious the disorder was likely to be. Hence the need for interpretation of the dreams by a physician, or one of the temple priests versed in such lore.

Under Christianity, the mind's eye picture of Aesculapius metamorphosed into Jesus. The temples fell into disuse, replaced by the shrines of saints and martyrs, to which people came hoping less for dreams than for miracles. Incubation faded out of medical practice, and was not brought back after the Renaissance. From time to time, however, there were indications that something of therapeutic value had been lost by this neglect. The mesmerists in the early 19th century reported that some 'somnambules' – subjects put into the mesmeric trance state, resembling sleep-walkers – showed remarkable skill in diagnosis. When the French Academy of Medicine set up a commission to investigate mesmerism in the 1820s, its members reported that one woman they had tested had shown that in her trances she was a better diagnostician than doctors, though she had no medical training. When a patient who, she insisted, was being given the wrong treatment had died, a post mortem had revealed that her diagnosis had been correct.

'Dreams are sometimes found to go before a severe bodily illness,' Henry Maudsley noted in his *Pathology of Mind* (1879), 'which they seem to foretell.' One of his patients, the victim from time to time of profound melancholia, always knew from her dreams when the attacks were about to come on, and when they were to terminate: 'so certain were these dream presages that they had never failed to occur and had never deceived her.' He was the more impressed because the dreams did not immediately precede either the attacks or the recovery. It seemed that her brain 'forefelt and foretold the impending calamity in its dreams before it had waking consciousness of it, just as it forefelt and foretold recovery.'

In the closing years of the 19th century it appeared possible that doctors, at least, might begin to take dreams seriously again as prognostic aids. Horace Hutchinson noted that a quasi-scientific explanation was being given – the same as the one in the Hippocratic treatise: that the psyche, in sleep, has access to information of a kind which the waking mind, owing to the demands put upon it by the information pouring in through the senses, is unlikely to enjoy. But in spite of the efforts of a few leading physicians, notably Maudsley, the mechanist concept of medicine prevailed, and with it a disposition to dismiss the therapeutic role of dreams as a superstition.

Interest in the therapeutic possibilities of dreams, apart from their role in psycho-analysis, was to be kept alive largely thanks to the career of the remarkable psychic, Edgar Cayce. As a child growing up in Kentucky Cayce had the reputation of being something of a 'seer', a faculty which he lost in adolescence. When in his early twenties he contracted what was thought to be an hysteric form of illness, suggestion under hypnosis was tried to see if it would remove the symptoms, without success. Still, it gave Cayce an idea. Suppose the suggestion he was to be given took the form of telling him, in his trance, to work out what treatment was required – auto-suggestion, in other words, to replace external suggestion? Not merely did this work for Cayce; he found that in his hypnosis-induced, and eventually self-induced, sleep, he could 'see' what was the matter with other people, and prescribe for their disorders.

Suspicious though local doctors were, when they investigated they had to concede that his gift was genuine. The method he used resembled the incubation procedures of old, except that his 'readings', as he called them, needed no interpretation except his own, when they were obscure. He would lie down and enter into a sleep-like trance state in which the required information would come to him – he could not explain how – enabling him to give a diagnosis even when he had no idea who the patients were, or where they lived, which might be at a distance. From 1902 to 1945, no fewer that 14,000 records of his readings were filed, with the relevant information about the cases available for inspection, and revealing an unparalleled success rate. Sceptics who hoped to expose him as a fraud – Hugo Muensterberg, Professor of Psychology at Harvard, among them – went away baffled.

In spite of the well-attested evidence, when Cayce died in 1945 his work had done little to remove the medical profession's prejudice against taking dreams seriously. However, the prospect that endoscopy's potential usefulness will again be recognised and exploited has improved, thanks to the research conducted in dream laboratories since the connection of rapid eye movements (REMs) with dreaming has been grasped. In 1975 one of the leading researchers in this field, Dr William Dement, observed that this was one of his hopes, and he cited one of his own dreams to show how important their prognostications could be.

> Some years ago I was a heavy cigarette smoker – up to two packs a day. Then one night I had an exceptionally vivid and realistic dream in which I had inoperable cancer of the lung. I remember as though it were yesterday looking at the ominous shadow in my chest x-ray and realising that the entire right lung was infiltrated ... Finally, I experienced the incredible anguish of knowing my life was soon to end, that I would never see my children grow up, and that none of this would have happened if I had quit cigarettes when I first learned of their carcinogenic potential. I will never forget the surprise, joy and exquisite relief of waking up. I felt that I was reborn. Needless to say, the experience was sufficient to induce an immediate cessation of my cigarette habit.

The dream, in other words, had not merely revealed the problem but had solved it. 'Only the dream can allow us to experience a future alternative as if it were real,' he observed, 'and thereby to provide a supremely enlightened motivation to act upon the knowledge.'

Although most psychoanalysts have tended to concentrate on the mental and emotional problems of their patients, paying little attention to possible physical disorders, Medard Boss recalled that he had encountered cases in which an impending illness was forecast in a dream; and in a few cases the dreams had given clues to a possible cure. How often such dreams are attributable to precognition remains in dispute; the mind in sleep may well be picking up warnings that the seeds of a disorder are already establishing themselves in the body. Again, though, from the dreamer's point of view the issue is academic, if from our dreams we can pick up warning signals and, better still, learn how to act upon them.

Dream groups

In the early 1970s a Virginian, Henry Reed, was so disturbed by a dream that he decided to give up drink – rescuing himself from alcoholism. Then, inspired by another dream, he founded the *Sundance Community Dream Journal*, linking the possibilities of group exploitation of dreams with the

American Indian tradition. 'Every dreamer,' he argued, 'is a researcher;' the fruits of the research needed to be distributed.

Experiments conducted with Robert Van de Castle, a professor in the University of Virginia Medical School, confirmed what Reed had already realised: that the function of groups was not merely to relate and discuss dreams, but actually to share them. If an individual had a problem, the rest of the group would be invited to help, without being informed what the problem was. The next morning, they found, their dreams would often relate to the problem in jigsaw fashion, each providing small pieces of relevant information. And out of Reed's pioneer efforts arose Bill Stimson's *Dream Network Bulletin*, published in New York, linking groups throughout America and in other countries.

At the same time, Montague Ullman had been pursuing a similar course. Dissatisfied with the standard psycho-analytic techniques he had practised, and in particular with dream interpretations along Freudian lines, Ullman began to explore the possibility of giving dreams a more important role in group therapy. 'When we are awake, we play games with the truth,' his reasoning was. 'We rationalise, suppress, deny and separate ourselves from any aspect of the truth that may be too painful for us to deal with at the moment. Because of this, the dreamer needs help to see the honest self-portrayal in the dream.'

This was all very well, Ullman realised, but it would not be easy for a group to help if the truths *were* painful for the dreamer. They would presumably be too painful for the dreamer to want to share them with the group, as its members might offer embarrassing interpretations. A method was needed which inspired trust, and would not represent an intrusion into the dreamer's privacy. The method Ullman began to use was dream *appreciation*, rather than interpretation. The members of the group would describe their feelings about the dream in much the same way as they would describe their feelings about a film, or a television drama, they had seen, the emphasis being on the aesthetic quality.

What the dreamer gets is a succession of commentaries, any or all of which may give him clues about the dream's significance for him. But he is not expected, as he would be in conventional group therapy, to bare his psyche to the other members if he is not ready to do so. He can leave at the end of the session and ponder what the appreciations have revealed to him. And the process, Ullman has found, can be both satisfying and therapeutic, as emotional blocks are broken down.

Freud's view that dreams are fundamentally selfish, Ullman has come to realise, was mistaken; dreams are a connecting force in human relationships. 'I was taught that dreams were very personal narcissistic indulgences,' he has written:

> I now view them quite differently. I believe that the source which informs dreaming consciousness includes but goes beyond issues of personal motivation. I have come to feel that our dreams are fundamentally concerned with the survival of the species, and only incidentally with the problems of the individual.

Prophetic dreams

The other type of interpretation requiring scrutiny is of dreams which foretell the future, but where the likelihood is that the divination is not so much precognitive as self-fulfilling: that they have nudged, pushed or pulled the dreamers into taking the courses which eventually make the dream come true.

In *The Understanding of Dreams* de Becker surveyed the remarkable record of dreams in the launching of religions and the making of famous leaders. 'The Buddha's vocation was announced, specified and defined by a series of convergent dreams;' 'dream activity was basic to the vocation of Mahomet and the Islamic adventure;' and although Jesus's dreams were not recorded, those which are related in the New Testament 'seem absolutely essential to the Christian adventure,' as the dreams in the Old Testament were for the Israelites, and for the future of the Jewish people. According to the Roman historian Valerius Maximus, Hannibal saw an angelic figure appear who claimed he had been sent from heaven to urge Hannibal to conquer Rome. Turning away from him in the dream, Hannibal saw a snake violently upsetting everything in its way, and behind it, the sky obscured by lightning flashes and smoke. What could it mean? What he was seeing, the dream apparition told him, was the destruction to follow in Italy: 'Go! The Fates must be fulfilled.'

Many other cases can be cited; but at this point the question arises whether prophetic dreams have done more harm than good. There was no need, Valerius felt, to recall the evils which Hannibal inflicted upon Italy; and even those who cannot withhold admiration for Hannibal's feats of arms can hardly deny that they brought little but misery, without achieving his goal.

In other cases there is room for doubt. In 1881 Bismarck proudly related a dream he had had in a letter to Kaiser Wilhelm I. Eighteen years before, 'in the worst days of the struggle' (Bismarck had suspended the sittings of the Prussian parliament), he had been unable to see any way out of his and his country's difficulties. At this point

> I dreamt (as I related the first thing next morning to my wife and other witnesses) that I was riding on a narrow Alpine path, precipice on the right, rocks on the left. The path grew narrower, so that the horse refused to proceed, and it was impossible to turn round or dismount owing to lack of space. Then, with my whip in my left hand, I struck the smooth rock and called on God. The whip grew to an endless length, the rocky wall dropped like a piece of stage scenery and opened out a broad path, with a view over hills and forests, like a landscape in Bohemia; there were Prussian troops with banners, and even in my dream the thought came to me at once that I must report it to your Majesty.

Bismarck had woken up, 'rejoiced and strengthened', and the difficulties were duly surmounted.

To patriotic Germans Bismarck's victories, first over Austria, and then in 1870 over the French, could be regarded as a sublime vindication of the prophecy. To the Austrians, the French, and ultimately the allies in the First and Second World Wars, the dream set in train a destructive sequence of events.

So, on a smaller scale, did the most recent prophetic dream in de Becker's catalogue. Appointed Prime Minister of Iran in 1950, Mahommed Mossadeq nationalised the oil industry, expropriating the Anglo-Iranian Oil Company's assets. In a speech the following year he described how before he took office, his doctor had advised him to rest for his health; but one night he had dreamed of a person shining with light, telling him it was not the time to rest: 'Arise, and break the chains of the people of Iran.' Mossadeq had decided he must obey and, thanks to his advocacy, his nationalisation programme was adopted; demonstrating, he felt, that the apparition in his dream had been an inspired guide. He spoke too soon; in 1953 a coup overthrew his government, Mossadeq was jailed, and the power which the Allies had stripped from the pro-German Shah in the First World War was handed back to his son, with ultimately dire consquences.

'As history-makers,' Horace Hutchinson observed in *Dreams and their Meaning* (1901), 'dreams have played a big part. "We are such stuff as dreams are made on" is scarcely as true as if it were a little inverted to "We are such stuff as dreams have made us."' What we cannot tell is how different the course of history would have been if the founders of religions or great warriors had *not* been influenced by their dreams. All that can be said is that such dreams have occurred; that the dreamers have felt them to be prophetic; and that in so far as the dream provided the decisive impulse, their historic influence has been staggering. Where interpretation is essential in such dreams is in separating out the element of wishful thinking: in treating them not as commands which must be obeyed, but as signposts showing us possibilities which are worth considering.

7

Burnished Horn

To go back to where we began: the evidence for the usefulness of dreams, surely, is far too impressive, historically and contemporaneously, to be brushed aside on the reductionist hypothesis presented in *Nature* by Francis Crick and Graeme Mitchison. Crick has, in fact, since retreated a few steps. 'It is unlikely that remembering dreams will do much harm unless carried to great excess,' he has told Liam Hudson in the course of correspondence, which Hudson uses in his *Night Life* (1985). Crick cites blood-letting as his analogy; useless as a therapy, 'but we would all agree that taking a small sample of blood for diagnostic purposes is useful.' Remembering dreams for the specific purpose of analysis, therefore, can be permitted. He even predicts the emergence, eventually, of 'a really scientific method of analysing dreams'.

Useful as the analysis of dreams for prognosis and diagnosis can be, it is only one of the facets of dream exploitation. If people are to be convinced that dreams are worth taking seriously, the more promising prospect is offered by the range of testimony, old and new, to their value as a source of inspiration, as problem solvers, and as indications that the mind in sleep has the capacity to pick up useful information not ordinarily available to us when we are awake.

Undoubtedly the main problem is that our dreams are for the most part irrational. So much emphasis is placed on reason as the only trustworthy guide through life that it is hard to fit dreaming into a suitable role. It can, though, be more easily understood if looked at in its evolutionary context.

Sleep, the great naturalist Georges Buffon pointed out in the 18th century, is the normal condition of primitive life. A vegetable 'is but an animal that sleeps':

Sleep, which appears to be a purely passive state, a species of death, is on the contrary the first state of the living animal and the foundation of life. It is not a privation, an annihilation; it is a mode of being, a style of existence as real and more general than any other. We exist in this state before existing in any other; all organised beings which have not the senses exist in this state only.

As life developed, however, sleep began to present a hazard. It offered the ideal opportunity for predatory species to prey on the sleepers, making sleep 'glaringly, almost insanely, at odds with common sense', as Christopher Evans noted in *Landscapes of the Night*. To explain its continuance, he thought, it must be credited with 'some function of transcending importance, comparable at least to the functions of eating, drinking and mating'. Simple recuperation is not enough; some species do without sleep. Dreams, perhaps, provide the essential clue.

The most likely function of 'transcendent importance' is the provision of some kind of help to the conscious mind, without which our consciousness would suffer serious deprivation. This was the theory put forward by Marie de Manaceine, the Russian investigator of the subject, in her *Sleep* (1897). Her belief was that Darwin's disciples were misguided in their refusal to accept the reality of psychological, as distinct from physiological, evolution. What our ancestors felt, she argued, must have been passed on down to us

not indeed as such, but in the shape of latent capacities and possibilities inherent in our neuro-cerebral system. And thus it may well be that during sleep, when the immediate personal consciousness is inactive, these latent characters of the psychic organism inherited from our remotest ancestors stir within us, and fill with strange images and unforeseen desires our inner world.

But why, if sleep and dreams are part of the evolutionary process, have dreams remained obscure, chaotic, often silly? Here, Halse Rivers was able to offer an explanation in his *Instinct and the Unconscious* (1920). As an unconscious activity, he pointed out, they are not subject to the same control as our waking thoughts. Inevitably they tend to display the characteristics of thought in early childhood, before control is achieved. 'The character of the dream finds a natural explanation if its appearance in consciousness is simply due to the removal in sleep of higher controlling levels, so that the lower levels with their infantile modes of expression come to the surface, and are allowed to manifest themselves in their natural guise.' The irrational character of dreams, he believed, resulted simply from the fact that the behaviour exhibited in them was of a kind held in check by the conditioning of adult life.

A distinction needs to be made, in other words, between the content of dreams and the manner in which it is presented. There is a parallel here with mediumship, where the information provided may be of deep interest while the manner in which it is conveyed – by a Red Indian spirit guide, or a planchette chasing around a ouija board – can appear ridiculous. As a working hypothesis, it can be argued that we all enjoy the potential, in our unconscious minds, of powers we rarely know how to exploit. Our normal waking consciousness tends to block them; but in sleep we have many intimations of their existence, such as the built-in alarm clock which wakes us up (if we want it to, and can train it). And sometimes, in dreams, the 'subliminal self', as Frederic Myers called it in his *Human Personality* (1903), is able to use a dream to solve a problem, or prompt us, or deliver some warning.

It seems very likely that dreams have a variety of other functions, such as the 'computer clearance' which Christopher Evans proposed. 'Sleep is the period when the brain comes off-line,' he suggested, facilitating the revision of programs. In *The Inner Eye* (1986) the psychologist Nicholas Humphrey has suggested that dreams can resemble charades, in which we put ourselves into roles which are not our own to teach ourselves lessons in psychology which otherwise we might never learn. It is no accident, he argues, that most dreams are 'the acting-out of relatively ordinary situations'; or that as children grow up, 'their dreams become increasingly oriented towards exploring those *social* situations which in waking life prey on the child's mind'; it is all part of the process of growing up within a society.

Doubtless the very common range of dreams in which, as adults, we find ourselves in embarrassing situations should also be looked at from this point of view. They may be reminding us that we have yet to come to terms with some aspect of ourselves we have declined to recognise because we have not quite 'grown up'. But the essential point is that the way our dreams present themselves, infantile though they often are, should not be allowed to delude us into dismissing them as unworthy of our attention. The appropriate metaphor, Liam Hudson argues, is not the rubbish bin but the bric-à-brac stall. 'On this are jumbled together a few objects that may be of real value with the many that are virtually but not quite useless; the tarnished caddy spoon that might have been silver, the begrimed oil painting that looks vaguely genuine.' And the analogy can be taken further; it admits individual differences. The objects may vary enormously in value to the passer-by, according to his taste.

One other doubt, frequently encountered, remains to be disposed of. Why, if dreams are potentially so useful, do most of us find such difficulty in recalling them?

In *Lucid Dreaming* (1985) Stephen LaBerge offers a plausible explanation. Anybody who has kept a pet is likely to feel sure that animals dream; but they have no way in which to distinguish dream from reality. Dream recall could be dangerous for them. Sleep and dreams, therefore, at the animal stage may have been assisting evolution (as, indeed, they may still be assisting it) without the dreams being recalled. 'But if the theory I have proposed for why dreams are difficult to recall is correct, then – contrary to Crick and Mitchison – remembering dreams should do humans no harm, precisely because we can tell the difference between dreaming and waking experiences.'

LaBerge goes on to echo Montague Ullman's idea that the way forward – the next evolutionary step, in this context – is to think of our dreams as we think of works of art: to be appreciated, rather than interpreted. The dream 'is not so much a communication as a creation,' he suggests. 'An uninterpreted dream is like an uninterpreted poem.' Independently, Hudson has come to the same conclusion. The thesis of his *Night Life* is 'that dreams can be interpreted if they are approached in the same spirit that we approach poems,' if we pay close attention to their waking context and if we allow for the fact that individuals differ 'both in how they dream and how they assimilate what they have dreamt to their waking lives'.

Hudson, though, distances himself from an element in dreaming which *does* require interpretation, and sometimes action. The terrain he explores in *Night Life* is 'dangerous', he fears, because the model may appear to be Jungian: 'as a matter of principle, the present argument is designed to avoid all mention of the occult and supernatural, the cast of mind that has earned Jung a bad name.' Among academic psychologists, extra-sensory perception is still widely regarded as 'supernatural', and to be avoided at all costs. Yet in connection with dreams this is an attitude tenable only by closing their minds to the mass of evidence pointing to the fact that in sleep 'we are not only able to scan backward in time and tap into our remote memory,' as Ullman has put it in *Working with Dreams* (1979), 'but are also able to scan forward in time and across space to tap into information outside our experience.'

It is immaterial, Ullman points out, that dreams in which time or space are no obstacle occur infrequently. Even if one occurs to us only once in a lifetime, it would still demonstrate the range of our psychic abilities, and compel us to accept that dreams demand a more complex frame of reference than we are accustomed to allow them. Nevertheless it is not necessary to accept the reality of paranormal intervention. Even if all the accounts which point to it are attributed to faulty memory, exaggeration and coincidence, the fact that the messages were heeded and acted upon has so often had beneficial consequences, to the point of sparing the dreamer from injury or death, as to be worth bearing in mind. The parallel here is with the old technique, for use in times of worry, of opening the Bible at random and jabbing a finger at the text – or the more commonly adopted method, these days, of consulting our horoscopes in the newspapers. The knowledge that the way in which the horoscopes are compiled is bogus can be unimportant, if what is written happens to trigger a useful response and set us on a course of reflection or action which meets our needs.

Many 19th-century writers, ironically, grasped this better than their 20th-century counterparts, who often have been either too much under the influence of the Freudian inheritance or too inhibited by rationalist and behaviourist preconceptions. There was a greater willingness then to appreciate what John Sheppard, in his essays *On Dreams* in 1847, described as 'the intellectual *inventiveness and power* occasionally exerted'. Again and again, that recognition of the potential of dreaming was to appear in the work of writers who, like Henry Maudsley, were not given to fantasy; 'dreams have been a neglected study,' he feared; 'nevertheless it is a study which is full of promise of abundant fruit.' And there was Professor J.R.L. Delboeuf, the Belgian who was one of the most enlightened exponents of the new discipline, psychology – striving to emancipate itself from the clutches of academic philosophy. The dream, he concluded from his investigations – the fruits of which were published in 1885 as *Le Sommeil et les rêves* – 'is a concealed aperture through which from time to time we can cast an eye over the immense treasures that nature amasses for us so indefatigably.'

The influence of rationalism proved too great for such opinions to establish themselves in the academic world. It needed the discovery of the link between rapid eye movements and dreaming to bring dreaming back into contention; and as the content of dreams, disclosed in laboratory experiments, has proved embarrassing – notably in the Maimonides research – the initial enthusiasm has faded, kept alive largely by individuals such as LaBerge, with his work on lucid dreaming, and Schatzman, investigating problem-solving in dreams. It is again left to the public – prompted from time to time by individuals who have made a study of dreams and become impressed by what they have to offer.

The most eloquent of these, in recent times, has been the psychiatrist Dr Alan McGlashan. 'In regard to dream-language we have behaved too long like day-trippers to the Continent, willing to learn only such phrases as will enable us to buy some trifle at a cheap rate of exchange and smuggle it home through Customs,' he has lamented in *Gravity and Levity* (1976). 'Dreams are the insights of the unconscious made visible. They should be treated with respect, handled with gentleness, for they are envoys from a land still as remote from us and as fabulous as the realm of Prester John.' Remote it is likely to remain, because conventional psychology lacks the means – and consequently also the impetus – to explore it. But this gives us the advantage. *We* can be the explorers.

Bibliography

A comprehensive bibliography of works on dreams would require a book. I have listed here those works which are relevant to my 'burnished horn' theme. Works referred to in the text in which the account of a dream is incidental – biographies, for example – are not included; if they are not in the text, they will be found in the source references. The place and date of publication are of the editions I have consulted.

Abercrombie, John, *Inquiries concerning the Intellectual Powers*, London, 1840.

A.E. (George William Russell), *The Candle of Vision*, London, 1918.

A.E. (George William Russell), *Song and its Fountains*, London, 1931.

Almansi, Guido, and Claude Béguin, *The Theatre of Sleep*, London, 1986.

Archer, William, *On Dreams*, London, 1935.

Aristotle, *Works*, Princeton, 1984.

Arnold-Forster, Mary, *Studies in Dreams*, London, 1921.

Aubrey, John, *Miscellanies*, London, 1857.

Baillet, Adrian, *La Vie de M. Des Cartes*, Paris, 1641.

Bergson, Henri, *On Dreams*, London, 1914.

Bigelow, John, *The Mystery of Sleep*, London, 1904.

Boss, Medard, *The Analysis of Dreams*, London, 1957.

Bridge, Ann, *Moments of Knowing*, London, 1970.

Brodie, Benjamin, *Psychological Inquiries*, London, 1855.

Brook, Stephen (ed.), *The Oxford Book of Dreams*, Oxford, 1983.

Browne, Sir Thomas, *Works*, iv, London, 1835.

Cox, Edward, *Sleep and Dream*, London, 1878.

de Becker, Raymond, *The Understanding of Dreams*, London, 1968.

de la Mare, Walter, *Behold This Dreamer*, London, 1939.

Delboeuf, J. R. L., *Le Sommeil et les rêves*, Paris, 1885.

de Manaceine, Marie, *Sleep*, London, 1897.

Dement, William C., *Some Must Watch While Some Must Sleep*, San Francisco, 1974.

Dunne, J. W. *An Experiment with Time*, London, 1934.

Eisenbud, Jule, *Psi and Psychoanalysis*, New York, 1970.

Eisenbud, Jule, *Parapsychology and the Unconscious*, Berkeley, 1983.

Eliade, Mircea, *Myths, Dreams and Mysteries*, London, 1968.

Ellis, Havelock, *The World of Dreams*, Boston, 1911.

Evans, Christopher, and Peter Evans, *Landscapes of the Night*, London, 1983.

Faraday, Ann, *Dream Power*, London, 1972.

Faraday, Ann, *The Dream Game*, London, 1976.

Flammarion, Camille, *The Unknown*, London, 1900.

Freud, Sigmund, *On Dreams*, London, 1952.

Garfield, Patricia, *Creative Dreaming*, New York, 1975.

Ghiselin, Brewster (ed.), *The Creative Process*, University of California, 1952.

Godley, John, *Living Like a Lord*, London, 1955.

Goodwin, Philip, *The Mystery of Dreams*, London, 1658.

Grant, A. H., *Literature and Curiosities of Dreams*, London, 1865.

Grant, John, *Dreamers: a Geography of Dream*, London, 1986.

Graves, Robert, *The Meaning of Dreams*, London, 1924.

Green, Celia, *Lucid Dreams*, London, 1968.

Greene, Graham, *Ways of Escape*, London, 1982.

Greene, Graham, *A Sort of Life*, London, 1984.

Greenwood, Frederick, *Imagination in Dreams*, London, 1984.

Gurney, Edmund, *et al.*, *Phantasms of the Living*, London, 1886.

Hadamard, Jacques, *An Essay on the Psychology of Invention in the Mathematical Field*, Princeton, 1945.

Hadfield, James H., *Dreams and Nightmares*, London, 1954.

Hall, Calvin S., *The Meaning of Dreams*, New York, 1966.

Harding, Rosamund, *An Anatomy of Inspiration*, London, 1948.

Harman, Willis, and H. Rheingold, *Higher Creativity*, Los Angeles, 1984.

Hervey de Saint-Denys, Marquis de, *Dreams and How to Guide Them*, London, 1982.

Hill, Brian, *Such Stuff as Dreams*, London, 1967.

Hudson, Liam, *Night Life*, London, 1985.

Humphrey, Nick, *The Inner Eye*, London, 1986.

Hutchinson, Horace, *Dreams and their Meaning*, London, 1901.

Jung, Carl, *Memories, Dreams, Reflections*, London, 1973.

Kerouac, Jack, *Book of Dreams*, San Francisco, 1961.

Kingsford, Anna, *Dreams and Dream-Stories*, London, 1888.

LaBerge, Stephen, *Lucid Dreaming*, Los Angeles, 1985.

Lang, Andrew, *The Book of Dreams and Ghosts*, London, 1897.

Lincoln, J. S., *The Dream in Primitive Culture*, London, 1935.

Lyttelton, Dame Edith, *Some Cases of Prediction*, London, 1937.

Macario, M., *Du Sommeil, des rêves, et du somnambulisme*, Lyon, 1857.

McGlashan, Alan, *The Savage and Beautiful Country*, London, 1966

McGlashan, Alan, *Gravity and Levity*, London, 1976.

MacKenzie, Norman, *Dreams and Dreaming*, London, 1965.

McNish, Robert, *The Philosophy of Sleep*, Glasgow, 1830.

Malcolm, Norman, *Dreaming*, London, 1959.

Maritain, Jacques, *The Dream of Descartes*, London, 1946.

Mattoon, Mary Ann, *Understanding Dreams*, Dallas, 1984.

Maudsley, Henry, *The Pathology of Mind*, London, 1879.

Maudsley, Henry, *Natural Causes and Supernatural Seemings*, London, 1939.

Maury, Alfred, *Le Sommeil et les rêves*, Paris, 1878.

Megroz, Rodolphe, *The Dream World*, London, 1939.

Monteith, Mary, *A Book of True Dreams*, London, 1929.

Murphy, Michael, and Rhea White, *The Psychic Side of Sport*, Reading, Massachusetts, 1980.

Myers, Frederic, *Human Personality*, London, 1903.

Owen, Robert Dale, *Footfalls on the Boundary of Another World*, London, 1860.

Parker, Julia and Derek, *Dreaming*, London, 1985.

Priestley, J. B., *Rain Upon Gadshill*, London, 1939.

Priestley, J. B., *Man and Time*, London, 1964.

Prince, Walter F., *Noted Witnesses for Psychic Occurrences*, New York, 1932.

Ratcliff, A. J. J., *A History of Dreams*, London, 1923.

Rhine, Louisa, *The Invisible Picture*, London, 1981.

Rivers, W. H. R., *Dreams and Primitive Culture*, London, 1918.

Rivers, W. H. R., *Instinct and the Unconscious*, London, 1920.

Rivers, W. H. R., *Conflict and Dream*, London, 1923.

Rycroft, Charles, *The Innocence of Dreams*, London, 1979.

Sabine, W. H. H., *Second Sight in Daily Life*, New York, 1949.

Seafield, Frank (pseudonym: see Grant, A. H.).

Sheppard, John, *On Dreams in their Mental and Moral Aspects*, London, 1847.

Stevens, William Oliver, *The Mystery of Dreams*, 1950.

Stevenson, Robert Louis, *Across the Plains*, London, 1909.

Symonds, John Addington, *Sleep and Dreams*, London, 1857.

Synesius of Cyrene, *Essays*, Oxford, 1930.

Taylor, Jeremy, *Dream Work*, New York, 1983.

Tyrrell, G. N. M., *Science and Psychical Phenomena*, London, 1938.

Ullman, Montague, and Stanley Krippner, with Alan Vaughan, *Dream Telepathy*, Baltimore, 1974.

Ullman, Montague, and Nan Zimmerman, *Working with Dreams*, New York, 1979.

Van de Castle, Robert, 'Sleep and Dreams', in B. B. Wolman, *Handbook of Parapsychology*, 1977, pp. 473–99.

Walsh, William S., *The Psychology of Dreams*, London, 1920.

Wolman, B. B., *Handbook of Parapsychology*, New York, 1977.

Woods, Ralph L., *The World of Dreams*, New York, 1947.

Yeats, W. B., *The Wind Among the Reeds*, London, 1899.

Yeats, W. B., *Autobiographies*, London, 1980.

Zohar, Danah, *Through the Time Barrier*, London, 1982.

Source References

The names, or words, in parentheses refer to the subject dealt with on the page. The source is identified by the author, the book (if it is not given in the text), the publication date, and the pages. Where the book is to be found in the bibliography, I have cited simply the author, the date of the edition I have consulted, and the pages. The letters 'p.c.' refer to personal communications.

INTRODUCTION: HORN – OR IVORY?

1 *Odyssey*, 1973 (E. V. Rieu's translation).
2 *Nature*, 14 July 1983, 111–14.
3 Medawar, *The Hope of Progress*, 1977, 104–5.
   Evans, 1983, 142–50.

CHAPTER 1: INSPIRATION FROM DREAMS

6 Bunyan, *Pilgrim's Progress*, opening lines.
   De la Mare, 1939, 97–8.
   (Lawrence), Brook, 1983, 254.
7 (Wells), p.c. Renée Haynes.
   Stevenson, 1909, 229–52.
9 Kingsford, 1888, Introduction.
10 (Poe) J. H. Ingram, *Poe*, 1981, 121.
11 (Priestley), Megroz, 1939, 295.
   Kerouac, 1961, Introduction.
   Greene, 1982, 210–11.
   Gaskell, *C. Brontë*, 1857, 243.
12 Scott, *Journal*, 1891, i, 113.
   (Ballantyne), Lockhart, *Scott*, 1928, iii, 88–9, 119–20.
15 (Yeats), U. O'Connor, *Celtic Dawn*, 1984, 323.
16 Archer, *William Archer*, 1831, 363–75.
17 Cocteau, Jean, *Le Foyer des artistes*, 1947, 57–9.

Bunuel, Luis, *My Last Breath*, 1985, 92–100.
18 (Lamb), Downey, 1929, 57.
   Coleridge, *Works*, 1895, 295–8; Evans, 1983, 223–4; de la Mare, 1939, 619.
19 (Goethe), Eckermann, *Conversations with Goethe*, 1935, 355–66.
   (Swinburne), Gosse, *Swinburne*, 1917, 241–2.
   Masefield, 1939, 767–8.
20 (Benson), Ratcliff, 1923, 221.
21 Kingsford, 1888, 77–82.
   (Hebbel), Almansi and Beguin, 1986, 155–6.
   Yeats, 1899, 94–5.
22 (Blake), Gilchrist, *Blake*, 1863, i, 68–9.
23 Hamerton, *Turner*, 1879, 81–2.
   Hervey, 1982, 162.
24 (Gauguin), Haftman, *Klee*, 1954, 131.
   (Breton), Haftman, *Klee*, 1954, 139.
   (Tartini), Harman and Rheingold, 1984, 36–7.
   (Beethoven), Ghiselin, 1952, 42–3.
25 (Wagner), Harman and Rheingold, 1984, 31–2.
   (d'Indy), Myers, 1903, i, 58.
   Cox, 1878, 85–6.
   Browne, 1831, 141–2.
26 Graves, 1924, 111.
   Keller, *The World I Live In*, 1933, 169–91.

27 Symonds, 1857, 56.
    Maudsley, 1879, 14–18.

CHAPTER 2: PROBLEM-SOLVING IN DREAMS

29 Browne, 1835, iv, 356.
    Abercrombie, 1840, 302–3.
30 Hervey, 1982, 88.
    Brodie, 1855, 151–2.
31 Greenwood, 1894, 27.
    Holmes, 1978, 47.
    Pauwels and Bergier, *The Morning of
        the Magicians*, 1960, 318; Taylor, 1983,
        7.
32 (Descartes), Baillet, 1641, 81–6.
34 De Becker, 1968, 96–100.
    Maritain, 1946, 12–13.
    (Kekulé), Koestler, 1964, 118, 169–71.
35 (Mendeleev), La Berge, 1985, 168–9.
    (Fabre), Megroz, 1939, 183.
36 (Hilprecht), Myers, 1903, i, 375–9.
37 (Agassiz), Stevens, 1950, 37.
    (Loewi), Harman and Rheingold, 1984,
        39; Koestler, 1964, 205–7.
38 (Ramanujan), *Scientific American*, June
        1948, 547.
39 Arnold-Forster, 1921, 104–7.
    Hervey, 1982, 92.
40 (Chladni), Hill, 1967, 22–3: *Biographie
        universelle*, viii, 168.
41 Evans, 1983, 223.
    Hadfield, 1954, 235.
    Kaempffert, *A Popular History of
        American Inventions*, 1924, ii, 381–2.
42 Arnold-Forster, 1921, 7.
44 Maury, 1878, 142–3.
    (Nicklaus), Murphy and White, 1980,
        161.
    Abercrombie, 1840, 272–87.
47 Hutchinson, 1901, 290–1.
    Cavendish-Bentinck, *Autobiography*,
        1937, 126–7.
48 Greenwood, 1894, 100–2.
49 (Allgood), Stevens, 1950, 242–4.
50 Stevens, 1950, 202–5.
52 (Dante), Stevens, 1950, 43–5.
53 Lang, 1897, 10.
    Lewis: *Proceedings SPR*, viii, 389.
54 (Bickford-Smith), Hutchinson, 1901,
        226; *Proceedings SPR*, viii, 389.
    Hutchinson, 1901, 235–7.
55 Megroz, 1939, 223–8.
56 Rhine, 1981, 42–3.
57 Priestley, 1964, 222.

    Sabine, 1951, 44–7.
58 (Dement), Evans, 1983, 230–2.
59 Schatzman, *New Scientist*, 11 August
        1983, 416–17.
61 (Hilprecht), Myers, 1903, i, 375.
    Gurney, 1886, i, 298.
    Evans, 1983, 138–9.
62 Flournoy, *Spiritism and Psychology*, 1911,
        130–1.

CHAPTER 3: SECOND SIGHT IN DREAMS

63 (Vaughan), Ullman *et al.*, 1974, 2–3.
    Ehrenwald, *American Society of Psychical
        Research Journal*, January 1984, 71.
64 Gurney, 1886, i, 332.
65 (McDougall), Gurney, 1886, i, 331–2.
    Taylor, 1983, 92–3.
66 Rhine, 1981, 44–6.
67 Aubrey, 1696, 58–9.
    Lang, 1897, 4.
68 (Graves), Megroz, 1939, 16.
70 Stevenson, *American SPR Journal*, 1960,
        153–71; 1965, 210–25.
    Greene, 1984, 24.
    Rhine, 1981, 39.
71 Heren, p.c.
    Tyrrell, 1938, 24–6.
73 (Garibaldi), Guerzoni, *Life*, i, 398–9.
    (Stanley), *Autobiography*, 1909, 207.
75 (Belasco), W. F. Prince, 1928, 150–1.
    Owen, 1860, 124–5.
76 (Twain), Paine, *Life*, i, 131–9.
    (Haggard), *Proceedings SPR*, xxxvi,
        219–27.
78 Romanes, 1896, 345.
79 Ullman and Zimmerman, 1979, 306–7.
    Le Brocquy, p.c.
80 Rhine, 1981, 46.
    Murray, *My First 100 Years*, 1963,
        179–80.
81 Boss, 1957, 177.
83 Bridge, 1970, 91–2.
84 Stockwood, *Light*, Summer 1984, 52.
    (Warburton), Gurney, 1886, i, 338.
86 (Marten), Priestley, 1964, 205;
        Chambers Edinburgh Journal,
        13 Oct, 1832.
    Carlyon, *Early Years*, 1856, i, 219;
        Owen, 1860, 120–4.
89 (Chaffin), *Proceedings SPR*, xxxvi,
        517–24.
    Jaffé, 1979, 130.
90 Yeats, 1980, 256–61.

91 Ermacora, *Proceedings SPR*, xi, 235–308.
93 (Aserinsky/Dement), Evans, 1983, 124–34.
94 Ullman & Krippner, 1974, *passim*.

CHAPTER 4: DREAMING THE FUTURE

98 McNish, 1830, 108–9.
99 Maury, 1878, 161.
100 Carpenter, *Principles of Mental Physiology*, 1974, 550–1; (Lehmann), Boss, 1957, 185.
Evans, 1983, 44–74.
101 Dunne, 1927, *passim*.
105 Mackenzie, 1965, 138.
Evans, 1983, 72.
106 Priestley, 1964, 220–1.
107 Sabine, 1949, 29–30.
108 Kipling, 1933, 215–16
109 Bridge, 1970, 36–40.
110 Forster, *Dickens*, 1874, iii, 484–5.
Hutchinson, 1891, 258–9.
111 *Proceedings SPR*, v, 343.
112 Greenwood, 1894, 196–8.
Priestley, 1964, 220.
113 Ullman, 1979, 308–11.
Targ and Puthoff, 1977, 107–9.
114 Forman, 1978, 91–2.
Boss, 1957, 179–81.
115 (Hone), Lang, 1897, 24–5.
116 Evans, 1983, 178.
117 Flammarion, 1922, i, 224–8.
118 (Bozzano), Flammarion, 1922, i, 230–3.
120 (Trevor), *Proceedings SPR*, v, 314–16.
121 *Country Life*, 26 December, 1947.
122 (Hudd), Randles, 1985, 54–5.
Sikorsky, 1939, Introduction.
124 Priestley, 1939, 197–8.
(Shelley), Megroz, 1939, 86–8.
125 (Schopenhauer), Flammarion, 1922, i, 268.
126 (André), Sargent, *Life of André*, 1861, 42; Stevens, 1950, 152–5.
127 Greene, 1982, 92.
128 Goddard, p.c.; Priestley, 1964, 192.
Jaffé, 1979, 36–7.
129 Rhine, 1981, 98–108.
130 Dunne, 1981, 54–6.
131 Jaffé, 1979, 38.
Aubrey, 1857, 54–60.
132 Walton, *Lives*, 1884, 104–5.
(Abercrombie), Owen, 1861, 103.

133 (Brighten), *Proceedings SPR*, viii, 400–2.
134 Saltmarsh, *Foreknowledge*, 1938, 22–6.
135 Bérard, *Revue*, 15 September 1895; Flammarion, 1900, 429–34.
136 (Kinsolving), *Proceedings SPR*, xi, 495; Lang, 1897, 43.
137 (Stanton), Zohar, 1982, 34.
138 Jaffé, 1979, 35–8.
139 MacKenzie, 1974, 105–6.
(Dunne), Lyttelton, 1937, 152–3.
140 Priestley, 1964, 209.
141 Rhine, 1981, 118–19.
142 (Foyt), Murphy and White, 1980, 62.
Rhine, 1981, 116–17.
143 ('Frau K.'), *Proceedings SPR*, v, 335–7.
144 Eckermann, *Conversations with Goethe*, 1875, 289–90.
145 Lyttelton, 1937, 53–4.
147 (de Lanyi), Boss, 1957, 187–8.
148 Livneh, *Journal SPR*, 1986, 383–6.
150 (Hellembach), Flammarion, 1922, i, 293–4.
(Maeterlinck), de Becker, 1968, 392–3.
151 (Williams), *Proceedings SPR*, v, 324–5; Lang, 1897, 41–2.
153 Rhine, 1981, 109–10.
(*Princeton*), Sabine, 1951, 65–6; Ebon, *True Experiences*, 1967, 58–60.
154 Lamon, W., *Recollections of Lincoln*, 1911, 114–18.
155 (Terriss), *Proceedings SPR*, xiv, 309–16.
156 Tenhaeff, *Journal SPR*, 1939–40, 2–6.
Cicero, *Treatises*, 1876, 168–9.
157 (Maeterlinck), de Becker, 1968, 391–2.
158 (Shoemaker), Murphy and White, 1980, 63.
159 Macario, 1857, 80–1.
160 Flammarion, 1922, i, 279.
161 Bridge, 1970, 94–5.
(Sitwell), MacKenzie, *A Gallery of Ghosts*, 1972, 126–7.
162 Megroz, 1939, 274–5.
163 (Murray), *Proceedings SPR*, xiv, 317–21.
Godley, 1955, 43–60; p.c.
167 Moss, 1974, 209–10.
Booker, p.c.
169 (Bessent), Ullman *et al.*, 1974, 170–9.

CHAPTER 5: LUCID DREAMING

171 Myers, *Proceedings SPR*, iv, 241.
172 Freud, 1900, 64.
Van Eeden, *Proceedings SPR*, xxvi, 431–61.

Arnold-Forster, 1921, 52–9.
174   LaBerge, 1985, *passim*.

CHAPTER 6: DREAM INTERPRETATION

177   Lincoln, 1935, 1–15.
      Eliade, 1970, 103–4.
178   Aristotle, 1984, 730–9.
      (Papyrus), de Becker, 1968, 200.
      Oneirocritica, passim; Freud, 1900, 21–2;
          Almansi and Béguin, 1986, 244–9.
179   Synesius, 1930, 330–49.
181   (Panurge), Almansi and Béguin, 1986,
          258.
      (Luther), Goodwin, 1658, 146–64.
      Thomas, 1971, 128–30.
      Hobbes, 1953, 6.
182   *Spectator*, 18 September, 1712.
      Hazlitt, *Plain Speaker*, 1894, 27.
      Maudsley, 1939, 9–16.
183   Greenwood, 1894, 78–9.
184   Jones, 1953, 384–99.
      Freud, 1952, 61–71.
185   Archer, 1935, 2–7, 91–5.
      Evans, 1983, 75–99.
      Marsh, *Ambrosia and Small Beer*, 1964,
          37.
186   Fordham, *Jungian Psychotherapy*, 1978,
          21.
      Van der Post, *Jung*, 146–7, 213.
187   Mattoon, 1984, 45–50.
      Jung, 1973, *passim*.
189   (Freud), Van Over, *Psychology and ESP*,
          1972, 109.
190   Eisenbud, 1970, 194.
191   Ehrenwald, *The ESP Experience*, 1978,
          52–3.
      (Van de Castle) Wolman, 1977, 483.
      Ullman and Krippner, 1974, 32–3.
      Rivers, 1923, *passim*.

194   Hall, 1966, 71–85, 221.
      Lincoln, 1935, 15.
195   Mattoon, 1984, 5.
      Hippocrates, *Writings*, 1978, 252–9.
196   Maudsley, 1879, 42.
197   Hutchinson, 1901, 65.
      (Cayce), Agee, *Edgar Cayce on ESP*,
          1969, *passim*; Stevens, 1950, 264–5.
198   (Dement), LaBerge, 1985, 173–4.
      Boss, 1957, 159–88.
199   (Reed/Stimson) *Omni*, December 1983,
          24.
      Ullman, *American SPR Newsletter*,
          April 1986; Ullman and
          Zimmerman, 1979, 12.
      Ullman, *Research in Parapsychology*,
          1983, 143.
200   de Becker, 1968, *passim*.
202   Hutchinson, 1901, 44.

CHAPTER 7: BURNISHED HORN

203   Hudson, 1985, 52–63.
      (Buffon) Bigelow, 1904, 50.
204   Evans, 1983, 18.
      de Manaceine, 1897, 319.
      Rivers, 1920, 230–1.
205   Evans, 1983, 142–3.
      Humphrey, 1986, 125.
      Hudson, 1985, 59.
206   LaBerge, 1985, 202–3.
      Hudson, 1985, 116, 160.
207   Ullman and Zimmerman, 1979, 314.
      Sheppard, 1847, 7.
      Delboeuf, 1885, 252.
208   McGlashan, 1976, 96.'

Mislaid: I would be grateful for the source
   reference to the dream of Mrs Bramly
   (p. 85).

Index

Abbey Theatre, Dublin, 14, 49
Abbotsford (Sir Walter Scott's house), 109
Abercrombie, John, 181; *Inquiries Concerning the Intellectual Powers*, 29–30, 44–5, 47, 132
Addison, Joseph, 181
A.E. (George William Russell): *Deirdre*, 15
Aesculapius, 194–5
Agassiz, Jean Louis, 37, 62
Allgood, Sara, 49–50
American Psychologist (journal), 96
Ames, Winthrop, 16
André, John, 126–7
Anglo-Iranian Oil Company, 200
Anstey, John, 3
Anthony, Susan, 137
Archer, Lieut.-Col. C., 16
Archer, William: *The Green Goddess*, 15–16; *On Dreams*, 184
Archives of General Psychiatry, 95
Aristotle, 29, 170, 177
Arliss, George, 16
Arnold-Forster, Mary: on lucid dreaming, 172, 174–5; *Studies in Dreams*, 39, 42, 171–2
Artemidorus of Daldus: *Oneirocritica*, 177–8, 180, 182
artists: inspiration from dreams, 22–4
Aserinsky, Eugene, 93
Atlay, Mrs James, 110–11
Aubrey, John: *Miscellanies*, 66, 131

Baillet, Adrien, 32
Ballantyne, James, 12–13
Baroda, Gaekwar of, 164–5
Battle, Mary, 90
Bedollière, Emile de la, 160
Beerbohm, Max, 50
Beethoven, Ludwig van, 24–5
behaviourism, 193, 207
Belasco, David, 75; *The Return of Peter Grimm*, 75
Benedict XIII, Pope (Pedro de Luna), 13–14

Bennett, F., 158–9
Benson, A.C.: 'The Phoenix', 20
Bérard, Ernest, 135–6
Bergson, Henri, 63–4
Bernhard, Prince of the Netherlands, 156
Bessent, Malcolm, 169
betting *see* gambling
Bevan, Archdeacon Hugh Henry Molesworth, 82, 158
Bickford Smith, Mrs A.M., 54
Biot, Jean Baptiste, 30
Bismarck, Prince Otto von, 200
Blake, Robert, 22
Blake, William, 18, 22–3
Blakeson, Don, 168
Bobin, Angèle, 159
Boccaccio, Giovanni, 52–3
Bohr, Nils, 32
Booker, Christopher, 167–8
Boss, Medard, 114, 147, 197; *The Analysis of Dreams*, 81–2
Bozzano, Ernesto, 118–120
Braid, James, 99
Brain/Mind Bulletin, The, 40–1
Bramly, Mrs (*née* Tyrrell), 85–6
Breton, André, 24
Bridge, Ann (Mrs O'Malley): *Moments of Knowing*, 82–4, 109, 160–1
Brighten, William E., 133–5
Britt, Edgar, 164–5
Brodie, Sir Benjamin: *Psychological Insights*, 30, 182
Bronowski, Jacob, 73
Brontë, Charlotte, 11
Brown, Harvey, 64
Browne, Sir Thomas, 29; *Religio Medici*, 25
Brownies: R.L. Stevenson on, 7–9
Buddha, 3, 199
Buffon, Georges, 203
Buñuel, Luis: *My Last Breath*, 17
Bunyan, John: *The Pilgrim's Progress*, 6

C.H.H., 54
Cabanis, Pierre, 30
Caesar, Julius, 177
'call' dreams, 80–6
Calpurnia, 177
Campbell, Mrs Patrick, 49–50
Cardan, Jerome, 30
Carlyon, Clement: *Early Years and Late Reflections*, 86, 87
Carpenter, William Benjamin, 99
Carr, G.S.: *Synopsis of Pure Mathematics*, 38
Carr, Harry, 168
Carroll, Lewis: *Alice in Wonderland*, 6, 11
Cayce, Edgar, 196
Chaffin, James S. (Senior and Junior), 88
chess, 39–40
Chicago, University of, 93–4
Chien Andalou, Un (film), 17
Child, Irvin L., 96
Chladni, Ernst: *Such Stuff as Dreams*, 40
Cicero, 156
clairvoyance, 99
Clarke, Captain, 75–6
Clemens, Henry, 76
Clemens, Samuel (Mark Twain), 76
Cocteau, Jean: *The Knights of the Round Table*, 17
coincidence, 100–1, 112–13, 140, 163
Coleridge, Samuel Taylor: *Kubla Khan*, 18
Collis, Mary, 159
Comte, Auguste, 99
Condillac, Etienne Connot de, 30
Condorcet, M.J.A.N. Caritat, Marquis de, 29
Corder, William, 86
Coué, Emile, 172, 174–5
Country Life, 121
Cox, Serjeant Edward, 25
Craig, Walter, 163
Craiglockhart Hospital (Scotland), 191–2
Crick, Francis, 2–3, 41, 60, 203, 205
Cunningham (friend of Anna Seward), 126–7

D'Acre, Joseph, 132
Daily Mirror, 165–6
Daniel (prophet), 177
Dante Alighieri: *Paradiso*, 52–3
Dante, Jacopo di, 52–3
de Becker, Raymond: *The Understanding of Dreams*, 194, 199–200
de la Mare, Walter, 6
de Trafford, Sir Humphrey, 168
Dean, Douglas, 94
déjà vu, 100, 116–25, 140
Delboeuf, J.R.L.: *Le Sommeil et les rêves*, 206
Dement, William, 58, 93, 196

Descartes, René, 32–4
Devereux, G.: *Psychoanalysis and the Occult*, 188
Dickens, Charles, 13, 110
'disaster' dreams, 69–72, 106
divination, 178–81
Drake, Mrs R.A., 114
Dream Network Bulletin, 198
Drummond family of Drumquaigh, 67
Dunne, J.W.: *An Experiment with Time*: on dreaming the future, 1, 105, 127, 130; Graves and, 167–8; accounts in, 101–7; and differences between dream and event, 113; and warning dreams, 139

Eckermann, Johann, 18, 144–5
Edward VII, King, 47
Eeden, Frederic van: 'A Study of Dreams', 171–3
Ehrenwald, Jan, 63–4, 106, 188–90
Eisenbud, Jule, 188–9
Eliade, Mircea: *Shamanism*, 176
Elliot, Mrs M.R., 66
'Elvira' (spirit control), 91–3
Emerson, Ralph Waldo, 25
endoscopy, 194, 196
Ermacora, Giovanni Battista, 90–3
euphonium, 40
Evans, Christopher, 3, 41, 61–2, 105, 116; *Landscapes of the Night* (with Peter Evans), 61, 100–1, 184, 204
Evans, Peter, 61; *see also* Evans, Christopher
Evans-Wentz, Walter Yeeling: *The Tibetan Book of the Dead*, 170
Ewart, Colonel Henry Peter, 47
Extra-Sensory Perception (ESP), 61–4; research and experiments in, 90–7; flaw- and need-directed, 106; psychoanalysis and, 188–90, 205
Eysenck, Hans, 184; *Learning and Behaviour Therapy*, 193

Fabre, Henri: *Souvenirs entomologiques*, 35, 41
'farewell' dreams, 72–80
Fay, Frank and W.G., 14–15
Fielding, Jean Eleanora, 64
Figueroa, Chevalier Giovanni de, 118–20
Flammarion, Camille: collects accounts of psychic experiences, 134, 160; *Death and its Mysteries*, 117
Flournoy, Theodore, 62, 86; *Spiritism and Psychology*, 62
Fordham, Michael, 185–6
foreknowledge, 131–46
Forman, Jean: *The Mask of Time*, 113
Forrest, Colin, 51

Forster, John, 110
Fox, John: *Book of Martyrs*, 131
Foyt, A.J., 142
Franklin, Benjamin, 30
Franz Ferdinand, Archduke of Austria, 146
Freeman, Marie L., 73
Freud, Sigmund: and Descartes' dream, 33; and dream material, 173; and dream censorship, 185; and Jung, 186–7; and ESP, 189, 192–3; Rivers and, 191, 194; Ullman on, 200; *The Interpretation of Dreams*, 2, 172, 179, 184, 192, 193–4

gambling, 160–9
Gardiner, Julia, 153
Garfield, Patricia: *Creative Dreaming*, 174
Garibaldi, Giuseppe, 73
Garnett, Edward, 6
Garnier, Canon, 117
Garrett, Eileen, 94
Gaskell, Elizabeth, 11–12
Gauguin, Paul, 23
Giardino, Piero, 52
Gilchrist, Alexander, 22
Gilmer, Thomas, 153–4
Glasfurd, Alec L., 13–14; *The Antipope*, 14
Goddard, Air Marshal Sir Victor, 128
Godley, John (*later* Lord Kilbracken), 163–7, 168
Goethe, J.W. von, 18
Gonne, Maude, 15
Gosse, Sir Edmund, 19
Grabinsky, Bruno, 147
Granville-Barker, Harley, 16
Graves, J.H., 155
Graves, Robert, 68–9; *The Meaning of Dreams*, 26
Green, Celia: *The Decline and Fall of Science*, 172
Greene, Graham: dreams stories, 11; *A Burnt-Out Case*, 11; *The Honorary Consul*, 11; *It's a Battlefield*, 11; *A Sort of Life*, 70; *Ways of Escape*, 11, 127
Greenwood, Frederick, 182; *Imagination in Dreams*, 31, 48, 112
Gregory, Augusta, Lady, 15
Griffith, Major and Mrs, 132
Griffith, Arthur, 15
Grisewood, Frederick, 121–2
Gurney, Edmund, 61, 64, 101, 136, 194

Hadfield, James: *Dreams and Nightmares*, 41
Haggard, Rider, 76–8
Hall, Calvin S.: *The Meaning of Dreams*, 193
Hamerton, Philip Gilbert, 23
Hamey, Dr Baldwin, the Younger, 131–2

Hannibal, 199
Hansel, C.E.M.: *ESP and Parapsychology*, 95
Harris, Naomi, 64
Hauer, Franz von, 149
Haynes, Edmund, 7
Hazlitt, William, 181
Hearne, Keith, 174
Hebbel, Friedrich: *Judith*, 20
Hellenbach, Lazar, Baron von, 149
Heren, Louis, 71
Hervey de Saint-Denys, Marquis, 170; *Les Rêves et les moyens de les diriger*, 23, 30, 39, 170
Hill, Brian, 40
Hilprecht, H.V., 36–7, 61–2
Hippocrates, 194–5
Hobbes, Thomas: *Leviathan*, 180
Hodgson, Richard, 136–7
Holmes, Oliver Wendell: *Mechanism in Thought and Morals*, 31–2
Hone, William, 115–16
horseracing *see* gambling
Howe, Elias, 41–2
Hudd, Roy, 122
Hudson, Liam: *Night Life*, 202, 204–5
Hudson, Mrs Sammie, 166–7
Hume, David, 98
Humphrey, Nicholas: *The Inner Eye*, 204
Hutchinson, Horace, 47, 54, 195; *Dreams and Their Meaning*, 110–11, 201
hyperaesthesia, 99–100, 134
hypnosis, 99, 195–7

identifying paramnesia, 100, 103, 116
Indy, Vincent d', 25
Iveagh, Lady, 64–5

Jaffé, Aniela, 137; *Apparitions*, 89, 128, 131
James I, King of England, 180
James, William, 62
Jerram, Douglas, 160–1
Jesus Christ, 195, 199
Johnson, Canon, 120
Johnson, Lionel C., 161
Jones, Ernest, 183
Joseph (Old Testament patriarch), 176
Joseph, St (husband of Virgin Mary), 3
Jung, Carl Gustav, 62, 172; dream interpretation, 185–8; and precognition, 187–8; *Memories, Dreams, Reflections*, 185, 187; *Modern Man in Search of a Soul*, 186; *Psychology of the Unconscious*, 185

Kaempffert, W.B., 41
Kekulé, Friedrich, 34–5, 40–1
Keller, Helen: *The World We Live In*, 26–7

Kennedy, Robert, 71
Kerouac, Jack: *Book of Dreams*, 11
Kilbracken, 3rd Baron *see* Godley, John
Kingsford, Anna, 9–10, 17, 20
Kinsolving, George, 136–7
Kipling, Rudyard: *Something of Myself*, 108–9
Koestler, Arthur: *The Act of Creation*, 4
Kurigalzu, Assyrian King, 36–7

LaBerge, Stephen, 207; *Lucid Dreams*, 173–5, 205
Lamb, Charles, 17
Lamon, Ward, 154
Lane, Frederick, 154–5
Lang, Andrew, 67, 137; *Dreams and Ghosts*, 53
Langland, William: *Piers Plowman*, 6
Lanyi, Monsignor de, Bishop of Grosswardin, 146–7
Larrey, Baron, 160
Lawrence, D.H., 6
Le Bas, Henry Vincent, 83–4
le Brocquy, Louis, 79–80
Lehmann, Alfred, 100
Leno, Dan, 122
Lewis, Herbert J., 53
Life magazine, 94
Lightfoot, William and James, 87–8
Lincoln, Abraham, 154
Lincoln, J.S.: *The Dream in Primitive Culture*, 176, 193
Livneh, Gilad, 149
Lockhart, John Gibson, 12–13
Loewe, Otto, 37–8
Lombroso, Cesare, 91
Longstaffe, Marjorie, 114
Lowe, Ralph, 157–8
lucidity, 171, 207
Luna, Pedro de *see* Benedict XIII, Pope
Luther, Martin, 180
Lyttelton, Dame Edith, 144

Macario, Maurizio: *Du Sommeil, des rêves et du somnambulisme*, 159–60
McCarthy, Eugene, 71
McDougall, Rev. A.B., 65
McGlashan, Alan: *Gravity and Levity*, 207
Mackenzie, Andrew: *Riddle of the Future*, 138
MacKenzie, Norman: *Dreams and Meaning*, 105
McNish, Robert: *The Philosophy of Sleep*, 98
Maeterlinck, Maurice, 157; *La Vie de l'espace*, 150
Mahomet the Prophet, 3, 199
Mahoney, Patrick, 49
Maimonides Hospital, New York, 94–7, 169, 207

Manaceine, Marie de: *Sleep*, 203
Mancini, Angelina, 91–2
Mancini, Maria, 91–3
Mansfield, Katherine: *Sun and Moon*, 10
Maritain, Jacques, 34
Marsh, Sir Edward, 184
Marten, Maria, 86
Martinique (island), 102–3
Mary, Virgin, 3
Mary I, Queen of England, 131–2
Masefield, John: 'The Woman Speaks', 19
mathematicians, 38–9
Mattoon, Mary Ann: *Understanding Dreams*, 186–7, 194
Maudsley, Henry, 181, 183, 193, 195, 206; *Pathology of Mind*, 27–8, 195
Maury, Alfred: *Le Sommeil et les rêves*, 44, 99–100
Maxwell-Scott family, 109
Medawar, Sir Peter, 3
mediumship, 204
Megroz, Rodolphe: *The Dream World*, 11, 55, 68–9, 161–2
Meir, Golda, 147–9
Mendeleev, Dmitri, 35, 175
Milton, John: *Paradise Lost*, 27
Mitchison, Graeme, 2–4, 60, 202, 205
Mnemonic Induction of Lucid Dreams (MILD), 174
Monitor (BBC programme), 4, 57
Morris, Robert, 169
Moss, Thelma: *The Probability of the Impossible*, 166
Moss, W.H., 42–3
Mossadeq, Mohammed, 200
Muensterberg, Hugo, 196
Murray, Donald, 162
Murray, Margaret, 80
musicians: inspiration from dreams, 24–5
Myers, Frederic, 61, 170, 194; *Human Personality*, 170, 204

Nagel, Lynn, 173
Nature (journal), 2, 174, 202
Nebuchadnezzar, King, 177
Newbold, W. Romaine, 61
Newman, James R., 38–9
Newton, William, 126–7
Nicklaus, Jack, 44
Nicolson, Harold, 184
Night My Number Came Up, The (film), 128
Nimblefoot (horse), 163
Norway, Edmund and Nevell, 86–8
Nursing Mirror (journal), 174

O'Casey, Sean, 15
O'Connor, Ulick: *Celtic Dawn*, 15
Odysseus, 1
Ogilvie family, 67
oneiromancy, 177
Osis, Karlis, 94
Ouspensky, Petr D., 172
out-of-the-body experiences, 171
Owen, Robert Dale, 45, 87–8, 132; *Footfalls*, 75–6

Paine, Albert Bigelow, 76
Pall Mall Gazette, 31
Palladino, Eusapia, 91
paramnesia *see* identifying paramnesia
Parapsychology Foundation, 94
Pauwels, Louis and Jacques Bergier: *Le Matin de magiciens*, 32
Pearl Harbor, 70–1
Pearson, Gordon, 48
Penelope, 1
Perceptual and Motor Skills (journal), 174
Perceval, Spencer, 152
playwrights: inspiration from dreams, 14–17
Podmore, Frank, 134, 155
Poe, Edgar Allan: *Gold Bug*, 58; 'The Lady Ligeia', 10
poets: inspiration from dreams, 17–22
Pollexfen, George, 90
Portland, William Cavendish-Bentinck, 6th Duke of, 47
positivism, 29, 98–100
predestination, 125–31
prevision, precognition, 98–100; Dunne and, 101–6; research for, 168–9
Priestley, J.B.: collects accounts of dreams, 4, 57, 105–6; dreams essays, 11; on Dunne, 105–6; and precognitive dreams, 112, 140–1; *I Have Been Here Before*, 2; *Rain Upon Gadshill*, 123; *Time and the Conways*, 2, 14
Princeton, USS, 153–4
prophetic dreams, 199–201
psi-induction, 190
psychoanalysis, 182–90
Puthoff, Harold *see* Targ, Russell and Harold Puthoff

Rabelais, François, 180
Ramanujan, Srinivasa, 38–9
Ramsay, Bertrand, 41
rapid eye movements (REMs), 93–5, 173, 198
rationalism, 29, 206
Redgrave, Michael, 128
reductionism, 2–3, 202
Reed, Henry, 197–8
Revue des Revues, 135

Rhine, Louisa: on disaster dreams, 70; on 'call' dreams, 80; on predestination and precognition, 129, 141–3, 153; *The Invisible Picture*, 56, 66
Rivers, W.H.R.: *Conflict and Dream*, 190–4; *Instinct and the Unconscious*, 203
Rocke, Alan, 41
Romanes, George J., 78–9
Rudofsky, Susanna, 40
Russell, George William *see* A.E.
Rutherford, Mr (Sir Walter Scott's dreamer), 45–6, 60

Sabine, W.H.H.: *Second Sight in Daily Life*, 57, 107–8
Saltmarsh, H.F.: *Foreknowledge*, 134
Sarajevo, 147
Sargent, Winthrop, 126
Sassoon, Siegfried: *Sherston's Progress*, 192
Schatzman, Morton, 59–60, 207
Schopenhauer, Artur, 125–6, 130, 157
Science (journal), 173
Scientific American (journal), 38
scientists: inspiration and problem-solving by dreams, 30–2, 40
Scott, Sir Walter, 12–13, 45–6, 60; *The Bride of Lammermoor*, 12
Seward, Anna, 126
shamans, 176
shared dreams, 64–9
Shaw, George Bernard, 16
Shelley, Mary, 125
Shelley, Percy Bysshe: *Catalogue of the Phenomena of Dreams*, 124–5
Sheppard, John: *On Dreams*, 206
Shoemaker, Willy, 157
Sidgwick, Eleanor, 143–4
Sikorsky, Igor: *The Story of the Winged 'S'*, 122–3
Sitwell, Sir Osbert: *Left Hand, Right Hand*, 161
sleep, 203–5
Smith, Mrs A.M. Bickford *see* Bickford Smith Mrs A.M.
Society for Psychical Research, 53–4, 62, 64, 85, 93, 162; Jung addresses, 187; *Journal*, 61, 133, 149; *Proceedings*, 111, 133, 171
Spectator (journal), 120
Stanford Research Institute, 113
Stanley, Sir Henry Morton: *Autobiography*, 73–4
Stanton, Elizabeth, 137
Stevens, Oliver: *Mystery of Dreams*, 50
Stevenson, Ian, 69–70
Stevenson, Robert Louis: on 'Brownies', 7–9; *Across the Plains*, 7–8; *The Strange Case of Dr Jekyll and Mr Hyde*, 8–9

Stimson, Bill, 198
Stockwood, Mervyn, Bishop of Southwark, 84
subconscious mind, 47, 62
Sundance Community Dream Journal, 197
Surrealist Manifesto, 1924, 24
Swinburne, Algernon Charles, 19
Symonds, Dr John Addington, 27, 30, 181
Symons, Arthur, 18
Synesius of Cyrene, 179–80, 183
Synge, John Millington, 15
Szent-Gyorgi, Albert, 38

Tallmadge, Nathaniel Pitcher, 153
Targ, Russell and Harold Puthoff: *Mind-Reach*, 113
Tart, Charles: *Altered States of Consciousness*, 172–3
Tartini, Giuseppe: 'Devil's Trill', 24
Taylor, Jeremy, 65; *Dream Work*, 32
Telegraph Sunday Magazine, 3
telepathy, 78, 84, 92–3
Tenhaeff, W.H., 155–6
Terriss, William, 155
Thomas, Keith: *Religion and the Decline of Magic*, 180
Titanic, SS, 70
Torrey Canyon (oil tanker), 72
Trevor, Thomas Warren, 120
Turner, J.M.W., 22–3
Twain, Mark *see* Clemens, Samuel
Tyler, President John, 153
Tyrrell, G.N.M.: *Science and Psychical Phenomena*, 71
Tyrrell, Robert Yelverton, 85–6

Ullman, Montague: and REMs, 94–5; hears accounts of dreams, 113; and Bessent's precognitive dreams, 169; and dreams in group therapy, 197–199; on dreams as works of art, 205–6; *Dream Telepathy* (with Stanley Krippner and Alan Vaughan), 63, 96, 189; *Working with Dreams* (with Nan Zimmerman), 79, 206
unconscious, the, 41
'unfinished business' dreams, 86–90
United Irishman (journal), 15

Valerius Maximus, 199
Van de Castle, Robert, 198; 'Sleep and Dreams', 189
Van der Post, Sir Laurens, 185
Vaughan, Alan, 63
Vonnegut, Kurt, 63

Wagner, Richard, 24
Waldron, P., 168
Walker, Dudley, 71–2
Walton, Izaak: *Life*, 132
Warburton, Canon Mark, 84–5
warning dreams, 131–46; unheeded, 146–59
Watson, James: *The Double Helix*, 3
Wells, H.G., 6
West, E.G., 43, 121, 140
Wilde, Oscar, 68
Wilhelm I, Kaiser, 200
Williams, Francis (*later* Lord Francis-Williams): *Dangerous Estate*, 31
Williams, John, 151–3
Wotis, John, 40
Wotton, Nicolas and Thomas, 132
Wren, Henry, 87
writers: inspiration from dreams, 7–14
Wyatt, Sir Thomas, 132

Yau, Marion, 72
Yeats, William Butler, 90; 'The Cap and Bells', 21–2; *Cathleen ni Houlihan*, 15–16

Zola, Emile, 127